GOD'S HUMAN SPEECH

God's Human Speech

A Practical Theology of Proclamation

Charles L. Bartow

WILLIAM B. EERDMANS PUBLISHING COMPANY
GRAND RAPIDS, MICHIGAN / CAMBRIDGE, U.K.

138228

© 1997 Wm. B. Eerdmans Publishing Co.
255 Jefferson Ave. S.E., Grand Rapids, Michigan 49503 /
P.O. Box 163, Cambridge CB3 9PU U.K.

Printed in the United States of America

02 01 00 99 98 97   7 6 5 4 3 2 1

Library of Congress Cataloging-in-Publication Data

Bartow, Charles L.
    God's human speech: a practical theology of proclamation/
Charles L. Bartow.
        p.   cm.
    Includes bibliographical references and indexes.
    ISBN 0-8028-4335-2 (pbk.: alk. paper)
    1. Preaching. 2. Word of God (Theology). 3. Bible — Inspiration.
4. Revelation. I. Title.
    BV4211.2.B263   1997
    251 — dc21   97-10577
                                                                        CIP

The author and publisher gratefully acknowledge permission to reprint material granted by
the following:

"Advent," by William Brower. Reprinted by permission of the author.

"Balloon," by Anna Jarrard. Reprinted by permission of the author.

Excerpt from "Little Gidding" in Four Quartets, copyright 1943 by T. S. Eliot and renewed
    1971 by Esme Valerie Eliot, reprinted by permission of Harcourt Brace & Company. British
    rights granted by Faber and Faber Ltd.

Excerpt from The Prayers and Meditations of St. Anselm, translated by Benedicta Ward (Lon-
    don: Penguin, 1973), p. 152. Reprinted by permission.

"Three Floors," copyright © 1962 by Stanley Kunitz, from Passing Through: The Later Poems
    New and Selected by Stanley Kunitz. Reprinted by permission of W. W. Norton & Company,
    Inc.

Unless otherwise indicated, all biblical quotations in this volume are taken from the New
Revised Standard Version of the Bible, copyright © 1989 by the Division of Christian Education of the National Council of Churches of Christ in the U.S.A., and used by permission.

For William Brower
Teacher, Colleague, Friend

Advent

by William Brower

Mired in blood and ashes,
Brushed by the burnt bone of the tormented,
We struggle for a footing.
Climbing crookedly along the edge of chaos
We reach our island.
It is slippery and shapeless
But ground and time enough
For a brief pretense of sanity, wisdom, peace.

So here, at Ground Zero and the zero hour,
We sit with the boiling, bloody sea around us,
With the ashes of brothers and sisters
Drifting among the antennas.
Shall we stir again?
Or die now, dirty and foolish . . .
It will soon be over.

Look there!
Through the gray shadows,
See him.
Hear him.
The little servant shape
Trembling, crying in his chosen emptiness.
It is a new-born child
Who has joined us in this vulnerable flesh
To place his Father's kiss upon our faces. (1970)

Contents

Preface

> *My God, where is that ancient heat towards thee,*
> *Wherewith whole shoals of Martyrs once did burn,*
> *Besides their other flames?*
>
> GEORGE HERBERT

I WAS TEMPTED TO GIVE this book the title *Positive Preaching and the Post-modern Mind.* Respect for P. T. Forsyth kept me from it. Nevertheless my concern is to encourage confidence in the Bible read and the sermon delivered as means of grace in an age of radical criticism of Scripture, creed, and confession. Can God speak an audible word with the words of Scripture and so be known among us as transcendent presence? Can the creeds and confessions of the church assist us in understanding a God so disclosed? Does knowledge of that God free us not only to the praise of God's glory, but to a deeper appreciation of ourselves and an appropriate care of the earth? These and other questions, perhaps beyond anyone's means to answer fully, at least can be addressed, however modestly. It is good to live with some answers, but it is wise never to forget the questions. *"Deus cognitus, Deus nullus,"* said H. H. Farmer. A God comprehended is no God, and the theology that pretends to know everything is a sham. Yet theology must know something or it cannot even recognize the aptness of what Farmer said.

What I seek, and invite the reader to seek with me, is knowledge more tantalizing than certain, more daring than determinate, sound but not settled knowledge, like the knowledge we have of loved ones that enables us to go on loving them even in the face of disappointment with them and with ourselves. No, I seek a bit more than that, to be honest. I seek assured knowledge, the "heat" of which Herbert wrote. I seek what must be known to live with loved ones and not lose them, to live with God and not lose God in the living. Does God live, and has God lived among us as one of us? Is God's human speech after all incarnate? Does God have a name, a particular name, a divine name, a human name? Or is God just whatever I yearn for God to be — if there is a God — or what I need God to be in order that I may be what I want to be?

These are very practical questions and therefore not inappropriate for a very practical theologian to ask. So I ask them, and I attempt answers, answers that will help me — and perhaps help others — to keep up the public reading of the Scriptures in worship, and to keep up the "attempt," as Barth called it, to preach. For I cannot hope to find the living God if the living God has not found me, and I cannot preach the gospel of the living God if the living God has not spoken to me. If God's speech is not human speech, *truly* human speech, then God might as well keep silent. Preachers might as well keep silent too.

I need to thank a number of people who have helped me get on with raising my questions and venturing some answers. William O. Harris, librarian for archives and special collections, helped track down sources. George Hunsinger gave me very useful bibliographical leads, as did Dennis T. Olson. Scott R. A. Starbuck, my pastor, provided solid scholarly critique. Dale E. Bussis, a former teacher and friend, read much of what I had to say and commented on it helpfully. Ulrich Mauser proofread the manuscript and gave me a number of helpful suggestions. My daughter, Rebecca, challenged successfully a number of my thoughts. Kristin E. Saldine prepared the indexes and the bibliography. Deirdre King Hainsworth proofread the galleys. My colleagues in *Preaching and Speech Communication in Ministry* at Princeton Seminary were, each in his or her own way, an inspiration: Thomas G. Long, G. Robert Jacks, James F. Kay, Nora Tubbs Tisdale, Janet L. Weathers, Henry Robert Lanchester, Nancy Lammers Gross. John W. Stewart took on the job of chair of the Department of Practical Theology while I was on leave writing. Cullen I K Story gave encouraging comments on my treatment of Psalm 27 in Chapter 3. Patrick D. Miller did the same. Richard F. Ward of Yale Divinity School has been a constant friend and conversation partner in performance theory and theology. To W. J. Beeners, my

predecessor in the Egner Chair in speech at Princeton, I owe nothing
less than my career. My longtime friend and colleague Jana L. Childers
graciously accepted my invitation to write a foreword to this book. She
also read and commented on every chapter. Without years of friendly
and vigorous exchange of views with scholars in the Speech Communication Association (Performance Studies Division), the Religious
Speech Communication Association, and the Academy of Homiletics, I
would nearly be at a loss for words. Without my students I would be at
a loss for ever fresh encouragement and insight. Without my secretary,
Lois F. Haydu, and my typist, Joan Blyth-Lovell, I would simply be lost.
To my former dean, Conrad H. Massa, to Dean James F. Armstrong, to
President Thomas W. Gillespie, and to the board of trustees of Princeton
Theological Seminary I am grateful for a generous sabbatic leave that
allowed me the time to read, think, and write. I am also grateful for a
Princeton Seminary Faculty Grant that provided funding for aspects of
my research. I am grateful, too, for the guidance and help of the editors
and staff of Wm. B. Eerdmans Publishing Company. As with everything
in life, so in this particular project, my wife Paula has been a constant
source of down-to-earth help, long-suffering affection, and wise counsel. She proofread every page of my handwritten manuscript! I have no
idea how to thank her — or God — for all she means to me.

PRINCETON, NEW JERSEY
APRIL 16, 1996

Foreword

HOW IS THE WORD OF GOD known here at the end of the twentieth century? Who gets to name God? Can human beings speak for God? How can we distinguish between our wishful thinking about God and legitimate construals? What will prevent us from confusing God's word of comfort with our own idolatrous longings? Does anybody believe any more that this is remotely possible? Does God still speak?

Preachers of the Modern Age who were concerned with such questions had several ready resources. They could turn to H. H. Farmer's *Servant of the Word*, Philip Brooks's *Lectures on Preaching,* or P. T. Forsyth's great classic, *Positive Preaching and the Modern Mind.* There they would find the great theological/homiletical questions, such as authority, revelation, and inspiration, treated thoughtfully. If they still harbored questions about such things as the precise relationship between preaching and theology, they had recourse to several additional works. Karl Barth, Dietrich Ritschl, and Heinrich Ott, for example, had each commented voluminously on the subject. If they were concerned still yet about the question of the preacher's personhood, or the preacher's proper role in the preaching event, there was no lack of comment in the homiletical textbooks of the day. H. Grady Davis or Clyde Fant made free to share their wisdom.

However, the preacher of the Postmodern Age who is burdened with such theological questions has had a great deal less help. She or he may even have come to feel that there is something wrong with the questions themselves. The most common effect of postmodernism on a preacher, after all, is to leave her with the feeling that all the cards are up in the air. One learns not to expect any two of one's friends to be able "to agree as to touching one thing." One learns to value the diversity of opinion, respect the experience of the individual, and keep one's questions about defensible interpretations of the Scripture to oneself. One learns about two-edged swords.

Onto this stage strides Charles L. Bartow, a big man with a big faith. The planks of postmodernism seem to wobble beneath his feet. "In Christ Jesus, God takes us as we are and presses us into the service of what God would have us be," he says. His inspiration for the saying is a Modern preacher — Paul Scherer — but Bartow finds in this kerygmatic statement a promise for the Postmodern Age. God's self-revelation in Jesus Christ still presses us, he claims. What's especially important to Charles Bartow about that (what is important to all who have recently come to be called "postliberals") is the direction of the pressing.

God speaks first, Bartow proclaims. Before, beyond, and during anything we have to say about who God is, God speaks and shapes us. Agreeing with Barth that one cannot speak of God by speaking of human beings in a loud voice, Bartow seems also to suggest that loud voices do little or nothing to faze the inexorable Word God is intent on speaking. "God is not an obscurantist" (p. 9 below). Neither is God just one of our more interesting cosmic projections, he insists. The Word God speaks is definitive and one that both confirms and disconfirms our expectations.

So saying, Charles Bartow does the church, or at least some sectors of it, an important service. He restores some tautness to one of those famous theological equations that cannot exist without it. In areas of the church where tension between idolatry and claiming one's own experience has flagged, Bartow suggests a tightening. Between the "definitive" and the "plural" — between the "context-specific" and the "protean" Word of God — Bartow turns the screws, and offers the faith community a chance to reaffirm its trust in the God who speaks — even the God who holds down divine hands "all the day long" to a sometimes contrary people.

But this book offers the church more than a thoughtful, passionate defense of the power of the Word of God; it offers a positive, practical homiletic. Bartow believes that preaching is a theological enterprise embodied at any given time in a human voice, body, and person. And Charles Bartow practices what he preaches. He makes a persuasive theological argument for Divine Presence — Real Presence — in the public reading of Scripture and in preaching, and he shows how a preacher's language, inflection, phrasing, and intonation are in service to that presence. No contemporary homiletician knows more about the mechanics of voice, the principles that govern the "vocal exegesis" of the biblical text, or the disciplines of oral performance. Bartow brings them all to bear here without leaving the reader the slightest chance to think for the shortest moment that effective preaching is merely a function of speech-communication technique.

In *God's Human Speech*, the Charles L. Bartow whom God has "pressed into the service of what God would have him be" uses his theological mind, his pedagogical know-how, and his preacher's heart to "encourage confidence" (p. ix above) in the public reading of the Scriptures and in preaching. It is easy to imagine that God is pleased with the effects of this conscription. No open reader will be able to come away from this book untouched by the blood and the fire of the gospel. This is not a book about a few safe principles and a couple of interesting concepts. This is a passionate book, which argues fiercely and tenderly — thoroughly and honestly — for something its writer believes in. You might even say for something its writer knows.

> [The Word of God] is not *verbum* but *sermo*, not *ratio* but *oratio*. . . . It is intentional and artful, poetic, crafting for itself a work, a dramatic narrative, a story. It is *actio divina*, God's self-performance, and, as such, it deploys language and languages, silence and sound, stillness and gesture, anything — even nothing — to its own ends. It is at no one's disposal. Instead, all persons, all things, all cultures, all systems of common life and governance, all events, all times, and all places are at its disposal. It is infinite; it is eternal. (pp. 26-27 below)

What more could we ask?

JANA CHILDERS
SAN ANSELMO, CA

Introduction

THIS BOOK REPRESENTS AN ATTEMPT to write a practical theology of the spoken word, that is, of proclamation. In my view, practical theology, as distinguished from biblical exegesis and dogmatics,[1] is always and of necessity local and performative, inductive and interdisciplinary. By local and performative I mean that practical theologians deal with specific forms of praxis, for example, the practice of worship, of congregational life, of mission, even of worldly embodiment of the gospel. Such praxis, or localized activity, is not just a necessary part of practical theological reflection, it is central to it. Practical theology in its descriptive, constructive, and critical moves always starts with concrete, performative acts, and it sticks with them. Even in its most theoretical moments those acts are kept in focus. Performative acts, as distinguished from more casual and spontaneous behaviors, involve an element of choice, of calculation, of commitment.[2] Most typically, though not exclusively, they are public too.[3] Anything may be a perfor-

---

1. For Karl Barth the three main branches of theology are biblical exegesis, dogmatics, and practical theology. See Karl Barth, *Homiletics* (Louisville, KY: Westminster/John Knox Press, 1991), p. 17.

2. See Ronald J. Pelias, *Performance Studies: The Interpretation of Aesthetic Texts* (New York: St. Martin's Press, 1992), pp. 47-63.

3. Pastoral care situations may not be public in the usual sense, though the counselee may be considered to be "going public" to an "audience" of one, namely the counselor. Also, both counselor and counselee are "framing" experience, not just emoting; e.g., see Pelias, pp. 95-98, for a discussion of empathy or strategic choice in the understanding and performance of the "other."

1

mative act,[4] but not everything is. When grief overtakes me, "now that I have my dead,"[5] and, suddenly, alone, I weep or pray or slump into quiet melancholy, that is not an instance of performative action. That is simply a case of my being myself, all unadorned and perhaps even shattered.

But when I step into the pulpit of a church, face the congregation, say: "Let us hear the word of God," and then proceed to read from the Bible and to preach, that *is* a performative action. The people of the church have chosen me, educated me, called me, and installed me in that pulpit. And I have chosen to accept that appointment. They have prayerfully considered what they want me to do for them. I have prayerfully calculated how to go about it. We are committed to one another, and, in that commitment, we understand ourselves to be mutually accountable to God for our deportment. In the pulpit I am no longer simply a private person. I am a public *persona.* I am still myself, no doubt, whatever that may be. But I am not in service to myself. I am not engaged in self-expression. Instead, I am in service to the words — and the Word — the people of God would hear. My weeping, melancholic, all unadorned and shattered self is not what people come to church to see and to hear. On their faces you can read it: "We wish to see Jesus" (John 12:21). And, for their sakes, I had better hope to see him too — however terrifying or comforting the prospect of doing that may be.

Practical theology is not only local and performative, it is also inductive and interdisciplinary. It is inductive because it seeks to understand the significance of the performative acts under consideration. Since those acts are usually public and calculated and a function of commitment, it may be assumed that they hold significance for those engaged in them — and perhaps for others as well. Practical theology seeks to explicate that significance, hold it up to scrutiny, and construct theory that may serve as a guide to further practice. Also, all that may be said about the significance of particular performative acts is implicitly interdisciplinary. In the reading of the Scriptures and in preaching, for example, theological considerations are bound up with other considerations, such as the semiotics of language and vocal and physical gesture,

4. Pelias, pp. 3-8.

5. Howard Nemerov, "The Snow Globe," *The Collected Poems of Howard Nemerov* (Chicago: University of Chicago Press, 1977), p. 129.

literary theory and rhetoric, even aesthetics. Mundane considerations such as vocal technique, articulation, diction, and pronunciation also come into play. Contemporary research in cognitive science makes it clear that content cannot be separated from form, abstract thought from bodily function, or intellectual grasp from emotional commitment.[6] Theology, art, and technique thus converge in any human performative enterprise. And if the divine self-disclosure in Jesus Christ is the primary (if peripatetic)[7] locus of performative action for practical theology (and other forms of theological study as well), it is imperative that we attend to that self-disclosure with all the varied means appropriate to it. Erasmus has said that the Word of God is not *verbum* but *sermo*,[8] it is not *ratio* but *oratio*. He was offering a translation of *logos* in John 1:1ff. in contradiction of the *Vulgate* translation. The Word of God is face to face, oral-aural situated, and suasory discourse. It is not a dead letter. It is not reason alone. It is an event of *actio divina* (God's self-performance, if you will). It is in fact God's human speech. To study the reading of the Scriptures and the preaching of sermons with particular focus upon the scriptural text as *spoken* text and the sermon as *spoken word* therefore is singularly appropriate. Such study takes us straight to the theological heart of the matter. It directs our attention to God's self-disclosure as performative event, and it prompts a careful review of our listening and of our speaking in the light of that event.

In chapter 1 of this practical theology of proclamation I use the rhetorical tropes of oxymoron, metaphor, and metonymy to explicate the significance of the statement "Let us hear the word of God!" I argue that the tropes give us a way to speak about "the human being–encountering God" and "the God-encountering human being"[9] without sacrificing either God's transcendence or God's immanence and without violating the integrity of human experience or claiming more than can be claimed

6. See Mark Johnson, *The Body in the Mind: The Bodily Basis of Meaning, Imagination and Reason* (Chicago: University of Chicago Press, 1987), esp. pp. 18-138.

7. The thought here is that the Jesus of Scripture is alive and not dead and is attested as such in Scripture itself. Thus he is a moving figure, not a fixed one; a subject, not an object of encounter; self-disclosive and not disclosed only through attempts at refiguration of him.

8. See Thomas O. Sloane, *Donne, Milton, and the End of Humanist Rhetoric* (Berkeley, CA: University of California Press, 1985), p. 79.

9. Karl Barth, *The Humanity of God* (Richmond, VA: John Knox Press, 1960), p. 55.

for the power of human discourse. The real presence and claim of God in Christ, through the agency of the Holy Spirit, with the words of Scripture, and by means of duly called and installed ministers of word and sacrament, is affirmed. Thus, as the *Second Helvetic Confession* asserts: "The preaching of the Word of God is the Word of God."[10] The real presence of the triune God in the reading of the Scriptures and in preaching is further explicated in chapter 2. Here it is seen as an event of *actio divina* (or divine self-performance), which instances an appropriate and faithful pluralism in the scriptural witness and in preaching. This pluralism, while disconcerting and powerful in its own way, is not without limits. And, while it challenges many traditional notions of authority in the exercise of the ministerial office, it clearly affirms others.[11] It also sets constraints upon the content of sermons. The chapter concludes with a discussion of how one may discern in the plural biblical witness a unifying gospel of divine initiative that is neither reductionist nor dictated by the ideological commitments and expectations of preachers and congregants. Scripture reading and preaching thereby may be guided by a norm that is intrinsic to the *kerygmatic* occasion. What this results in theologically, and in terms of the art of the spoken word, is a view of Scripture reading and proclamation of the gospel that understands the preacher's work as an act of interpretative speech.

In the next two chapters a move is made from description to constructive proposals for guiding practice. Chapter 3 explores the public reading of the Scriptures as an act of proclamation of the gospel as well as a work of interpretative speech. Scriptural texts are shown to be "arrested performances,"[12] which come to life through the reader's and congregation's embodiment of their sense and significance, their denotation and connotation, their intellectual and emotional content. But the movement is not along a one-way street from indwelling and understanding of the text to public utterance of it. Instead the movement is along a two-way street; for the art of the spoken word itself provides means to indwell the text and to come to an understanding of it that

10. "The Second Helvetic Confession," *The Book of Confessions* (Louisville, KY: Presbyterian Church [U.S.A.], 1994), C5.004, pp. 55-56.

11. See Walter Brueggemann, "Preaching as Reimagination," *Theology Today* 52, no. 3 (Oct. 1995): pp. 313-29, esp. p. 324.

12. Beverly Whitaker Long and Mary Frances HopKins, *Performing Literature: An Introduction to Oral Interpretation* (Englewood Cliffs, NJ: Prentice-Hall, 1982), p. 2.

can shape performance. This process is made concrete through a performative analysis of selected passages from the Bible and classical and contemporary literature. The chapter concludes with a detailed performative analysis of Psalm 27.

Chapter 4 deals with the sermon as a refiguring of the world of the preacher and of the congregation through an encounter with the biblical and apostolic witness to the Word incarnate in Jesus Christ. The interpretative effort to make sense of this encounter is guided by the confessional tradition of the church. Yet that confessional tradition, like the world of the preacher and of the congregation, is subject to critical assessment and refiguration in light of the scriptural witness. Thus the doctrine of *sola scriptura* is operative in hermeneutics and in preaching. But it is not seen as a device of intimidation inhibiting interpretative efforts. Instead it is looked upon as a means to provoke and direct them. The sermon, growing out of the preacher's interpretation of the encounter of Bible, creedal tradition, and contemporary life, will take the form of a dramatic narrative with prose commentary, a performative action with beginning, middle, and end. It will feature moments of orientation, disorientation, and reorientation.[13] It will not be a shapeless series of verse by verse and word by word expository comments and incidental insights. Yet the outcome of the drama for those involved in it, while objectively settled in the once for all salvific work accomplished by God in Jesus Christ, will not be subjectively settled in the individual lives of preachers and congregants. Nor will it be settled in the corporate life of the church. Regarding those experiential outcomes, no one can tell. Who knows what is in store for us as a result of what we hear from the pulpit? When we enter the preaching moment, when we take to the homiletical stage, so to speak, frankly, "our beginnings never know our ends."[14]

13. See Walter Brueggemann, *The Message of the Psalms: A Theological Commentary* (Minneapolis, MN: Augsburg Publishing House, 1984), pp. 25-123. Brueggemann uses Ricoeur's notion of orientation, disorientation, and reorientation in hermeneutics to classify selections from the psalter. However, the concept is dynamic, and what *functions* as an instrument of orientation in one setting may function as an instrument of disorientation or reorientation in another. Use of the concept in discussing sermon composition, then, refers not to a stereotypical outline of sermonic content, but to a deep movement of dramatic force running beneath the surface of the sermon, whatever its formal structure.

14. T. S. Eliot, "Portrait of a Lady," *The Complete Poems and Plays*, 1909-1950 (New York: Harcourt, Brace and World, 1952), p. 11.

In chapter 5 we assume a critical stance for assessing practice. Such critique, of course, may well lead to modifications in constructive homiletical theory and to changes in homiletical practice. But the movement from constructive theory to practical effort to critical reflection is not merely circular. The process is goal oriented. It has an end in view. It has an eschatological tug drawing it forward toward that definitive act of judgment and mercy beyond time, which already in time has been effected in Jesus Christ. In that moment (our name for it is eternity) Scripture reading and preaching will cease and all will be eucharist. In the meantime, no triumphalism! Congregations — as they should — will take the measure of every attempt at the reading of Scripture and preaching. To paraphrase W. H. Auden, the words of the preacher, like the words of the poet, will be "modified in the guts of the living."[15] As part of the congregation of the faithful, preachers themselves, and academic homileticians, will become engaged in reverent, yet unsparing, critique of the church's proclamation. This means paying attention to one's own efforts and to various contexts and acts of proclamation and not just to the efforts of pulpit "stars" and decontextualized summaries of kerygmatic content and the state of the church and world. Those who read this book also — and immediately — get a crack at homiletical criticism, if they wish to take it: Chapter 6 consists of sermon manuscripts by the author — "arrested performances" of earlier homiletical "attempts."

A caution: A couple of years ago, a friend of mine and I exchanged views on a controversial issue facing the church. We were on opposing sides. In one of his letters my friend warned me that I was "in over my head." Indeed I was, as I am, as we all are when it comes to matters of faith and what we take to be the truth. Certainly that is the way it is when it comes to the reading of the Scriptures and to preaching. Is there anyone fit for the task? Is there someone somewhere who can handle it with aplomb? Demosthenes said that the entire rhetorical enterprise could be summed up thus: "Delivery, delivery, delivery!" Citing Demosthenes approvingly, Calvin, quoting Augustine, averred that the Christian life — and all the theologizing that goes with it — could be summed up this way: "*Humility, humility, humility.*"[16] There is enough

15. W. H. Auden, "In Memory of W. B. Yeats," *Selected Poetry of W. H. Auden* (New York: Random House [The Modern Library], 1958), p. 53.
16. John Calvin, *Institutes of the Christian Religion*, 2.2.11, ed. John T. McNeill, Jr., trans. Ford Lewis Battles (Philadelphia: Westminster Press, 1960), pp. 268-69.

to the theology and art of Scripture reading and preaching to prove Calvin right. But humility can hold its heart high even as its head is bowed. And it can press ahead with what is commanded of it despite the magnitude of the task, for it knows down deep what pride can never fathom, that "Christ rises! Mercy every way/Is infinite, — and who can say?"17

17. Robert Browning, "Christmas Eve and Easter Day," XXXIII, *Browning's Complete Poetical Works*, ed. Horace E. Scudder (Boston: Houghton Mifflin Co., 1895), p. 335.

1. Hear the Word of God!

IN OUR LORD'S DAY WORSHIP, before we read the Scriptures and preach, we say this: "Hear the word of God!" It is not an invitation — take it or leave it — to pay attention to the preacher. It is not a request that people bend every effort to discern in what is about to be said something agreeable to their own sense of the divine. It is not mere encouragement to "listen for God's Word" in what otherwise may be vague, elusive pulpit chatter, as though it were up to congregations to decide when and whether God has spoken. God is not an obscurantist, however incoherent those who speak the Scriptures and preach may be. And God does not vouchsafe the divine presence only to those who have been led to expect it. "Hear the Word of God" is, rather, an echo of Yahweh's call to the sons and daughters of Abraham and Sarah, Rebekah and Isaac, Jacob and Rachel: "Hear, O Israel" (Deut. 6:4).[1] It resonates with the challenge of Jesus to any and all who would follow him: "Let anyone with ears listen" (Matt. 13:43b)! So we speak it not simply to urge people to do their best to make something of what we are about to say. More importantly, we speak it to alert people to the fact that, with what we say, God is about to make something of them.

We need to be clear about this. "Hear the word of God" should not be thought of as a magical formula for conjuring God's presence. It is not up to preachers to call upon deity to make itself known when they speak

---

1. What Israel was to hear in the *Shema* was the word that constituted the people as a people of God, as a people of Yahweh alone. It is a restatement of the first commandment of the Decalogue.

any more than it is up to congregations to determine when and whether
God has spoken. God is free of divinely appointed "ordinary means"[2] of
grace even if we human beings are not. In any case, the absence of God
may be as much God's word to us human beings at any given moment as
the divine presence. Likewise, silence from God may be precisely what
people now and then are expected to "hear." It was so in Samuel's day. "The
word of the Lord was rare in those days" (1 Sam. 3:1), we read. It was *yāqār*,
"precious" (KJV), as a jewel, hard to come by, priceless. Likewise, Amos:

> The time is surely coming, says the Lord GOD,
>   when I will send a famine on the land;
> not a famine of bread, or a thirst for water,
>   but of hearing the words of the LORD.
> They shall wander from sea to sea,
>   and from north to east;
> they shall run to and fro,
>   seeking the word of the LORD,
> but they shall not find it. (Amos 8:11-12)

At other times God's word broke out everywhere, like a rash, even a
deadly rash. There was no escaping it. So Isaiah spoke to a disobedient
people and to that people's errant governors:

> Hear the word of the LORD,
>   you rulers of Sodom!
> Listen to the teaching of our God,
>   you people of Gomorrah! . . .
> cease to do evil,
>   learn to do good;
> seek justice,
>   rescue the oppressed,
> defend the orphan,
>   plead for the widow. (Isa. 1:10, 16d-17)

But the rulers of Judah did not hear, and the people did not listen. The
oppressed were not rescued. Orphans were not defended. Nobody
pleaded for the widow. Instead, justice went to the highest bidder, to

2. See "The Shorter Catechism," *The Book of Confessions* (Louisville, KY: Presbyterian Church [U.S.A.], 1994), C.7.088, where the "ordinary means" of grace are stated
specifically as "Word, sacrament, and prayer."

the "haves" instead of the "have nots." Therefore the rulers of the people were deposed, and the people themselves were scattered. The land of Judah was despoiled. Said Isaiah:

Your country lies desolate,
    Your cities are burned with fire;
in your very presence
    aliens devour your land;
    it is desolate, as overthrown by foreigners.
And daughter Zion is left
    like a booth in a vineyard,
like a shelter in a cucumber field,
    like a besieged city. (Isa. 1:7-8)

In the hours before his arrest and trial and crucifixion, Jesus faced a people who had turned a deaf ear to God:

Jerusalem, Jerusalem, the city that kills the prophets and stones those who are sent to it. How often have I desired to gather your children together as a hen gathers her brood under her wings, and you were not willing! (Matt. 23:27)

Not willing, one may suppose, because Jesus was not exactly what was expected in Jerusalem by way of a Messiah: no turning of stones into bread, no leaping from the pinnacle of the temple, no appearance among the people "heaven sent and unhurt,"[3] no kingdom gained through accommodation of the will of God to humanity's penchant for playing God (Matt. 4:1-11). The producers of *Napoleon*, an old, soundless, classic film, got it right. After announcing to the governing body of a freshly liberated France that he himself was the revolution, Napoleon gathered an army thrilled to bask in its commander's glory, and he marched that army up through the French Alps to look out over the vulnerable plains of Italy. The text beneath the cinema scene read: "Then the tempter took them to a high mountain and showed them all the kingdoms of the world and their splendor" (Matt. 4:8, para.). First here, then there, even now, the scene repeats itself, though with great variation in hue and color and personnel — God in Christ, by the power of the Spirit, waiting to embrace the "least"

3. Paul E. Scherer, *The Word God Sent* (Grand Rapids, MI: Baker Book House, 1977), p. 144.

among us while the "greatest," not hearing, not seeing, would prevent it: "Lord, when was it that we saw you hungry or thirsty or a stranger or naked or sick or in prison, and did not care for you?" (Matt. 25:44).

The word of God is not always what we think it should be. Often we cannot imagine — much less re-imagine — it, so totally does it disconfirm instead of confirm our expectations concerning it. We can gesture toward it in the figure of speech called oxymoron, a wise foolishness, an impossible possibility.[4] Thus Moses heard the word of God spoken from a bush that was "blazing, yet . . . not consumed" (Exod. 3:2b). Elijah came upon it in "a sound of sheer silence" (1 Kings 19:12b).[5] In psalmists' laments it greets us "like a solemn joy,"[6] a hopeful despair, a doubt-filled faith. Still more startling, in the New Testament, it confronts us in a virgin mother whose first-born son, fully human, fully divine, we call "God of God, Light of Light, Very God of Very God."[7] We call him Jesus, too, the "Nameless of the hundred names,"[8] "for he will save his people from their sins" (Matt. 1:21b). He is crucified, yet risen, an apparent Absence, yet a real Presence in the breaking of bread, in the drinking of the cup. He reigns in earth and heaven. Yet the symbol of his reign is not a scepter only, but also a cross. He rules the church, yet as one who is the servant of all (Matt. 20:26-28). St. Paul calls him God's wisdom *(sophía);*[9] "For God's foolishness is wiser than human wisdom" (1 Cor. 1:25).

Yet, "Hear the word of God" is not always and only a warning to get ready for the utterly unexpected. God, after all, while not at our beck

---

4. For a thorough and superbly nuanced treatment of the significance of the oxymoron in biblical hermeneutics see Stephen Prickett, *Words and the Word: Language, Hermeneutics and Biblical Interpretation* (New York: Cambridge University Press, 1986), pp. 4-36, esp. p. 7. Oxymoron is derived from *oxys* (sharp) and *moros* (dull, foolish). Thus it is a smart saying that at first seems foolish.

5. Prickett, pp. 149-73.

6. Robert Browning, "Paracelsus V," *Browning's Complete Poetical Works,* ed. Horace E. Scudder (Boston: Houghton Mifflin Co., 1895), p. 41:

Festus: God! Thou art love! I build my faith on that. . . .
   I know Thee, who hast kept my path, and made
   Light for me in the darkness, tempering sorrow
   So that it reached me like a solemn joy;
   It were too strange that I should doubt thy love. . . .

7. "The Nicene Creed," *The Book of Confessions,* C.1.1.

8. Alfred Tennyson, *The Ancient Sage,* stanza 1, ln. 49.

9. Rebecca Pentz, "Jesus as Sophia," *Reformed Journal* 38 (Dec. 1988): pp. 17-22.

and call, surely is not capricious, does not toy with us, has no interest in playing hide and seek with us. That, in fact, may be a bit more typical of our carrying on, so to speak, ever since our storied ancestors tried their hand at the game in the Garden of Eden. We do not need to get into a Barth vs. Brunner debate[10] about a point of contact in the human condition for the divine word — whether there is or is not such a thing — to realize that there are times when God comes to us and speaks to us a word precisely suited to our deepest needs and most fervent hopes, not crushing our human spirit, but enabling it,[11] not squelching our imagination, but firing it. It is not surprising, therefore, that the history of our forebears in the faith should be told largely in stories, that their prayers, even their prophecy, should be set to verse, and that variant readings of oft-told tales and oft-sung hymns should crop up, now here, now there, throughout the Scriptures and throughout the preaching those Scriptures have inspired. As H. H. Farmer pointed out some decades ago, not everything is discontinuity when it comes to revelation.[12] There is continuity, too. There is confirmation of our previous experience of God and not only disconfirmation. There is the shock of recognition and not merely the shock.[13] There is metaphor and not only oxymoron.

Jesus preached in parables — extended metaphors,[14] Sallie McFague has called them. Therefore we meet God, see Christ, hear the divine word — in all its strangeness and difference — in and through the mundane events of everyday life: Planting seed and reaping harvest,[15] cleaning house[16] and tending business,[17] yearning for the return of wayward children.[18] Certainly Jesus himself is profoundly different from us. He is truly divine. We are exclusively human. Further, even in his likeness to us, he is

10. For a most helpful contemporary analysis of the Barth-Brunner debate see Garrett Green, *Imagining God: Theology and the Religious Imagination* (San Francisco: Harper and Row Publishers, 1989), pp. 28-29.

11. George S. Hendry, *The Holy Spirit in Christian Theology* (Philadelphia: Westminster Press, 1956), pp. 96-117, esp. pp. 114-15.

12. H. H. Farmer, *Revelation and Religion* (New York: Harper and Bros., 1954), p. 60.

13. Fred B. Craddock, *Preaching* (Nashville: Abingdon Press, 1985), pp. 44-47.

14. Sallie McFague, *Speaking in Parables: A Study in Metaphor and Theology* (Philadelphia: Fortress Press, 1975), pp. 72-80.

15. See Matt. 13:3ff., Mark 4:3ff., Luke 8:5ff.

16. See Luke 15:8.

17. See Luke 16:1-9.

18. See Luke 15:11-32.

without sin, we are told, while we are full of it. In McFague's terms, we may construe that as the *difference* in his similarity to us,[19] the *is not* in his being for us in some sense a living metaphor of our own life before God. Yet, though remaining sinless, Jesus has been "in every respect . . . tested as we are . . ." (Heb. 6:15b). Therefore we can see in him what God has called us to be. That is the similarity, the *is* in Jesus as a living parable[20] of our life before God. If Jesus were fully human and only seemingly divine, that would be of no help to us, for there would be nothing in him to lift us above what keeps us low and compromised: aspiring to the good, but chasing after evil, wanting God, but at the same time wanting to be "the gods of God,"[21] yearning for the affection of our fellow human beings, yet half the time treating them rather shabbily. Harry Emerson Fosdick stated the situation memorably, half a century ago: "If Jesus is only a good man, he towers there, solitary and alone, an isolated phenomenon in human history."[22] Who could presume to be anything like him or to see in him anything remotely akin to what they themselves might hope to become?

Yet, if Christ Jesus is truly God, but only seemingly human, if, in Paul Scherer's phrase, he has not actually "entered this life of ours to bear himself the weight of it,"[23] then we are left still godless in our sins and successes, our joys and sorrows, our laughter and our tears. George Arthur Buttrick saw clearly how much is at stake:

> For this is true: if God had kept the whole heaven between us and Him, if always He had been only ultimate Truth, like snow on some inaccessible mountain, how would we know Him to be "good"? Or if He had come near as an angel, how could we have worshipped? What do angels know about human tears and laughter?[24]

19. Sallie McFague, *Metaphorical Theology: Models of God in Religious Language* (Philadelphia: Fortress Press, 1982), p. 13.

20. Leander E. Keck, *The Bible in the Pulpit: The Renewal of Biblical Preaching* (Nashville, TN: Abingdon Press, 1978), pp. 136-37.

21. Helmut Thielicke, *Between God and Satan,* trans. C. C. Barber (Grand Rapids, MI: Wm. B. Eerdmans Publishing Co., 1958), p. 4.

22. Harry Emerson Fosdick, "What Does the Divinity of Jesus Mean?" *Riverside Sermons* (New York: Harper and Bros., 1958), p. 273.

23. Paul E. Scherer, a prayer in *Worship Resources for the Christian Year,* ed. Charles L. Wallis (New York: Harper and Bros., 1954), p. 333.

24. George Arthur Buttrick, "The Name of the Nameless," *Sermons Preached in a University Church* (Nashville, TN: Abingdon Press, 1959), p. 169.

If, however, God joins us in this "vulnerable flesh to place his Father's kiss upon our faces,"[25] if, in fact, Jesus really is one of us, a down-to-earth man among us women and men, then everything is changed. We are not alone. We are not cut off from God or our own best future. We also "can account for the love in us, for our love might then be the broken image of His love. We [can] account also for the running fire of glory, beneath the deceit, in any Jacob."[26] Once again, Dr. Buttrick:

> The name "Jesus" is manifestly a human name. "Jesus" or "Joshua" was as common a name then as "John" or "William" in our time. There were two or three "Joshuas" then in the wider family of the High Priest, and manuscript evidence hints that Barabbas was also Jesus; for Barabbas, as it stands, means only "son of Abbas," the first name is missing. Did Pilate ask: "Whom do you want me to release for you: Jesus son of Abbas or Jesus who is called Christ?" The name is human. Jesus looked out of the window and said, as we say, "I wonder if it will rain." When his mother cried because in their poverty a coin was lost, he wept with her so poignantly that in man's estate he remembered and turned that desolate moment into a deathless story. When word came that a caravan from Damascus was passing through the valley just over the hill back of Nazareth, he begged to go see it. He laughed. He prayed. He worked day by day. How else could we know God's real nature toward us? A musician, when he was asked to compose a new national anthem for a European land, is reported to have said: "How can I? I wasn't born there." Jesus was born here. He lived among us. "The word became flesh and dwelt among us."[27]

The word become flesh may be known still in the public reading of the Scriptures and in preaching. It is not a "real absence" as a wag once spoke of Zwingli's doctrine of Christ in the sacrament, but a real presence. We can trace it in still another trope or figure of speech, metonymy.[28] Metonymy is a figure closely related to (yet distinct from) synecdoche.[29]

25. William Brower, "Advent" (unpublished poem); see dedication page.
26. Buttrick, p. 168.
27. Buttrick, pp. 168-69.
28. Arthur Quinn, *Figures of Speech: 60 Ways to Turn a Phrase* (Salt Lake City: Gibbs M. Smith Inc., 1982), pp. 52-56.
29. Quinn sees synecdoche as a type of metonymy. Burke (see note 31) sees synecdoche as a trope related to metonymy. That is the position taken here. Quinn, however, aptly delineates the transposition of these figures of speech from the realm of

In synecdoche the part stands for the whole. For example, this sentence: "I saw tall sails trailing a rainbow wake up the Hudson." The person actually saw ships. But the term for one part of a ship, the sail, is used in the sentence to represent the ship as a whole. Take note: The sail is *necessarily* a part of the tall ship. You cannot have a workable tall ship without a sail. In metonymy you also have the term for a small thing related to a larger whole being used in place of the term that directly names the greater object. But the small thing has *no necessary* relationship to the greater reality it represents. For instance, the term "scepter" may be used in a sentence instead of the term "sovereign." This can be done because we all know that scepters typically are part and parcel of any king's or queen's exercise of power. Real sovereigns, however, actually have no need of scepters to be who they are and to enforce their rule. Yet because sovereigns choose to carry scepters, those scepters are identified with the sovereigns' persons and authority. Thus, in metonymy, objects of little import in themselves stand for other objects or persons of great import, but they do so by *appointment and tradition*, not out of necessity. In Shakespeare's *Merchant of Venice*, when Portia uses the words "sceptered sway"[30] we all know that she is referring, metonymically, to the king's — any king's — brute power, person, and presence. In psalmodic material, a twist is given to this: The *Lord* sends out the scepter from Zion; the king himself does not. The Lord rules through the king or the king does not rule (Ps. 110:2).

Some have called both synecdoche and metonymy reductionist tropes.[31] This is because a term for a part of a whole (synecdoche) or a term for a lesser object associated with a greater object (metonymy) is being used in place of a term (or number of terms) inherently more rich, complex, and sizeable. Grammatically and logically, of course, that is precisely the case. There is more to a ship than a sail and there is more to kings and queens than the scepters they carry. Nevertheless, because sovereigns wield scepters, and because, by appointment of their majesties and by tradition, scepters have come to represent sovereign sway; even if the king or queen

---

language to the realm of persons, things, and experienced interactions between them. *Thus the figures become symbols shaping consciousness and providing the conditions for perception.*

30. William Shakespeare, *The Merchant of Venice*, 4.1.193. For a discussion of the scepter of the Lord, see Scott R. A. Starbuck, "And What Had Kings? The Reappropriation of Court Oracles Among the Royal Psalms of the Hebrew Psalter" (unpublished Ph.D. dissertation, Princeton Theological Seminary, 1996), pp. 170-77.

31. Kenneth Burke, *On Symbols and Society*, ed. Joseph R. Gusfield (Chicago: University of Chicago Press, 1989), pp. 247-55.

is not literally present, nobles gathered to do the sovereign's will had better get on with it. When the scepter is set down in the midst of the company of nobles, those nobles know they are obligated to conduct their sovereign's affairs and not their own. They also know that they are obligated to conduct those affairs with fidelity to their sovereign's publicly declared precepts, laws, and ordinances. Life itself — their own life! — depends on it. Metonymy thus is not simply a reductionist trope or figure of speech. It is a trope of real presence in the face of apparent absence.

Before exploring the figure of metonymy as a way to understand real presence in preaching, it may be of some help to consider its use for understanding real presence in the Lord's Supper. John Calvin used the trope in just that way.[32] In contrast to the Roman Catholic doctrine of transubstantiation and Lutheran teaching regarding consubstantiation, Calvin understood the relationship of the bread and the cup to Christ's presence in the sacrament metonymically. In other words, Christ appointed the bread and the cup to signify his presence in the worshiping assembly. The liturgy of the sacrament in the Reformed tradition makes this clear. Before the Great Prayer of Thanksgiving the presiding minister says:

> And now, in His name, I take these elements to be set apart by prayer and thanksgiving to the holy use for which *He has appointed them.*[33]

The bread and the cup, having just been brought in or uncovered, prayerfully are set apart from their common use "to this holy use and mystery,"[34] according to the command of Christ. The phrase "holy use and mystery" is to direct the hearts and minds of the faithful to him who is "seated at the right hand of power" (Matt. 26:64). Yet the resurrected and ascended Christ also is known in the breaking of the bread, in the pouring of the cup, and in the communication in both kinds of presiders, servers and congregants. The bread and the cup do not localize Christ's presence. Yet, with them, Christ Jesus makes himself known among his people. He exercises his Lordship, and nourishes his people, indeed makes himself one with them and they with him.[35] Therefore,

---

32. John Calvin, *Institutes of the Christian Religion*, 2.4.17, ed. John T. McNeill, Jr., trans. Ford Lewis Battles (Philadelphia: Westminster Press, 1960), pp. 1370-74.

33. *The Book of Common Worship* (Philadelphia: Presbyterian Church in the U.S.A., 1946), p. 171.

34. *The Book of Common Worship*, p. 161.

35. *The Book of Common Worship*, p. 173. Italics mine.

at the conclusion of the eucharistic service, the congregation, led by the
presiding pastor, boldly prays:

> We give Thee thanks, O Lord, for Thy rich mercy and invaluable
> goodness, vouchsafed to us in this sacred Communion, wherein we
> have assurance that we are very members of the mystical Body of Thy
> Son, and heirs through hope of his everlasting Kingdom. *So enrich us
> by Thy continual grace that the life of Jesus may be made manifest in
> our mortal body,* and Thy Kingdom be furthered through all such
> good works as Thou hast prepared for us to walk in.[36]

Here the metonymic figure is extended (see italics above) to include the
entire worshiping assembly, so that the church gathered and dispersed
becomes a living metonym of the presence of Christ in the midst of the
world.

What a strange thing, though, to represent one's majesty and reign
not with a sovereign's scepter (or even a moderator's gavel!) primarily, but
with the bread and wine of common folk! How odd to break the bread of
the presence and pour out the cup, and share them with all who belong to
Christ, without regard to rank or station or intellect, as though he who sat
at the "right hand of power" governed the church, "his body,"[37] not with
a show of strength, but in humility, not as some Napoleon wading through
blood to dominance, but as a suffering servant: "he had no form or
majesty that we should look at him, nothing in his appearance that we
should desire him" (Isa. 53:2b). How peculiar that his people, "baptized
into his death" (Rom. 6:3), should eat this bread and drink this cup with
thanksgiving and even joyful anticipation! As though women and men,
the circling planets, the countless galaxies, had no other future except the
one he brings! Not one of the ages measured by human achievement, past
or present, has believed it. Always there have been those who would take
by force what is given to them. "From the days of John the Baptist until
now the kingdom of heaven has suffered violence . . ." (Matt. 11:12a),
Jesus said. Well might he say it, given what was in store for him! Helmut
Thielicke has painted the scene vividly, unsparingly:

> So all the defenselessness of God's Son and his grace is a prophecy
> . . . for the open Lordship of God, which here has only begun, and is

---

36. *The Book of Common Worship,* p. 38. Italics mine.
37. See esp. 1 Cor. 12:12-31 and Eph. 4:1-16.

only secretly present, while he waits at the back door of the world as a scorned Lazarus, because the rich lord in the house does not want him to pass his threshold. It waits and trembles in secret power; for all belongs to it. It has trickled already through the framework of the house; and a tremor as of abysmal powers shakes the pillars and facades again and again. But the rich man thinks that it is the stamping of his mighty foot that does this. And he lays costly carpets on the stone, so that the growling of the depths no longer disturbs him.[38]

In communion, as living metonym of the reign of Christ, the church bears witness to all that. St. Paul captured the thought in a single sentence: "For as often as you eat this bread and drink the cup, *you proclaim (or declare, kataggéllō) the Lord's death until he comes*" (1 Cor. 11:26).

However, what the *laos* (the laity, the people of God) proclaim as, at table, they eat the bread and drink the cup of remembrance and anticipation, is that gospel which already has been proclaimed to them from the pulpit. If the saying is true — and it surely is — that "you cannot give what you haven't got," it also is surely true that you cannot proclaim what you have not heard. Saint Paul stated the issue plainly:

[H]ow are they to believe in one of whom they have never heard? And how are they to hear without someone to proclaim him? And how are they to proclaim him unless they are sent? (Rom. 10:14b-15a)

Paul, of course, understood himself to have been sent: "a servant of Jesus Christ, called to be an apostle, set apart for the gospel of God" (Rom. 1:1). Paul was to proclaim (or herald, *kērússo*, Rom. 10:14) the gospel (or evangel, *euaggélion*, Rom. 1:1). Clearly Thomas G. Long is correct when he observes that preachers do not come into the church out of the blue, from some exalted place apart, from some venue of privileged *gnōsis* (or special, secretive knowledge) concerning deity. Preachers come from the church itself, from among the *laos* of God, out of the pew, into the pulpit.[39] On the other hand, what preachers preach does not come from the people. Nor does it come from preachers themselves. What preachers preach comes from God via the apostolic testimony of servants of Jesus Christ who, like Paul, have been appointed by Christ to bear witness to all that

38. Thielicke, p. 74.
39. Thomas G. Long, *The Witness of Preaching* (Louisville, KY: Westminster/John Knox Press, 1989), pp. 10-11.

they have learned and received and heard and seen in him. Those who receive the gospel of God from the apostles, then, receive it from him who sent them. Further, as in their own preaching they strive to be faithful to the apostolic testimony, Jesus, who once "came . . . proclaiming the good news of God" (Mark 1:14), proclaims it again. James F. Kay, in his important study, *Christus Praesens* (a treatment of Rudolf Bultmann's Christology), put it clearly and succinctly:

> Jesus Christ . . . is not simply the object of discourse, but, rather, the essential agent of proclamation. Only his presence as the proclaimer enables a creaturely word to become kerygmatic. Christ himself, as the One in whom God acts, is the eschatological condition, the saving content of the kerygmatic occasion.[40]

What the apostles learned and received and heard and saw in Christ, however, has been made available to the whole church, and not to preachers alone, in the Holy Scriptures. The Scriptures, of course, include the books of the Old Testament as well as the New, for Jesus explicitly indicated that to understand who he was and to appropriately interpret his mission, people had to begin "with Moses and all the prophets . . ." (Luke 24:27a), as he himself did. The proclamation of the gospel cannot commence with the preaching of sermons, therefore. Instead it must commence with the public reading of the Scriptures upon which those sermons are based. It is the Scriptures, after all, that provide us with the testimony of those appointed by Christ to herald his presence, purpose, and power among us. As the bread and the cup serve metonymically to draw attention to the real presence of Christ in communion, so the Holy Scriptures of the Old and New Testaments, by inspiration of the Holy Spirit, direct the hearts and minds of the faithful to Christ Jesus who alone "is the one Word of God which we have to hear and which we have to trust and obey in life and in death."[41] God in Christ, by the power of the Holy Spirit, and with the words of Scripture, speaks today, as always, in command and succor, in holiness, justice, and compassion. "Let anyone with ears listen" (Matt. 13:43b)! Therefore, before the reading of the Scriptures and the preaching of sermons we can say, and we *do* say: "Hear the word of God!"

40. James F. Kay, *Christus Praesens: A Reconsideration of Rudolf Bultmann's Christology* (Grand Rapids, MI: Wm. B. Eerdmans Publishing Co., 1994), p. 114.
41. "The Theological Declaration of Barmen," *The Book of Confessions,* C.8.11.

We have explored the topic of the real presence and power of Christ in the public reading of the Scriptures and in preaching with reference to three rhetorical tropes or figures of speech: oxymoron, metaphor, and metonymy. Oxymoron is a linguistic, vocal, and physical gesture given in response to an event of divine self-disclosure when that event seems to disconfirm previous experience of the divine. Yet we bring that incongruous moment of revelation into the history of inter-pretation of human experience of God through metaphorical accounts of similarity in difference. Revelation thus evokes within us awareness of God's distance from us and nearness to us, God's accessibility to us and hiddenness from us, God's coming and God's going, God's speech and God's silence. The history of revelation, therefore, is marked by episodes of continuity and discontinuity. There is sufficient continuity to enable us to speak to each other about God and to have some idea of what we are talking about when we do. But there is sufficient dis-continuity to keep us aware of the fact that we can never sum it all up. "*Deus cognitus, Deus nullus,*" said H. H. Farmer.[42] A God comprehended is no God, and the theology that pretends to know everything is a sham. Further, revelation is a felt action upon and within us mediated by human speech. It is a statement made. It is a story told. It is a poem sung. God in Christ, through the agency of the Holy Spirit, with the words of Scripture, and by means of duly called and installed ministers of word and sacrament,[43] gives the church something to believe and to do and to say. God forms and reforms the church so that — despite its weakness, its brokenness, and even its little faith — it may effectively bear witness to the love and justice of God in the midst of the world.[44]

42. H. H. Farmer, *The Servant of the Word* (Philadelphia: Fortress Press, 1964), p. 63.

43. See "The Second Helvetic Confession," *The Book of Confessions,* C.5.004. The point is that preachers are not self-appointed, but appointed by God via the voice of the church.

44. *The Book of Order,* Presbyterian Church (U.S.A.), G.18.0100, has this state-ment: "The Presbyterian Church (U.S.A.) would be faithful to the Lordship of Christ and to its historic tradition of the Church reformed always reforming, by the Spirit of God." Yet, in fact, it would seem more true to the Reformed tradition to say that the church reformed must always be reformed according to the Word of God. The initiating agent in reform is God in Christ as he is attested in Holy Scripture. The Holy Spirit directs us to Christ as the one who reforms the church. It does not direct our attention, at least in the first instance, to the preachers and ordered bodies through which Christ reforms his church. The Scriptures thus are kept central to reform and, through properly

The hearts and minds of congregants are directed to this presence, power, and action of God in Christ *via* the metonymic function of the Scriptures in preaching and the elements of bread and wine in communion. God, that is to say, in total freedom, but nevertheless in fidelity to his own promise, uses these "ordinary means" of grace to prosecute his will. Gardner Taylor, for decades African American preacher laureate of the church, summed up the gospel in these words: "God is out to get back what belongs to him."[45] The figures of speech just discussed, oxymoron, metaphor, and metonymy, give us a way to say that God is still at it.

To my mind, these figures of speech also give us a way 'round the conflict of so-called theologies from above (e.g., Barth) and theologies from below (e.g., Schleiermacher).[46] They do this by providing us with a way to speak of objective revelation (revelation "out there") and subjective revelation (revelation "in here," i.e., in human experience) in terms of one historical, yet always contemporaneous, normative reality, which is Jesus Christ as he is attested for us in Holy Scripture. Objectively we are addressed by God and claimed by God in Jesus Christ from *without.* Subjectively we appropriate that address and claim through an act of faith, which is the work of God's own Spirit *within* us.

> When we cry, "Abba! Father!" it is that very Spirit bearing witness with our spirit that we are children of God, and if children, then heirs, heirs of God and joint heirs with Christ — if, in fact, we suffer with him so that we may be glorified with him. (Rom. 8:15b-16)

Here there is no subject/object split.[47] Yet here, also, there is no collapse of the one into the other so that everything is either sheer

---

adjudicated interpretations, function as a means of discernment concerning what is and what is not of the Spirit of Christ: *ecclesìa reformata, semper reformanda, secundum verbum Dei,* "the church reformed must always be reformed according to the Word of God." See Edward A. Dowey, "The Reforming Tradition: Presbyterians and Mainstream Protestantism: A Review," *The Princeton Seminary Bulletin* 14 (1993): p. 9.

45. Gardner C. Taylor, "The Sweet Torture of Sunday Morning," *Leadership* 3, no. 3 (Summer 1991): p. 20.

46. See Karl Barth, *The Humanity of God* (Richmond, VA.: John Knox Press, 1960), pp. 11-33 and 37-65.

47. See Joseph Sittler, *Essays on Nature and Grace* (Philadelphia: Fortress Press, 1972), pp. 1-50.

objectivity or sheer subjectivity. Here, instead, we know ourselves known of God in ways that go clear beyond our understanding in the very same instant (and by the very same means) that we know the divine reality itself intimately as the Heart of our hearts, as the Soul of our souls, as the Strength of our strength, as the Mind of our minds. We know God in our neighbor too, and our neighbor knows God in us. Yet neither we nor our neighbors know ourselves *as* God. We are only *human* beings, and even what that means is unclear to us except as we see what it means to God in him who is the accommodation of God's own majesty to our poor necessity. Said St. Paul — or did he sing it?

> Let the same mind be in you that was in Christ Jesus,
> who, though he was in the form of God,
>> did not regard equality with God
>> as something to be exploited,
> but emptied himself,
>> taking the form of a slave,
>> being born in human likeness.
> And being found in human form,
>> he humbled himself
>> and became obedient to the point of death —
>> even death on a cross.
>
> Therefore God also highly exalted him
>> and gave him the name
>> that is above every name,
> so that at the name of Jesus
>> every knee should bend
> in heaven and on earth and under the earth,
> and every tongue should confess
>> that Jesus Christ is Lord,
>> to the glory of God the Father. (Phil. 2:5-11)

There you have no "ruthlessly unennobled view of human nature."[48] There you have human nature divinely conceived, divinely lived, divinely commended to us. Why the music? Because a flattened literalism alone can never say what needs to be said. We speak in figures because what has been revealed to us from without, and yet simul-

---

48. Lance Morrow, "Fifteen Cheers for Abstinence," *Time*, Oct. 2, 1995, p. 90.

taneously within, requires it. We sing even because we truly know more than we can say.[49] We cannot measure up to the task of putting it all in straightforward prose. In fact all our gestures in figures of speech fall wide of the mark, and our music too must fail at last. Barth was right: we only can "attempt"[50] to preach. Yet we press on, we keep up the attempt —

> by the love impell'd,
> that moves the sun in Heaven and all the stars.[51]

When we say, "Hear the word of God," and then proceed to the public reading of the Scriptures and to preaching, all that is at stake — or there is nothing at stake at all.

49. Michael Polanyi, *The Tacit Dimension* (Garden City, NY: Doubleday and Co. [Anchor Books], 1967), p. 4. For an exposition of Polanyi's thought stressing its import for theology and proclamation, see: John V. Apczynski, *Doers of the Word*, Dissertation Series 18 (Missoula, MT: Scholars Press, 1977).

50. Karl Barth, *Homiletics* (Louisville, KY: Westminster/John Knox Press, 1991), pp. 43-44. Definition 2, p. 44, reads: "Preaching is the attempt enjoined upon the church to serve God's own Word, through one who is called thereto, by expounding a biblical text in human words and making it relevant to contemporaries in intimation of what they have to hear from God himself."

51. Dante Alighieri, *The Divine Comedy*, canto XIII, ln. 129.

2. A Gospel for "Interesting Times"

IN THE PREVIOUS CHAPTER an attempt was made to show how the Bible speaks of human bafflement before God's self-disclosure and self-attestation in history, among the people of God and, most especially, in Jesus Christ, God's Word made flesh. Prototypically[1] this bafflement, and what causes it, is indicated by oxymoronic signs and statements: a bush on fire that does not burn up, a sound of sheer silence, a virgin mother, a foolishness wiser than any human wisdom, a strength made perfect in weakness. An attempt also was made to show how the Bible records efforts to make sense of these discontinuities in human experience of God. So Jesus, again prototypically, gives account of the incommensurable through metaphors that provide a shock of recognition and not just a shock: "The kingdom of heaven is like treasure hidden in a field" (Matt.

---

1. Prototype here refers both to the content of biblical figures of speech and to their appointment as loci for constructive Christian thought regarding deity. In a word, the figures are instanced by revelation itself and are appointed, by the One disclosed with them, to define human beings in relationship to Godself. They are not primitive models of speech to be dispensed with. They are definitive models. All subsequent speech concerning God thus is to be conformed to them in their plural specificity. Even discursive speech concerning God, speech not self-consciously and patently figurative, must be held accountable to these divinely appointed figurations. So Colin Gunton observes: "At the heart of the modern rediscovery of metaphor is the recognition that the difference between the literal and the metaphorical is a matter of usage, not reference." Colin Gunton, "Proteus and Procrustes," in *Speaking the Christian God: The Holy Trinity and the Challenge of Feminism*, ed. Alvin F. Kimel, Jr. (Grand Rapids, MI: William B. Eerdmans Publishing Co., 1992), p. 71.

13:44), or "Again, the kingdom of heaven is like a merchant in search of fine pearls" (Matt. 13:45), or yet again, "the kingdom of heaven is like a net that was thrown into the sea" (Matt. 13:47).[2] Not least of all an attempt was made to show how the scriptural witness as a whole, not because of its intrinsic merit or immanent powers, but because of divine appointment, metonymically signals the contemporaneous presence, self-disclosure, and self-attestation of God. As the Bible is read aloud in worship and as sermons are preached that seek, however falteringly, to follow the lead of the prophetic and apostolic testimony, God, in Christ, through the agency of the Holy Spirit, speaks to those with "ears to hear," forming and reforming them as a people of God, the church.[3] Just so is the Bible God's word to us, and just so may we say that "the preaching of the Word of God *is* the Word of God."[4] This matter warrants further elucidation, and so we proceed to it.

Already it has been noted that the Word of God is not *verbum* but *sermo*, not *ratio* but *oratio*. It is lively, face to face, aural-oral discourse and suasory action. It is not a "morph" (a minimum unit of meaning in a linguistic system, e.g., a word), nor is it reason alone (though there is no need to think of it as utterly unreasonable and simply emotive). It is intentional and artful, poetic, crafting for itself a work, a dramatic narrative, a story.[5] It is *actio divina*, God's self-performance, and, as

---

2. Gaventa points out that there is much debate about *how* metaphor influences cognition, but that there is virtually no debate about the fact that it *does* influence cognition. It forces us to look at things differently; it invites our participation in a strange structuring of the familiar or in a familiar structuring of the strange. In so doing it rearranges the furniture of the mind. Beverly Roberts Gaventa, "Our Mother St. Paul: Toward the Recovery of a Neglected Theme," *Princeton Seminary Bulletin* 17, no. 1 (Feb. 1996): pp. 29-57. Technically the "is like" phrase indicates *simile;* simile in effect, however, is indistinguishable from metaphor and so may be thought of as a type of metaphorical construction.

3. Wilson states: "God initiates relationship and restores identity through preaching. The sermon offers love for the unloved, and justice for the downtrodden — in other words, God acts in and through preaching. We begin to conceive of the sermon as an intimate and personal event in a communal context with community-shaping power. It is God's salvation breaking into the world." Paul Scott Wilson, *The Practice of Preaching* (Nashville, TN: Abingdon Press, 1995), p. 23.

4. "The Second Helvetic Confession," *The Book of Confessions* (Louisville, KY: Presbyterian Church [U.S.A.], 1994), C.5.004, pp. 55-56.

5. James A. Sanders, *God Has a Story Too: Sermons in Context* (Philadelphia: Fortress Press, 1979). For Sanders the Bible especially celebrates the theological maxim

such, it deploys language and languages, silence and sound, stillness and gesture, anything — even nothing — to its own ends. It is at no one's disposal. Instead, all persons, all things, all cultures, all systems of common life and governance, all events, all times, and all places are at its disposal.[6] It is infinite; it is eternal. "In the beginning was the Word and the Word was with God and the *Word* was God" (John 1:1).[7] The Word was not less than God, or other than God, or a mere faculty of God. It was — and is — "very God of very God."[8] And, "when the fullness of time had come" (Gal. 4:4), the Word "became flesh and lived among us" (John 1:14).

It could be construed as an embarrassment: the particularity of Israel, the particularity of Jesus, the appointment of apostles, and the cultural borrowing done by the God and Father of our Lord Jesus Christ to make the divine self known among us.[9] However, if God is one, and if the God, who is one, alone is to be acknowledged as God (as the *Shema* expresses it) then the logic of self-disclosure, of self-attestation, and self-performance (i.e., *actio divina*) warrants our overcoming the embarrassment we may have concerning the aforementioned particularities. Let us dare to think of it in human terms. How does our friend and colleague Sally define herself, make herself known, if not through her relationships to — yet differentiation within — the circumstances, events, and human communities with which she is involved?[10] Sally has parents and siblings. She loves them. In fact she refuses even to imagine life without them. But Sally is not her parents, and she is not her siblings. Furthermore days come when she needs to let them know that. Motherly love turns to maternalism, fatherly love to paternalism, and the affection of brothers and sisters is tainted with rivalries unsought and unavoidable. At such times, since she has gumption, Sally stands up for

---

"*errore hominum providentia divina*": "God's providence works in and through human error and sin." See p. 23.

6. See C. H. Dodd, *The Apostolic Preaching and Its Developments* (London: Hodder and Stoughton, 1936), p. 96.

7. Emphasis mine.

8. "The Nicene Creed," *The Book of Confessions*, C.1.2, p. 3.

9. For a discussion of the dangers inherent in eschewing the particularity of revelation, see Blanche A. Jenson, "The Movement and the Story: Whatever Happened to 'Her'?" in Kimel, pp. 282-85.

10. Carol Simpson Stern and Bruce Henderson, *Performance: Texts and Contexts* (New York: Longman, 1993), pp. 253-316.

herself against her parents, against her siblings. But her being against them is the only way she really can be *for* them, for if she was daughter to them and sister to them exclusively on their terms, what they would end up having would not be Sally at all, but somebody else, another Sally, the invention of their own wants and needs, a cipher for their own purposes.[11] Those of us who are Sally's friends and colleagues may feel the sting of her being for us and against us at the same time too. And we may say: "Sally's not herself today!" But, of course, Sally is precisely herself, though we may be rather shocked at our "never really having known her before." Perhaps we even are daunted by the mystery left in her when all along we thought we knew her completely, "had her pegged" so to speak. From now on we will keep it in mind that Sally is more "her own person" than we ever thought. By word, by deed, for us and yet against us (perhaps even in contradiction of her own sense of herself),[12] she has performed herself, "come through"[13] to us truly, named herself. She is *this particular Sally* and no other. She is not simply the daughter of Maxine and Carl, not just the sister of Peg and David, not just "good old Sally," our friend and colleague. She is Sally "in her own right," Sally herself.

No attempt will be made to draw a direct analogy between Sally's self-performance and what I have called *actio divina*, God's self-perfor-mance. For one thing, to speak of God, as Barth noted, is not simply to speak about humanity in a loud voice.[14] God is wholly other than humanity and entirely different from what human beings might con-ceive divinity to be.

11. Contrast this view of persons in relationship to one another with Farmer's view of speech as an event in which self-conscious, self-directing wills condition one another through claim and shared meaning and so relate to each other with integrity. H. H. Farmer, *The Servant of the Word* (Philadelphia: Fortress Press, 1964), pp. 26-30.

12. Bonhoeffer asserts that, for the self, as known to itself, "Who am I?" remains a question, and, whatever sense of self one has, is a gift of God: "Whoever I am, thou knowest, O God, I am Thine!" Dietrich Bonhoeffer, *Letters and Papers from Prison* (New York: Macmillan, 1953), p. 222.

13. Performance may be defined as "form coming through." See Richard F. Ward, *Speaking from the Heart: Preaching with Passion* (Nashville: Abingdon Press, 1992), p. 77. See also Victor Turner, *From Ritual to Theatre: The Human Seriousness of Play* (New York: PAJ Publications, 1982), p. 13.

14. Daniel L. Migliore, *Called to Freedom: Liberation Theology and the Future of Christian Doctrine* (Philadelphia: Westminster Press, 1980), p. 68.

For my thoughts are not your thoughts,
    nor are your ways my ways, says the LORD.
For as the heavens are higher than the earth,
    so are my ways higher than your ways
    and my thoughts than your thoughts. (Isa. 55:8-9)[15]

For another thing, divinity has total freedom to act as itself, to disclose itself, to name itself, whereas human beings such as Sally, her family, her friends, and her colleagues, have only limited freedom to do so. Notice that Sally *must* "perform herself" at times in contradiction to her parents', her siblings', and others' expectations. In fact, to come to grips with all she may be and become, Sally may have to act in ways out of keeping with her own expectations concerning herself. Her relationships, as they bear upon self-definition, are not all freely chosen. Some are simply given. And her self is not a continuing possession of hers, but is, instead, something realized in and through acts that she performs in relation to others and in relation to her own (often less than fully comprehended) possibilities. In other words Sally is not a fixed but an enacted and becoming person. Her self, furthermore, is as much received as attained, and it consequently may be thought of as a gift no less than as an accomplishment. At times even Sally may say, "I'm just not myself today." But others already have learned what she later may come to know, namely, that at such times, she is more herself than she could have imagined.

Divine reality, on the other hand, is free in itself to be itself. It is perfect: a whole, complete, uncreated community of being,[16] Father, Son, and Holy Spirit, not needing, yet freely choosing — and so conditioning its own life by — relationships with other, created, not perfect, not whole, not complete communities of *human* being composed of people like Sally and her parents and her siblings, as well as Sally's friends and colleagues. It is not human beings who create God in their own image. Just the opposite is in fact the case. The "divine community,"

15. Especially the biblical word concerning the transcendent otherness of God's thought emphasizes grace; e.g., Hosea 11:1-8, a lament of God over his wayward people, and Romans 1:16-32, where "the gospel that reveals God's righteousness and wrath is also God's power of salvation." Charles L. Bartow, "Speaking the Text and Preaching the Gospel," in *Homosexuality and the Christian Community,* ed. Choon-Leong Seow (Louisville, KY: Westminster/John Knox Press, 1996), p. 95.
    16. Migliore, pp. 72-77.

God the Father, Son, and Holy Spirit, creates humanity in *its* own image, though there are those who apparently would not have it so. For instance, Miriam Therese Winter, in a sermon entitled "I AM Has Sent Me To You," seeks to convince us that Yahweh (the great I Am) gave Moses (and the rest of us) *carte blanche* to name divine reality in any way agreeable to us. Proclaims Winter:

> Names define and, by definition, limit, but I Am is infinite, not only in reality, but also in name. I Am is without limits, but not absolutely beyond them, for the name invites participation. . . . Our naming of I Am is never exhausted, for the fullness of I Am always dances beyond our comprehension. Indeed, the name "I Am Who I Am" is also translated as "I Will Be What I Will Be." There is always infinitely more to God than we can ever grasp, so why are we so hesitant to name and rename? . . .
>
> How gracious of God not to impose a limited or limiting name. God seems to be saying, "You fill in the blanks. Whoever you think I Am, I Am. . . .
>
> Whoever we need God to be *for* us, however we need God to be *with* us, God will be "for" and "with" us. . . . From our own experience we lift up, not idols, but icons that plant us on holy ground and have the capacity to facilitate our encounter with the living God.[17]

But Moses did not plant the bush that burned but was not burned up. He came upon it — or was led to it. And he did not receive permission to name God however he might for himself and for captive Israel. Quite to the contrary, he was instructed, when asked to name God, to repeat what he had been told, "I AM has sent me to you" (Exod. 3:14) — not Baal, not Astaroth,[18] and not "the queen of heaven" (Jer. 7:18; 44:15-28), but the One who would name and define himself as circumstance required. So Jesus said, "I am the bread of life" (John 6:48), "I

17. Miriam Therese Winter, "I AM Has Sent Me to You," *Princeton Seminary Bulletin* 16, no. 2 (1995): pp. 218-20.
18. Astaroth is a general designation for the female gods of the Canaanites. John D. Davis and Henry Snyder Gehman, *The Westminster Dictionary of the Bible* (Philadelphia: Westminster Press, 1944), p. 46. Note that in Genesis humanity got to name everything *except* God. For a discussion of early Israel's worship in relation to not bringing God under human control, see Israel Knohl, "Between Voice and Silence: The Relationship Between Prayer and Temple Cult," *Journal of Biblical Literature* 115, no. 1 (1996): pp. 17-30.

am the way, the truth and the life" (John 14:6a), "I am with you always, to the end of the age" (Matt. 28:20), indicating that in himself — and not elsewhere — could be found the fullness of the unsearchable God. Back in Moses' time, and earlier, to have a god's name was to have that god's power ready for one's own use. No wonder Jacob pleaded with his divine wrestling mate there at the ford of the Jabbock, "Please tell me your name" (Gen. 32:27). The great supplanter was always after power, wherever he could get it. To have a god, and especially *the* God, at one's beck and call, to name God however one might wish, to get God at one's disposal in a way that Sally, bless her heart, would let none of her friends or relations get her at their disposal, who could ask for anything more? No, for Israel, the name of the Holy One at last became the unpronounceable name, and the presence of I Am the presence of promise and not the presence of command performance. Jesus, with his disciples, kept the initiative with God even when he asked his disciples, "Who do you say that I am?" (Matt. 16:15). Contrary to Winter's assertion that "who do you say that I am" means whatever one might want it to mean,[19] Jesus affirmed only the response of Peter, "You are the Messiah, the Son of the living God" (Matt. 16:16). Further, Jesus' affirmation of Peter's naming of him was expressed this way: "Blessed are you, Simon son of Jonah! *For flesh and blood has not revealed this to you, but my Father in heaven*" (Matt. 16:17).[20] To the extent that Winter is asserting everybody's — and especially women's — right to identify their own unique and personal way of construing their *experience* of God, of course, she is on target. Who could identify our personal construal of inner experience of God if not we ourselves? To Moses and Israel *I Am Who I Am* meant "Deliverer." To Pharaoh *I Am Who I Am*, one can dare to conjecture, meant "Terror." But to name our experience is not to name God. Furthermore, our self-identified personal experience of God must be assessed in the light of *actio divina* as the Scriptures bear witness to it. If to Pharaoh the name of his experience of God was terror, that much he got right, but he got everything else wrong. Par-

19. Winter, p. 218.
20. Italics mine. On the right of divinity alone to name itself, see Janet Martin Soskice, "Can a Feminist Call God 'Father'?" in Kimel, pp. 88-93. Soskice further argues that it is precisely God's self-naming as "Father" in relation to Jesus Christ, the "Son," that undermines patriarchy.

ticularly he failed to recognize that God was naming Godself by word and deed with Moses' speech and action, and he paid the price.

The name of God — who God will be, what God will be, with us, for us, against us — comes not from our experience but into it. For example, when Joseph learned that his betrothed was with child "from the Holy Spirit" (Matt. 1:18d), the angel in his dream said to him, "you are to name him Jesus, for he will save his people from their sins" (Matt. 1:21b). God's self-performance, as we have called it, makes use of our language, our experience, our concepts, even our names. It will be recalled from chapter 1 that the name Jesus once upon a time was about as common a name as could be found. But God's self-performance is not determined by the purposes to which we put language, experience, and conceptualization. Instead, God's self-performance is determined by God's own purposes. Upon God's lips, as it were, our names assume a significance even for us that we could not dream of, and our languages, experiences, and concepts are put to uses we could never intend. The specificity of revelation thus is a function of revelation itself. It is not a function of any human determination — much less competence — to limit God. That specificity or particularity, in any case, sets no limit to how divinity has or will name itself among us. Quite to the contrary, it indicates God's freedom in self-disclosure and God's capacity to limit what we may say and do in the divine name. It keeps us humble, dependent upon God's Word, God's human speech, and not upon our own. And it keeps us from taking the name of the Lord our God in vain.[21] Karl Barth stated it well:

> That is the Word of God: the work of God upon us: for us and therefore against us: the work of the kindness which we cannot grasp, which we have outraged, which does good to us, as to those who always do evil. Where it is heard as such, there is still an active will to assert and help ourselves, to maintain and justify and advertise ourselves, but it has been fundamentally broken and its vital power is destroyed. At any rate it cannot exist in face of the Word of God — so that fundamentally it cannot exist at all. It can exist only as and

21. Exod. 20:7; Deut. 5:11. "God swears by his great name to carry out his purpose" (Jer. 44:26), that is, he swears by his attested power to accomplish his word. To know the name of God is to witness the manifestation of those attributes and apprehend that character which the name denotes (cf. Exod. 6:3 with v. 7; 1 Kings 8:43; Ps. 91:14; Isa. 52:6; 64:2; Jer. 16:21). Davis and Gehman, p. 415.

to the extent that we exist under the Word. If that means humiliation, it also means comfort. If it means limitation, it also means liberation. If it means law, it also means gospel.[22]

God's name, which is defined by the operations of God's might in making and keeping promises, receives its fullest expression in him who is given "the name that is above every name" (Phil. 2:9b). In Jesus, that is, we come to know God not just as the Father of Israel, but as "our Father," whom we may approach as children approach their mother (Isa. 66:13; Matt. 23:37; Luke 13:34)[23] or their father. And in him we know ourselves as women and men called out of slavery into friendship with God (John 15:15). Further, as we do the will of the One who sent him, Jesus calls us his "brother and sister and mother" (Mark 3:35). Beyond that, as Beverly Roberts Gaventa has pointed out, St. Paul, "called to be an apostle, set apart for the gospel of God" (Rom. 1:1b), apparently caring not a whit what might be thought of him, broke through culturally mandated gender roles, and depicted himself (and sometimes his coworkers) in maternal terms:

> But we were gentle among you, like a nurse caring for her own children. (1 Thess. 2:7)

> And so, brothers and sisters, I could not speak to you as spiritual people, but rather as people of the flesh, as infants in Christ. I fed you with milk, not solid food, for you were not ready for solid food. (1 Cor. 3:1-2)

> My little children, for whom I am again in the pain of childbirth until Christ is formed in you . . . (Gal. 4:19).[24]

Gaventa also has brought to our attention the fact that Paul uses maternal imagery to speak of the eschaton when, "at the name of Jesus

---

22. Karl Barth, *Church Dogmatics* I/2, trans. G. T. Thomson and Harold Knight (Edinburgh: T. & T. Clark, 1956), p. 278.

23. In the Isaiah passage the metaphor of "mother" is used of both a restored Jerusalem and God. In Matthew and Luke the irony is that Jesus would have the people of Jerusalem come to him as chicks to a mother hen; but the people would not come. God's name is "Father," but the Father and the Son both depict the steadfast love of the triune God as an act of mothering.

24. Gaventa, pp. 30-31.

every knee should bend, in heaven and on earth and under the earth, and every tongue should confess that Jesus Christ is Lord, to the glory of God the Father" (Phil. 2:10-11).

> When they say, "There is peace and security," then sudden destruction will come upon them, as labor pains come upon a pregnant woman, and there will be no escape. (1 Thess. 5:3)

> We know that the whole creation has been groaning in labor pains until now. (Rom. 8:22)[25]

So, in the eleventh century, Anselm of Canterbury could write of Paul:

> O St. Paul, where is he that was called the nurse of the faithful,
>   caressing his sons?
> Who is that affectionate mother who declares everywhere
>   that she is in labor for her sons?
> Sweet nurse, sweet mother,
> Who are the sons you are in labor with, and nurse,
> but those whom by teaching the faith of Christ
>   you bear and instruct?
> Or who is a Christian after your teaching
>   who is not born into the faith and established in it by you?
> And if in that blessed faith we are born and nursed
>   by other apostles also,
> it is most of all by you,
> for you have labored and done more than them all in this;
> so if they are our mothers, you are our greatest mother.[26]

In light of all this, could the case be made that the specificity, the particularity of *actio divina*, and the givenness of the oxymoronic, metaphoric, and metonymic figures that attend God's self-disclosure and self-attestation in Jesus Christ (as the sacred Scriptures bear witness to him through the action of the Holy Spirit) should be thought of as a source of celebration instead of embarrassment? This writer thinks so, for God's self-figuration in holy writ, through appointed witnesses, refigures human possibilities in such a fecund way

---

25. Gaventa, p. 31

26. *The Prayers and Meditations of St. Anselm*, trans. Benedicta Ward (London: Penguin, 1973), p. 152. Quoted in Gaventa, p. 27.

that none of us need any longer think of ourselves less highly than
we ought — or *more* highly than we ought (Rom. 12:3)! Humanity's
giving up of any license to imagine God out of its own resources frees
it to think God's thoughts after God and to come to grips with God's
amazing imaging of women and men as children of one divine parent;
parents, siblings, and friends of Christ; brothers, mothers, fathers,
sons, and daughters of each other. The obedience of Christ for which
we are captured in the proclamation of the gospel thus is an obedience
of liberation. Because of it we can consider ourselves "dead to sin and
alive to God in Christ Jesus" (Rom. 6:11). Ralph Waldo Emerson once
boasted: "His own Culture, the unfolding of his nature, is the chief
end of man."[27] *The Shorter Catechism*, on the other hand, had this to
say: "What is the chief end of [humanity]? [Humanity's] chief end is
to glorify God, and to enjoy [God] forever."[28] Somehow, to this writer,
and no doubt to others as well, *The Shorter Catechism*, St. Anselm,
and St. Paul, unembarrassed by what some may regard as the crude
particularity of the gospel, seem to have chosen the better part. The
richer pluralism of figuration lies with *actio divina*, the self-
performance of divinity, and with God's creation of humanity in the
divine likeness. It does not lie with humanity's self-invention and with
its construal of God in the image of the human. So John Goldingay
observed:

> I once thought that the preachers' job was . . . to create new symbols
> [to bring] everyday life and the gospel together in our culture. I now
> doubt whether this can be done. . . .[29]

Looked upon as God's self-attestation, then, pluralism in revelation is as limitless as God's own eternal Word is protean in its power to
accommodate itself to humanity's poor necessity. By it the God of the
Old Testament and of the New, the God of the prophets and the apostles,
the God and Father of our Lord Jesus Christ, discloses who he is and
what he expects of humanity and of the rest of creation. Furthermore,

27. Lloyd Rohler, *Ralph Waldo Emerson: Preacher and Lecturer* (Westport, CT:
Greenwood Press, 1995), p. 30.
28. "The Shorter Catechism," *The Constitution of the Presbyterian Church (U.S.A.)*
(Louisville, KY: Presbyterian Church [U.S.A.], 1994), C.7.001, p. 181.
29. John Goldingay, *Models for Interpretation of Scripture* (Grand Rapids, MI:
William B. Eerdmans Publishing Co., 1995), p. 282.

in Jesus Christ, by the power of the Holy Spirit, with the words of
Scripture, and with the faithful exposition (or opening up of the meaning) of those scriptural words in preaching, God does this specifically,
contextually, definitively — and not provisionally — in every epoch of
cosmic and human history, and among all sorts and conditions of
humanity,[30] that men and women of all times and places might hear
the Word that stands forever (Isa. 40:8), that justifies the ungodly (Rom.
5:6), that makes the earth an inheritance for the meek (Matt. 5:5), and
that turns the confession of the broken-hearted to eternal praise (Ps.
51:17):

> Glory be to the Father and to the Son and to the Holy Ghost; As it
> was in the beginning, is now, and ever shall be, world without end.
> Amen.

The plural self-attestation of God is self-limiting in this sense,
however, that it seeks our understanding and obedience, and we are
finite, not infinite, and our powers of imagination are grounded, cultured, embodied, and self-interested.[31] Even Garrett Green, who writes

30. Diogenes Allen, *Christian Belief in a Postmodern World: The Full Wealth of
Conviction* (Louisville, KY: Westminster/John Knox Press, 1989), pp. 9-19. Allen argues
that a postmodern (i.e., postfoundationalist) perspective does not require a collapse
into an uncritical pluralism and relativism. It does not require — or even allow — a
collapse into fideism either. It rather occasions responsible interpretation. What is being
argued in this chapter of mine is that pluralism in experience of God is grounded in
revelation itself understood as *actio divina*, and this plural self-disclosure of God, while
giving rise to provisional interpretations, itself is definitive. Thus people of faith may
have both assurance (through a reverence for the word) and conviction (reasoned
confidence): "That mind and soul, according well, May make one music as before."
Alfred Tennyson, 1850. See "Strong Son of God, Immortal Love" in *The Hymnbook*, ed.
David Hugh Jones (Philadelphia: John Ribble, 1955), p. 202, No. 228.
31. One of the strongest contributions of feminist interpretation of scripture to
hermeneutical theory, for example, is its demonstration of the socio-culturally condi-
tioned (and committed) stance of all interpretation, including the wide varieties in
feminist interpretation. Says Russell of feminist and liberation theologians: "Reading
the Bible from the perspective of the oppressed, they note the bias in all biblical interpretation and call for clear advocacy of those who are in the greatest need of God's
mercy and help: the dominated victims of society." Letty M. Russell, ed., *Feminist Interpretation of the Bible* (Philadelphia: Westminster Press, 1985), p. 12. Also, the literary
critic Wayne Booth demonstrates the plausibility, and sometimes mutually enriching
character, of different critical understandings of literary works due to critics' varied, and
perhaps even conflicting, purposes and methods. See Wayne C. Booth, *Critical Under-*

movingly and compellingly of people's imagination as the locus of divine self-disclosure,[32] notes the fragility of all human powers of figuration apart from the strength provided them by *actio divina* as the Scriptures bear witness to it.[33] Jesus' word to Peter therefore is his word to all who call him the Messiah, the Son of the living God: "Blessed are you . . . ! For flesh and blood has not revealed this to you, but my Father in heaven" (Matt. 16:17). Apart from the witness of holy Scripture and "the inward work of the Holy Spirit, bearing witness by and with the Word in our hearts,"[34] there is no hope of either understanding or obedience. The Word of God is free, and its imaginative use of human speech to express who God is and what God expects of those to whom he speaks is unfettered. But human beings are not free, and their imaginative use of language in service to divine truth is not unfettered, least of all when they most think so. The proverb "Pride goes before destruction, and a haughty spirit before a fall" (Prov. 16:18) is quite correct. Indeed, pride *is* the fall, and human beings are at no time more in danger of utter misunderstanding and disobedience than when they think themselves most competent to imagine God, to imagine God's will, to imagine God's church and God's kingdom, without each other, without the creeds and confessions of the church, without the public reading and corporate hearing of the Scriptures, without preaching, without the sacraments, without diligent use of the means

standing: The Powers and Limits of Pluralism (Chicago: University of Chicago Press, 1979), esp. chs. 3, 4, 5. The argument in this chapter, however, is that the scriptural witness itself has more power to disclose the full range of life at the margins of society — and of the gospel — than even feminist and liberationist hermeneutical theories. Also, while God indeed may be on the side of the poor and marginalized, God may not be there always *as the poor themselves suppose* (the definition of *holy* justice finally remains with the Word of God, not with the assumptions and methodologies of the Bible's interpreters, whatever their socio-cultural situatedness). Gustavo Gutiérrez said, "To know God is to do justice." *A Theology of Liberation* (Maryknoll, NY: Orbis Books, 1973), p. 194. But to do justice is *not* automatically to know God.

32. Garrett Green, *Imagining God: Theology and the Religious Imagination* (San Francisco: Harper and Row Publishers, 1989), esp. pp. 28-40.

33. Garrett Green, "The Gender of God and the Theology of Metaphor," in Kimel, pp. 44-63. Green argues against a "projectionist" theory of religion and the "role model" theology to which it leads. He includes a lengthy critique of Sallie McFague's *Metaphorical Theology* and *Models of God.*

34. "The Westminster Confession of Faith," *The Book of Confessions*, C.6.005, p. 12.

of grace, in a word, without God where and as he has made himself most clearly known.[35]

The divinely appointed plural witness to God's self-disclosure in Jesus Christ (specifically the prophetic and apostolic witness of Scripture) expects of us that we take it seriously[36] and seek to understand it *as the Holy Spirit speaks* in it.[37] The divine reality itself, that is to say,[38] directs our quest for understanding and obedience, for the words of Scripture are not unearthly and magical. They have not descended to us from heaven on angel's wings. They are not *seemingly* human, docetic. Instead, they are really human through and through. God picked the words of Scripture right off the streets of our often mean and mundane life. And God set them to divine purposes sometimes (perhaps *most* times) contrary to the intentions of those who first used them. In a provocative (and not uncontested) construal of the formation of the canon, Robert B. Coote and Mary P. Coote observe:

> Most significant for understanding the Bible, the cults of the rich and powerful had the skill of writing and produced Scriptures intended

---

35. See Avery Dulles, S.J., "The Symbolic Structure of Revelation," *Theological Studies* 41, no. 1 (March 1980): pp. 51-73.

36. To take the Bible seriously means to take it critically, but to take it, not reject it. To put it another way, we interpret Scripture even as Scripture interprets us. Further, the Bible in the mouth of God (that is, as it addresses us through the agency of the Holy Spirit) may surprise us as it interprets us, and it may do so with texts we might initially regard as not only strange, but irrelevant to the gospel of Christ and perhaps a threat to any redemptive view of that gospel. In a word, when Scripture seems least congenial to us, it may speak to us most profoundly and salvifically. To take the Bible uncritically, however, is not to take it seriously at all. It is to patronize it.

37. The Westminster divines said: "The Supreme Judge, by which all controversies of religion are to be determined, and all decrees of councils, opinions of ancient writers, doctrines of men, and private spirits, are to be examined, and in whose sentence we are to rest, can be no other but the Holy Spirit speaking in Scripture." "The Westminster Confession of Faith," *The Book of Confessions,* C.6.010, p. 128. Contrary to what D. Buttrick alleges, this is no static view of biblical authority or interpretation. Indeed it is quite dynamic and even vocal, focusing on the *Holy Spirit* who *speaks* in Holy Scripture. Surely if the Holy Spirit does not speak there (when and as it chooses and with what texts it will), it cannot be presumed to speak in contemporary human experience either to confirm the scriptural witness to Christ or to transform our understanding of it. See David Buttrick, *A Captive Voice: The Liberation of Preaching* (Louisville, KY: Westminster/John Knox Press, 1994), pp. 5-32, esp. p. 25.

38. See John 15:26.

to legitimate the institutions of state and temple. Because these Scriptures, like their strong and wealthy sponsors, made protection of the poor in theory an essential platform, declaring God's option for the poor, they could be turned against the rulers or institutions that commissioned them, or read with profit after their demise. As a result of such reversals, bouncing the Scriptures from rulers to ruled, we have the Bible.[39]

The Cootes further contend that while the New Testament writings have as their theological theme Christocentric[40] interpretation of the Old Testament,[41] their implicit legal theme as a collection is "the legitimacy of Roman jurisdiction."[42] One need not subscribe fully to what might be called the principle of social realism governing the Cootes' depiction of the formation of Scripture as canon. For instance, were the authors of Scripture *intent* on legitimating the reign of their regal sponsors, or was this more often than not simply the *effect* of their compositions? Also, if portions of the New Testament writings seem to legitimate Roman jurisdiction, other portions of it appear to call the exercise of Roman rule into question.[43] Despite such caveats, the Cootes call our attention to the fact that the contest of wills between God as God would be known and human beings as they would have God known (to their personal, political, social, and cultural advantage) was there from the beginning in the composition of the documents that make up the Bible and in the appointment of certain scriptural documents as canon, or formal rule for faith and life in the church.

As a result of all this, there are those who have come to practice

---

39. Robert B. Coote and Mary P. Coote, *Power, Politics and the Making of the Bible: An Introduction* (Minneapolis, MN: Fortress Press, 1990), p. 18.

40. Coote and Coote, p. 10.

41. I am using the terms "Old Testament" and "New Testament" for want of suitable alternatives. "Hebrew Bible" will not do unless we are prepared to call the New Testament the "Greek Bible." To call the New Testament the "Christian Bible" implies a Marcionite tendency. Some now use the terms "First Testament" and "Second Testament." This avoids making the Old Testament seem passé, but it does not quite eliminate the problem of apparent supersession.

42. Coote and Coote, p. 11.

43. See, for example, the introduction to the Revelation to John in *The New Oxford Annotated Bible with Apocrypha,* ed. Bruce M. Metzger and Roland E. Murphy (New York: Oxford University Press, 1991), p. 364.

what Leander E. Keck calls the hermeneutics of alienation.[44] The Bible
cannot be *for* us, they argue, or at least a good many of its texts cannot.
Therefore we need to silence Scripture (particularly where it speaks
with a voice that profoundly offends us) and look for God's self-
disclosure elsewhere: for example, in our quest for personal integrity
and group solidarity, liberation, and empowerment,[45] or in the advancement of science and technology,[46] or in ourselves as "new born
bard(s) of the Holy Ghost."[47] The gain for us all in such proposals, as
Goldingay has pointed out,[48] is that the proposals often powerfully
disclose to us how our readings of *actio divina,* as the Scriptures bear
witness to it, may be woefully inadequate or maybe even dangerous.
For instance, a feminist sorting out of text dealing with the fatherhood
of God may alert us to the fact that Jesus' calling God his father and
telling us to pray to God as "our Father" (Matt. 6:9b; Luke 11:2) does
not validate patriarchal hegemony in church leadership. Indeed, the
Holy Spirit, speaking in the Scriptures, directs our attention to Scripture's own controversy with itself in this matter.[49] To discern the

44. Leander E. Keck, *The Church Confident* (Nashville, TN: Abingdon Press,
1993), pp. 59-65.
45. For example, Fiorenza: "I would . . . suggest that the revelatory canon for
theological evaluation of biblical androcentric traditions and their subsequent interpretations cannot be derived from the Bible itself but can only be formulated in and
through women's struggle for liberation from all patriarchal oppression." Elisabeth
Schüssler Fiorenza, *In Memory of Her: A Feminist Theological Reconstruction of Christian
Origins* (New York: Crossroad Publishing Co., 1983), p. 32.
46. George Arthur Buttrick notes: "Auguste Comte, who is still quoted in our
humanisms, argued that we have progressed from religious mythology . . . , through the
abstractions of philosophy, to the certainties of logic and science. The fallacy in the
description is the word 'progressed.' Progressive shallowing is not progress; and we have no
right to assume, under euphoric words such as 'evolution' that flow of time necessarily
means enrichment of mind. For myself, I do not find in Buchenwald, or in the inanities of
our advertising, Exhibit A of an evolving nobility." Buttrick, "Dimension of Depth,"
Sermons Preached in a University Church (Nashville, TN: Abingdon Press, 1959), p. 204.
47. From Ralph Waldo Emerson, quoted in Jaroslav Pelikan, *The Melody of Theology: A Philosophical Dictionary* (Cambridge, MA: Harvard University Press, 1988), p. 69.
48. Goldingay, pp. 233-47, esp. p. 247.
49. Russell calls our attention to the tension in Pauline texts: "In Rom. 16:1,
Phoebe is called not only *diakonos* (minister, missionary, servant), but also *prostatis*
(leading officer, president, governor, superintendent)." Letty M. Russell, *Church in the
Round: Feminist Interpretation of the Church* (Louisville, KY: Westminster/John Knox
Press, 1993), p. 61.

"whole counsel of God"[50] regarding obedience therefore necessitates our being ready to hear challenges from within and from without the church that may cause us considerable disquiet. Yet more important, it also necessitates our grappling with biblical texts we may have avoided inadvertently or because they offended, or worse, terrified, us. Thus we may manage to escape a too hasty resolution in our own favor of the conflict of interpretations within the Bible.

The potential loss in such proposals, on the other hand, is that they may themselves lead to a domestication of the Spirit so that it can speak no contrary word. They also may encourage that embarrassment before the plural and crude particularity of *actio divina* that leads to inattention to it or rejection of it. It is worth remembering that lies can be put to the service of just causes and that truth can be put to the service of tyranny. Prayers, too, Kierkegaard somewhere has said, can be offered to an idol as to the true God and to the true God as to an idol. As Emerson has noted, let the one praying beware![51] What is a lie, is a lie, whatever happy ends it may serve, and truth concerning God is still truth, though it may have been penned in order "to legitimate the institutions of state and temple."[52] So, too, the true God remains the true God even when prayed to as a false God. The Apostle Paul said it: "Although everyone is a liar, let God be proved true . . ." (Rom. 3:4b). Bruce Metzger, on behalf of the NRSV translation committee, remarked:

> The Bible carries its full message, not to those who regard it simply as a noble [or ignoble?] heritage of the past or who wish to use it to enhance political purposes and advance otherwise desirable goals, but to all persons and communities who read it so that they may discern and understand what God is saying to them.[53]

---

50. "The Westminster Confession of Faith," *The Book of Confessions*, C.6.006, p. 127.

51. Said Emerson: "Since . . . we are . . . , by the inevitable law of our being, surrendered unreservedly to the unsleeping observation of the Divinity, we cannot shut our eyes to the conclusion, that *every desire of the human mind is a prayer uttered to God and registered in heaven*" (italics Emerson's). Ralph Waldo Emerson, "Pray Without Ceasing," Rohler, p. 77.

52. Coote and Coote, p. 18.

53. Bruce M. Metzger, "To the Reader," *The New Oxford Annotated Bible with Apocrypha*, p. xiv.

It would behoove us, then, to be careful of the beam in our own eye even as we attempt to remove the speck from the eye of Scripture, or from the creeds and confessions of the church that in various times and places has attempted to read the Bible's witness to *actio divina* in a way that leads to faithful understanding and obedience.

Another reason for not being overzealous in separating the wheat from the weeds in Scripture has to do with the fact that God typically sows the wheat among the weeds, precisely there, a divine intrusion into enemy territory in a kind of reversal of Jesus' well-known parable of the wheat and the weeds, where an enemy sows weeds among the wheat (Matt. 13:26). For instance: Abraham, in whom God promised to bless all the nations of the earth (Gen. 18:18), was not in all matters a paragon of virtue and rectitude. He even went so far as to bargain his wife's favors for his own safe passage through alien territory (Gen. 20:2-18). Jacob, renamed Israel, or "God rules" (Gen. 32:28; 35:10), was a liar and a supplanter (Gen. 25:27-34; 27:1-36). David, whose name suggests "Beloved of God," was, among other, better things, a wily and ruthless ruler who plotted the death of Uriah the Hittite, a loyal soldier in his army (2 Sam. 11:2-26). Moses, initially an unwilling servant of God (Exod. 4:10-17), yet the greatest of Israel's prophets (Deut. 34:10), was prevented from entering the promised land because of the rebellion of his followers against God (Deut. 1:37; 3:23-26). Israel itself, we are told, was "stiff-necked" (Exod. 32:9; 33:3; 33:5; 34:9; Deut. 9:6; 9:13; Acts 7:51). Jeremiah felt himself "deceived" or "enticed" by the very God who required the prophet to speak in his name (Jer. 20:7). The prophet's complaint, as the NRSV Bible notes, bordered on blasphemy.[54] Even the most worthy of Jesus' disciples seemed slow to comprehend him (John 12:16). James and John, the sons of Zebedee, were notoriously self-seeking (Mark 12:35-45). Simon, whose great confession of faith led Jesus to say:

> [Y]ou are Peter, and on this rock I will build my church, and the gates of Hades will not prevail against it. (Matt. 16:18)

was so indignant about Jesus' talk concerning the cross that Jesus had to upbraid him:

---

54. *The New Oxford Annotated Bible with Apocrypha*, p. 999 n.

Get behind me, Satan! You are a stumbling block to me; for you are setting your mind not on divine things but on human things. (Matt. 16:23)

Jesus' own parables reflect his readiness to use tales of disreputable persons and tragically conflicted situations to communicate theological truth and to give spiritual advice: so the parable of the unjust steward (Luke 16:1-9), of the importunate widow and the judge who "neither feared God nor had respect for people" (Luke 18:1-8), and of the laborers in the vineyard (Matt. 20:1-16). The entire Gospel according to Mark ends — by either design or happenstance, we cannot be sure which — with the desertion of Jesus' disciples and the fear of the women at the tomb to speak the good, if disquieting, news of Jesus' resurrection:

So they went out and fled from the tomb, for terror and amazement had seized them; and they said nothing to anyone, for they were afraid. (Mark 16:8)

Let it be said that none of this implies a willingness on God's part to wink at moral failure and condone infidelity. But it does represent God's willingness to bend what is worst in human beings to the service of what is best for them. To use the language of the liturgical theologian, Gordon Lathrop, God "breaks"[55] the texts of Scripture and the texts of contemporary life to make the divine will known and to make the divine presence felt. Had God chosen not to do this, it would appear unlikely that anyone at any time could understand him at all. The Bible, like the preaching it enables (as God wills), is God's *human* speech. In it we encounter divine reality on the turf of human and natural history, and so we encounter ourselves as we are, as we would be, and as God would have us be. So the Bible does not simply contain God's Word. It *is* God's Word, God's human speech *with* us, *about* us, *against* us, and thereby *for* us. It is in just this sense that we can say that God authors Scripture[56] and authorizes preaching.

55. Gordon Lathrop, *Holy Things: A Liturgical Theology* (Minneapolis, MN: Fortress Press, 1993), pp. 27-31, 80-81, 139, 154, 157, 196, 199-200, 201.

56. "The Westminster Confession of Faith," *The Book of Confessions*, C.6.004, p. 126. That Westminster's notion of divine authorship does not necessarily entail a naive assumption about divine dictation is made clear by Hendry in his illuminating exposition of the confession. See George F. Hendry, *The Westminster Confession for Today: A Contemporary Interpretation of the Confession of Faith* (Richmond, VA: John Knox Press, 1960), pp. 19-39.

Preachers do not have license to speak from the pulpit what they or their congregants want to hear. Instead they are obligated by the office to which they have aspired and been called and by their ordination vows to preach that truth which belongs to Christ as he is attested in Scripture. The authority of preachers thus rests not in their persons, nor in their experiences, nor in their rhetorical or elocutionary abilities, nor in their credibility among their contemporaries, but in their faithful witness to that to which the Scriptures themselves bear witness.[57]

It is clearly evident, as Walter Brueggemann has pointed out, that preaching occasions reimagining,[58] reimagining of the world in which we live, reimagining of humanity and its place in that world, reimagining of the cosmos and its destiny. In the first instance, however, this reimagining is not a reimagining on the part of human beings but a reimagining on God's part of human beings in relation to Godself in the face of humanity's penchant for idolatry. God's reimagining of humanity's relationship to Godself is not simply some sort of divine response to contextual pluralism and textual polyvalence,[59] though it takes place in and through them. It is *actio divina,* God's plural (yet definitive) self-performance, disrupting the machinations and imaginations of the heart intent on worshiping a god fashioned in its own image and likeness (Jer. 3:17; 7:24; 9:14; 11:8; 13:10; 16:12; 18:12; 23:17). It is the accommodation of divinity to humanity's desperate necessity. And, as already has been indicated, this self-performance, self-definition, and self-attestation of God is protean in its power. Divinity's way of dealing with humanity's propensity to idolatry is to name itself in a number of specific ways and times and places. It is to give human beings scriptured figures of speech to contend with, that with them people might pursue an understanding of God on God's own terms and not their own. It is to confront people with a distinct storied past to displace the hegemony of their own stories. It is to shake the foundations people have set in sand until those foundations crumble. And it is to replace those foundations with an immovable and irreplaceable foundation set in rock (Matt. 7:24-27). "For no one can lay any foundation other than the one that has been laid; that foundation is Jesus Christ" (1 Cor. 3:11). What reimagining *we* do is based upon the reimagining that has been done in

57. Charles L. Bartow, "Speaking the Text and Preaching the Gospel," in Seow, p. 86.
58. Walter Brueggemann, "Preaching as Reimagination," *Theology Today* 52, no. 3 (Oct. 1995): pp. 313-29.
59. Brueggemann, p. 315.

Scripture. Preaching follows that scriptural reimagining as the creeds and confessions of the church attest.[60] For what we are given with the scriptural word is true God and true humanity, the Wholly Other, others, and we ourselves, face to face. We are given grace and our abuse of it, faith and our flight from it, truth and our denial of it, divinity and our helpless need of it. O gracious God, "Thou hast made us for Thyself, and our heart is restless until it repose in Thee!"[61]

In the reading of the Scriptures and in preaching we seek to be faithful to the One who has borne — and who continues to bear — faithful witness to himself with the words of prophets and apostles. We cannot get out in front of the Bible[62] because the Bible is God's

60. In the Protestant church generally, and in the Reformed tradition particularly, creeds and confessions are subordinate standards, timely summations, in the face of controversy, of the church's proclamation of the gospel attested in Scripture. That gospel, and no other, is the canon within the canon, an interpretative key provided in Scripture itself. Thus Barth remarks: "The revealed Word of God we know only from the Scripture adopted by Church proclamation, or from Church proclamation based on Scripture. The written Word of God we know only through the revelation which makes proclamation possible, or through the proclamation made possible by revelation. The proclaimed Word of God we know only by knowing the revelation attested through Scripture, or by knowing the Scripture which attests revelation." Karl Barth, *Church Dogmatics*, I, 1, trans. G. T. Thompson (Edinburgh: T&T Clark, 1936), p. 136.

61. *The Confessions of Saint Augustine,* trans. Edward B. Pusey (London: Collier-Macmillan Ltd, 1961), p. 11.

62. In a provocative chapter on "Preaching and the Bible," D. Buttrick argues that the printed page — and the "biblical theology" and "biblical preaching" that are bound to it — is a weight on preaching now more than it is a pair of wings to give flight to the Word. What is needed is a use of the Bible that sees it as a resource for preaching that starts not with the biblical witness but with the redemptive word of the gospel. Says Buttrick: ". . . let us reaffirm our heritage: Preaching is God's Word to us. Preaching is the Word of God because it functions within God's liberating purpose and *not* necessarily because it is per se biblical." Buttrick, p. 31. Ironically, Buttrick makes his point by reference to specific texts of Scripture that help to support it. If the Bible is not functioning as authority for him at this point, it surely is being used as a resource for strengthening his ethos. His pattern of argumentation also suggests that his knowledge of God's "liberating purpose" itself springs from that burdensome page and from the people of God who, across the years, have attended to it. On the other hand, Buttrick's claim that the Bible *is* proclamation in its oral form (that is, as it is publicly read aloud) is fully consonant with the essential theme of this book. In any case, if the scriptural word — all of it — cannot be used by God to speak the redemptive Word of the gospel, it is unlikely that *our* words — *any* of them — can be so used. Further, if the redemptive Word of the gospel, as defined by us, is not tested against the full counsel of God in Scripture as a whole, what is to keep that redemptive word from being in the end more *our* word than God's, or Scripture's, or the church's?

way of staying ahead of us, yet with us. It bears in upon us eschato-logical judgment, the "Beyond Time" in time, the Christ to be in the Christ who was, and is, and is to be "the same, yesterday and today and forever" (Heb. 13:8). We trust the Bible (not uncritically) and use it as a means of grace because God in Christ, through the agency of the Holy Spirit, has entrusted it to us and has promised to keep on dealing with us by means of it. We have the Bible because it has taken hold of us through its "unique and authoritative witness to Jesus Christ."[63] We have it, too, because Jesus Christ himself bears unique and authoritative witness to it. God has spoken, and God has promised to speak again. So we read the Bible and preach from it in faith and hope. Said Barth:

> [I]nnovations which have their norm [elsewhere than in Scripture] are achieved only outside the church and . . . apart from Jesus Christ, as he has already made himself known to us.[64]

Who Jesus Christ is and what the kingdom is like that he preaches, inaugurates, and rules[65] has been received by us and understood by us in the context of our personal-corporate life in the church and in the world. Therefore, before we ever come to the Bible, we have precon-ceived notions about what it is likely to say. We have defined for our-selves, however inarticulately, the gospel. We think we know what the good news is, at least in part. And we think we know why it is good

---

63. In the Presbyterian Church (U.S.A.), when women and men are ordained to the ministry of word and sacrament, they are required to answer affirmatively this question: "Do you accept the Scriptures of the Old and New Testaments to be, by the Holy Spirit, the unique and authoritative witness to Jesus Christ in the Church universal, and God's Word to you?" *Book of Order* (Louisville, KY: Presbyterian Church [U.S.A.], 1995-96), G.14.0405. The question is adapted from "The Confession of 1967," *The Book of Confessions,* C.9.27, p. 265.

64. Barth, *Church Dogmatics,* I/2, p. 228.

65. D. Buttrick makes an eloquent and impassioned plea for a humble but fervent proclamation of the realm and rule (i.e., kingdom) of God, the new humanity in Jesus Christ. Buttrick, pp. 49-52. Indeed the attestation of Christ in Scripture *is* an attestation of him as the eschatological judge and ruler of our world and all creation. Yet the initiative in such proclamation belongs with God, not with us, and so the scriptural word once again must be received as "unique and authoritative," God's own, a check on our understandings of Christ and kingdom and an impetus to continual transfor-mation of communal and personal life.

news for us and for everybody — at least potentially. In this sense every
preacher has his or her own personalized *kerygma*.[66] Every congregation
does too,[67] and so does every person inside or outside the church. We
often have favorite texts as well. For example: Luke 4:16-21, John 3:16,
1 Corinthians 13, Psalm 23. This favorite text tends to identify us with
a theological stereotype also. For instance, one is unlikely to find a lover
of Luke 4:16-21 holding the text up as a banner between goalposts at a
football game during "point after" and "field goal" tries on nationally
televised contests. With John 3:16, however, just the opposite is the case.
Texts also have a way of being identified (perhaps appropriately or not
so appropriately) with certain moments in the drama of human life:
1 Corinthians 13, weddings; Psalm 23, funerals. Even people who reject
the claims of Christ have some notion of what he is purported to be.
That is why they reject him. They do not reject him for nothing. They
reject him for something. Years ago, James E. Sellers observed that there
is something of the unbeliever in every believer, something of the outsider in every insider. Therefore there is a need to preach the good news
as new news even inside the church.[68] Probably Sellers is still correct.
But how shall we go about it? What will help us to hear good news as
new news as we read the Scriptures and preach from them when we are

66. Charles L. Bartow, *The Preaching Moment: A Guide to Sermon Delivery*
(Dubuque, IA: Kendall/Hunt Publishing Co., 1995), pp. 59-68.

67. Just as preachers themselves have kerygmatic expectations, so their congregants too will have preunderstandings of the gospel as they approach the preaching
moment when the Scriptures are read aloud and the Word is proclaimed. The traditional
kerygma (or apostolic preaching/teaching) of the church has been summarized in sche-
matic form by Metzger:
    (1) The promises of God made in Old Testament days have now been fulfilled,
        and the Messiah has come:
    (2) He is Jesus of Nazareth, who
        (a) Went about doing good and executing mighty works by the power of
            God;
        (b) Was crucified according to the purpose of God;
        (c) Was raised by God from the dead;
        (d) Is exalted by God and given the name "Lord";
        (e) Will come again for judgment and the restoration of all things.
    (3) Therefore, all who hear the message should repent and be baptized.
Bruce M. Metzger, *The New Testament: Its Background, Growth and Content* (Nashville,
TN: Abingdon Press, 1965), p. 177.

68. James E. Sellers, *The Outsider and the Word of God: A Study in Christian
Communication* (Nashville, TN: Abingdon Press, 1961), esp. pp. 13-34.

inclined to think that we already fully know who God is and what God has done — and will do — for us in Jesus Christ as he is attested in Scripture? Here we move toward a stance for the preacher vis-à-vis the text that I have called "a gospel for 'interesting times.'" "Interesting times," of course, refers to the ancient Chinese curse: "May you live in interesting times."[69]

We do! Whether or not one is inclined to use the labels "post-enlightenment," "postmodern," "postfoundationalist," or "postcritical," there can be little doubt that, in the present era, what matters most to us is up for sharp debate. The gospel itself is debated outside and inside the church. What is it? What does it mean? Have those who would sum it all up in the words of Luke 4:16-21 or John 3:16 anything to say to each other? Or is their "conflict of interpretations"[70] a conflict of incommensurables? In the poet Robert Frost's terms, are we fated to a process of "walling in and walling out"[71] without question, without precise critique? If Richard Rorty is right in insisting that there can be no single metanarrative to instruct common life[72] in the "global village,"[73] are people simply destined to repeat over and over again their own version of things? At least when it comes to the reading of the Scriptures and to the preaching of the gospel, this writer thinks not. Since *actio divina*, God's self-performance and self-attestation in Jesus Christ, in the power of the Holy Spirit, and with the words of Scripture, is both definitive and plural, context-specific and protean, it has the capacity again and again to instigate fresh construals of it on our part.

---

69. David Tracy, *Plurality and Ambiguity: Hermeneutics, Religion, Hope* (San Francisco: Harper & Row, 1987), p. 8.

70. Paul Ricoeur, *The Conflict of Interpretations: Essays in Hermeneutics,* ed. Don Ihde (Evanston, IL: Northwestern University Press, 1974). See esp. pp. 381-497.

71. Robert Frost, "Mending Wall," *The Poetry of Robert Frost,* ed. Edward Connery Latham (New York: Holt, Rinehart and Winston, 1969), pp. 33-34.

72. Richard Rorty, *Contingency, Irony, and Solidarity* (New York: Cambridge University Press, 1989), p. 173. See also a helpful treatment of Rorty's thought in relation to contemporary journalistic communication in James Stewart Ettema, "Discourse That Is Closer to Silence than to Talk: The Politics and Possibilities of Reporting on Victims of War," *Critical Studies in Mass Communication* 2, no. 1 (March 1994): pp. 1-21.

73. Marshall McLuhan, *Understanding Media: The Extensions of Man* (New York: The New American Library Signet Books, 1964), p. 298. In McLuhan's own words: "With instant electric technology, the globe itself can never again be more than a village. . . ." McLuhan saw this initially more as threat than as promise, an end to traditional securities.

Our construals are not definitive. Our definitions of the gospel, freighted as they are with ideology and self-interest, are bound to be broken open again and again to what the Bible has to say in all its varied, and often disturbing, specificity. Our need, then, is to articulate a predisposition toward the scriptural witness that avoids the following:

1. Proscription of the initiative of God;
2. Prescription in advance of what the text itself must say;
3. Walling out of threats to any preunderstanding of the gospel;
4. Silencing of the creedal and confessional story of the church;
5. Silencing of congregants' questions and concerns;
6. Limiting of the range of the gospel's concerns to "helpful hints for hurtful habits"[74] when what it has in view is the life of humanity and the fate of the cosmos.

In a word, we need to articulate a preunderstanding of the gospel that is open to the possibility of radical (i.e., thoroughgoing or to the roots) transformation. Pursuant to that objective, I recommend that preachers approach every text to be read and preached from with what I have called "a gospel for 'interesting times.'" My own way of wording such a preunderstanding of the gospel, or kerygmatic expectation, is as follows:

> *In Christ Jesus, God takes us as we are and presses us into the service of what God would have us be.*

In chapter 3, public reading of biblical texts will be explored in the light of such a kerygmatic expectation. In chapter 4, homiletic theory and practice will be discussed. In chapter 5, the focus will shift to homiletical criticism. For now it only remains to be said that a transformational kerygmatic expectation, such as the one just articulated, necessitates a proclamation of the gospel that involves preachers in acts of interpretative speech. This does not mean that there are no rhetorical or suasory dimensions to the public reading of the Scriptures and preaching. And it does not mean that in reading the Scriptures and in preaching we are concerned only with conceptual clarity. Al-

---

74. "Helpful hints for hurtful habits" is a phrase coined by Paul E. Scherer, renowned Lutheran homiletician and preacher of the mid-twentieth century. He was deriding topical/therapeutic preaching.

ready it has been argued that *actio divina* itself is rhetorical. Since it is, it must be assumed that it speaks to the whole person and not just to the mind.[75] However, it does mean that we cannot avoid the plural specificity of the Bible's witness to *actio divina*, its raising of the questions that trouble our answers. And it means, too, that we cannot dismiss the precise figuration and refiguration of human life in the divine image *actio divina* entails. Texts make sense as we make sense with them.[76] We interpret texts as we speak texts and preach from them. We also interpret the gospel itself, seeking to make whatever sense of it the text will allow. Not least of all, we do this in humility, expecting, and ready to receive, from colleagues, congregants, and others, such fresh insights into the definition and significance of text and gospel as "the Holy Spirit speaking in the Scripture"[77] may give.[78] And we pray!

> My God, my God, thou art a direct God, may I not say, a literal God, a God that wouldest be understood literally, and according to the plain sense of all that thou saiest? But thou art also (Lord, I intend it to thy glory . . .) a figurative, a metaphorical God, too: a God in whose

---

75. Wilson, pp. 63-81, esp. 73.

76. Goldingay, pp. 36-55. Goldingay's discussion of audience-centered, meaning-producing reading is helpfully nuanced, granting a measure of freedom to interpreters yet granting a measure of authorizing power to the text as well. For example, "One can grant that there are very many aspects to a story's meaning but still assume that there are limits to what can be read out of a story, and it may be that interpreters can agree on meanings that do not belong to a story — not so much because author or audience could or would not have envisaged them but because they are not a natural understanding of this actual story" (p. 52).

77. "The Westminster Confession of Faith," *The Book of Confessions*, C.6.010, p. 128.

78. Russell makes mention of Calvin's statement regarding the marks of the true church: "For whenever we find the word of God purely preached and heard, and the sacraments administered according to the institution of Christ, there, it is not to be doubted, is a Church of God." Russell, *Church in the Round*, pp. 137-38. From a feminist perspective Russell then asserts that a pure word will be a word of solidarity and that what is "pure" must be determined via the inclusion of the whole church in a process of critique. This is in opposition to the privileging of any one group (e.g., clergy) in the decision-making process (p. 139). But, in my view, added to this is a need to have an understanding of all groups, and the church as a whole, under the whole counsel of God understood as the Holy Spirit speaking in all of Scripture, not apart from critical understanding and explication (i.e., interpretation), but through them.

words there is such a height of figures, such voyages, such peregrinations to fetch remote and precious metaphors, such extensions, such spreadings, such curtains of allegories, such third heavens of hyperboles, so harmonious elocutions . . . as all profane authors seem of the seed of the serpent that creeps; thou art the dove, that flies.[79]

79. John Donne, "Expostulation 19," in *Devotions Upon Emergent Occasions*, ed. Anthony Raspa (Montreal & London: McGill-Queens University Press, 1975), p. 99. Quoted in Ellen F. Davis, "Holy Preaching: Ethical Interpretation and Practical Imagination," in *Reclaiming Faith: Essays on Orthodoxy in the Episcopal Church and the Baltimore Declaration*, ed. Ephraim Radner and George R. Sumner (Grand Rapids, MI: William B. Eerdmans Publishing Co., 1993), p. 221.

3. Turning Ink into Blood

THE GOSPEL FOR "INTERESTING TIMES" — or kerygmatic expectation — with which chapter 2 ended provides the frame of reference for speaking and hearing the Scriptures in public worship. That kerygmatic expectation was stated as follows: In Christ Jesus God takes us as we are and presses us into the service of what he would have us be. *In Christ Jesus* indicates the locus of God's initiative and our response. We are baptized into Christ, and the Christ who attests the Scriptures as the Scriptures attest him is the Christ of apostolic testimony and ecumenical creed. He is God's

> only Son, our Lord; who was conceived by the Holy Ghost, born of the virgin Mary, suffered under Pontius Pilate, was crucified, dead, and buried; he descended into hell. The third day he rose again from the dead; he ascended into heaven, and sitteth on the right hand of God the Father Almighty; from thence he shall come to judge the quick and the dead.[1]

Further, the God who takes initiative in self-disclosure and self-figuration in Christ, whom we know in Christ as providential presence,[2] and

---

1. "The Apostles' Creed," *The Book of Confessions* (Louisville, KY: Presbyterian Church [U.S.A.], 1994), C.2.1-3, p. 7.

2. For Calvin true wisdom consisted of the knowledge of God and of ourselves. This is not "knowledge about," but "knowledge of." According to Wood, "It is a sustained personal awareness or existential apprehension of God, which profoundly determines one's existence." Charles M. Wood, *The Formation of Christian Understanding: An Essay in Theological Hermeneutics* (Philadelphia: Westminster Press, 1981), p. 32. Benjamin

who, by the Spirit — yet through very human servants of the word —
speaks to us in Scripture, forming and reforming us as a people of God,
the church, is as the creed makes clear, "God the Father Almighty, maker
of heaven and earth."

The *us* referred to in the kerygmatic expectation we bring to the
public reading and hearing of Scripture is not just a collection of
individuals having no common identity. It is, instead, that body or
ecclesial community chosen by God — and by God alone — to bear
witness to the divine presence in the midst of the world through word
and sacrament. This body is not made up of "the best and the bright-
est," those who are wise and powerful according to worldly standards;
nor is it made up of people of noble birth (1 Cor. 1:26). It is, instead,
a motley group, a representation of all sorts and conditions of humanity. Its diversity is not without limit, however, for the ecclesial community chosen by God is made up of those who confess what is
confessed in the creed concerning God and Christ. The people of the
church confess the rest of the creed too, of course. They "believe in
the Holy Ghost, the holy Catholic Church, the communion of saints,
the forgiveness of sins, the resurrection of the body, and the life ever-
lasting." God, through the voice of the church, also calls certain of the
church's members, as a matter of vocation, to preach the word and
administer the sacraments.[3] These women and men share the church's
confession. They, with all the others, have heard and believed the
prophetic and apostolic report.[4] As Thomas G. Long has said, they

---

Reist further argues that God's providence is precisely this presence of God in human
life. Benjamin A. Reist, *A Reading of Calvin's Institutes* (Louisville, KY: Westminster/John
Knox Press, 1991), pp. 19-21.

3. As I have elsewhere stated, there is a sense in which the whole church
proclaims the gospel. (Charles Bartow, *The Preaching Moment: A Guide to Sermon
Delivery* [Dubuque, IA: Kendall/Hunt Publishing Co., 1995], pp. 59-68.) Further,
baptism into Christ means that all Christians are called upon to bear witness to him
and to make known, proclaim, the good news concerning him. The appointment,
training, examination, and ordaining of persons to particular responsibility in this
regard does not compromise this exercise of responsibility by the whole people of
God. Instead, ordination of some to the vocation of proclamation of the gospel is a
gift to the church to enable its faithful witness. What is crucial is that this vocation in
principle be open to all who are baptized, for, by the voice of the church, God freely
chooses, disciplines, and equips women and men for the exercise of the office of servant
of the Word.

4. Isaiah 53:1; Romans 10:16; John 12:38.

come to the pulpit from the pew,[5] and they preach "the righteousness of God . . . revealed through faith for faith" (Rom. 1:17), urging the body to "contend for the faith that was once and for all entrusted to the saints" (Jude v. 36).

The reformative or transformational thrust of our kerygmatic expectation, signaled by the phrase "and presses us into the service of what he would have us be," thus is far from simply ever changing, progressive, revisionist, a matter of keeping up with the temper of the times. In fact, it has little if anything to do with establishing the gospel's relevance to the world as we construe it and experience it on our own terms. But it has everything to do with the gospel's keeping *us* relevant to the purposes of God whatever the vicissitudes of life. The Reformed tradition puts it this way: *"ecclesia reformata, semper reformanda, secundum verbum Dei"* — "the church reformed must always be reformed according to the word of God."[6] For Christ attested in Scripture is the only Christ there is. He is historical presence and eschatological judge. He is one who came, who is coming again, and who may be known now in the proclamation of the word and the administration of the sacraments. In word and sacrament he is present experience, but also, as David Tracy remarked, he is a "dangerous memory,"[7] calling into question all contemporaneous attempts to make of him what men and women might wish from God and expect of themselves. Yet, not in contradiction of that fact, but precisely because of it, he is our "only comfort in life and death"[8] as well.

So in speaking the Scriptures from the pulpit and preaching

5. Thomas G. Long, *The Witness of Preaching* (Louisville, KY: Westminster/John Knox Press, 1989), pp. 10-11.

6. Edward A. Dowey, "The Reforming Tradition: Presbyterians and Mainstream Protestantism: A Review," *The Princeton Seminary Bulletin* 14 (1993): p. 9. See also Michael D. Bush, "The History and Meaning of *Semper Reformanda*," *The Presbyterian Outlook* 178, no. 32 (September 23, 1996): pp. 5-6. Johannes Hoornbeek (1617–1666), a Utrecht theologian, appears to be the original source of the thought. Bush points out that *reformanda* is a gerundive in Latin grammar, and the gerundive is always in the passive voice. "*Ecclesia reformata, semper reformanda* proposes a limit on every extravagance in the Reformed church through the Protestant principle: *sola Scriptura*, Scripture alone. . . . It is a call not to innovation, but to modesty, exegesis and self-examination" (p. 5).

7. David Tracy, *The Analogical Imagination: Christian Theology and the Culture of Pluralism* (New York: The Crossroad Publishing Co., 1981), p. 279.

8. "The Heidelberg Catechism," *The Book of Confessions*, C.4.001, p. 29.

from them we heed God's promise to use[9] the Bible as a means of grace to shape, lead, set the terms for our theological, homiletical, hermeneutical efforts, to the end that every thought may be brought into captivity to the obedience of Christ (2 Cor. 10:15b). True liberation is liberation for such obedience. For this reason we privilege the biblical word over our own words, Scripture's social construction of reality in depicting the Christ over other social constructions past or present,[10] the Bible's plural and particular figuration of divine self-disclosure (also confirmed in the creedal and confessional witness of the church over time) over any privatized and idiosyncratic contemporary "readings" of the Christian God. Here we are not denigrating human experience. We simply are reminding ourselves — as the early church reminded itself, in the writings of the evangelists and apostles — "that experience is the point at which theology is grounded in history."[11] As G. B. Caird and L. D. Hurst note, it is an error to assume

9. Charles M. Wood makes the case that human use of the Scriptures in the church is decisive for understanding and meaning. The Bible is a means of grace *we* use. Wood, p. 19. Thomas G. Long picks up this same approach to biblical interpretation in dealing with (and settling?) disputed issues in the church. Thomas G. Long, "Living with the Bible," in *Homosexuality and Christian Community,* ed. Choon-Leong Seow (Louisville, KY: Westminster/John Knox Press, 1996), pp. 67-72. Wood and Long obviously are correct. We do use the Bible, and the purposes for which we use it bear upon how we understand its witness. What I wish to emphasize, though, is that all the while *we* are making use of Scripture *God also* is making use of it, and has made use of it, and that use is not only relevant to but determinative for our use. Local and particular contemporary experience thus does not have the final word in matters that in fact pertain to the whole life of the larger church. Instead, the last word is the word of the Holy Spirit speaking in the Scriptures and heard in the church at large (in the case of the Reformed/Presbyterian tradition, via appointed and constituted representative bodies, the record of whose discernment can be found in confessional standards).

10. Peter L. Berger, *The Sacred Canopy: Elements of a Sociological Theory of Religion* (New York: Doubleday [Anchor Books], 1967). Pages 3-51 discuss religion as social construction, though with Berger this does not seem to be a response to an objectively other, self-disclosing God. The result appears to be that individuals and churches (in fact all religious traditions) are left to adjudicate the claims of subjective experience of the sacred without anything more rigorous as a norm than intersubjective conversation in the direction of solidarity to preserve meaningful existence in the face of the ultimate threat to such a project, namely, death.

11. G. B. Caird, *New Testament Theology,* completed and ed. L. D. Hurst (New York: Oxford University Press, 1994), p. 348.

that the Jesus of history is a different person from the Christ of the church's faith:

> The New Testament writers . . . put enormous weight upon the actuality of the events they describe. "We cannot give up speaking of the things we have seen and heard" (Acts 4:20). "This is supported by an eyewitness, whose evidence is to be trusted" (John 19:35). The Fourth Gospel uses a blind man to convey that approach to simple fact that always triumphs over dogmatic theorizing: "All I know is this: once I was blind, but now I see" (John 9:25). Luke's Gospel begins with the claim that the author was "following the traditions handed down to us by the original eyewitnesses" (Luke 1:2). Those aspiring to apostleship were required to have been eyewitnesses (Acts 1:21-2). And the terms *euaggelizo* and *kerusso* connote the proclamation of news, not an invitation to a mystical, creative experience.[12]

It is clear that the church early on thought that it had in its midst the eternal Son of the Father, the heavenly Christ. Yet "the evidence equally demonstrates that [it] knew well that his character was known to them only through their memories of the earthly Jesus; and the First Epistle of John was written to demonstrate that it was heresy to think otherwise (I John 1:1-2)."[13]

This does not mean that the church of the past in every case should have — or that the church of today consistently must — harshly condemn every unique claim to experience of Christ expressed by individuals or groups inside or outside its membership. Nor does it mean that diverse, critical theological projects must be dismissed out of hand in favor of earlier formulations. As Thomas Gillespie has argued, the quest for orthodoxy (and orthopraxis) does not have to be stingy. It can be generous.[14] But it does mean that those chosen to proclaim the gospel and to read the Scriptures in public, corporate worship must not be in thrall to any particular popular opinion or school of thought, or the hermeneutical "methodology of the month,"[15] but must assess what they and others might make of the scriptural witness with which God

12. Caird, p. 347.
13. Caird, p. 348.
14. Thomas W. Gillespie, "A Generous Orthodoxy," *The Princeton Seminary Bulletin* 16, no. 3 (1995): pp. 268-71.
15. Caird, p. x.

addresses them on the basis of what that witness itself has to say. The object of the Scriptures' attention must be the object of our attention, recognizably so. The Bible itself is a record of human experience of God. That much at the very least we have in common with it. "All such experience would be illusory, however, unless it was accompanied by a rational confidence in the objective reality of that which occasioned it; it must be grounded in the existence of something which is independent of the experience itself."[16]

In this connection let us return for a moment to a consideration of the prototypical figures of speech used to designate the plural specificity of *actio divina* as the Scriptures bear witness to it. The oxymoronic statements of Scripture — the bush burning but not consumed, the silent sound "heard" by Elijah, the virgin mother, and the strength made perfect in weakness — are not without referent. Their referent is precisely that which is incommensurable with the predisposition to human experience of God possessed by those who coined those figures of speech. In other words, what they encountered, or understood others to have encountered, was not merely discontinuous with their previous experience of God. It was disconfirming of it. Atop Mount Carmel Elijah's expectation concerning God was confirmed. God, there, *was* a God of wind and storm and fire, vindicating the prophet.[17] Atop Mount Horeb, however, all that was previously confirmed was disconfirmed. Elijah no longer could expect God always to be and do what God was and did at the moment of the prophet's triumph. Similarly, for those expecting a messiah, Mary's child grew to be a troublesome enigma, somehow related to earlier prophecy, yet not quite exactly the fulfillment of that prophecy in any direct and predictable sense.[18] And for Paul, God's might was displayed to perfection atop Golgotha, where Jesus suffered rejection and crucifixion, what could only be called in strictly human terms defeat, utter and complete.[19] That is not simply paradoxi-

16. Caird, p. 348.

17. 1 Kings 18:17–19:18. For a discussion of disconfirmation concerning this story see Stephen Prickett, *Words and the Word: Language, Hermeneutics and Biblical Interpretation* (New York: Cambridge University Press, 1986), pp. 4-36.

18. Paul E. Scherer highlights the disparity of messianic expectation and actual fulfillment in his sermon "Let God Be God." Paul E. Scherer, *The Word God Sent* (Grand Rapids, MI: Baker Book House, 1977), pp. 143-52.

19. For Paul the power of God is manifest not only in the suffering of Christ, but in and through the struggles and infirmities of the apostle himself (2 Cor. 12:1-10). The

cal (against accepted or conventional teaching). It is utterly unthinkable. Oxymoronic statements, then, do not just make room in consciousness for entertaining the novel. They indicate that something has happened that truly is novel, requiring a change in consciousness itself (conversion or paradigm shift) so that human beings might perceive what was previously imperceptible, not heard, not seen, not smelt, not touched, not there!

Jesus' metaphors of the kingdom also have a referent: the kingdom of God, a distinctive, a unique way of being in the world.[20] But one cannot enter that kingdom if she or he is inattentive to Jesus or turns a deaf ear to his parables as recorded in Scripture; for the kingdom, while in this world, is not of it.[21] As Caird and Hurst have pointed out, "if the Synoptic Gospels are right to insist that Jesus spent much of his time explaining what *he* meant by the Kingdom, would it not follow that he did not mean what everybody else meant by it?"[22]

Caird and Hurst go on:

> For Jesus, entering the Kingdom was synonymous with the life of discipleship — of submitting to the demands of the God who is king. His teaching is dominated by the central burning conviction that God's rule is now actively present in the affairs of individuals, kings, and nations. . . . Jesus never questions the close link between the reign of God and Israel's election; but he insists on making God's sovereignty the primary consideration. First let Israel discover what it means for God to reign over Israel; then they will know what part Israel is to play in the plan of God.[23]

First let the church discover what it means for God to reign over the church; then the church will know what part it is to play in the plan of God. To that end let the church attend to the public reading of the Scriptures. As we have noted, the Bible, read and preached from, met-

---

almightiness of God asserted in the creed ("I believe in God the Father almighty") therefore needs to be understood in the light of Jesus' suffering under Pontius Pilate and in the light of the sufferings and persecutions endured by those who bore — and who bear — faithful witness to him in contexts of oppression.

20. Paul Ricoeur, "Biblical Hermeneutics," *Semeia: An Experimental Journal for Biblical Criticism* 4 (1975): p. 87.

21. See esp. John 18:36-38.

22. Caird, p. 367.

23. Caird, p. 369.

onymically signals the presence of the one who, with it, confronts us with what H. H. Farmer has called divine claim and succor.[24] The referent of the Bible as metonym is God speaking in the speaking of the biblical text. Our conviction is that we have heard God there before — as God has promised — and that we will hear God there again. Failing that, logic would seem to dictate that we can expect to hear God nowhere.

When we speak the stories, poems, parables, epistles of Scripture, we always are speaking God's word metonymically and not directly. When we speak passages containing oxymorons, metaphors, and other tropes, we are speaking specific figurations that have as their referents particular experiences of God, experiences not fully capable of expression in other terms, but only, and precisely, in the terms given. What may not be so obvious is that when we speak literally of God, we also are speaking experientially, indirectly, and by way of figuration. We are speaking of the infinite in finite terms, of *actio divina* in the discourse of *homo performans*.[25] We are using vocal and physical gesture[26] to sound forth and body forth (enact) human experience of the divine. Literal speech, then, is neither more nor less referential than figurative speech. Literal speech is simply a taken-for-granted form of figuration. It is common sense talk as opposed to talk that is uncommon or even unique. It is conventional, "old hat," conservative. Literal speech is vitally important too. Indeed it is indispensable. Without it, without already agreed-upon ways of indicating what matters — perhaps even what

---

24. H. H. Farmer, *The Servant of the Word* (Philadelphia: Fortress Press, 1964), pp. 44-49.

25. Victor Turner, *The Anthropology of Performance* (New York: PAJ Publications, 1982), p. 81.

26. Wallace Bacon, in a passage of startling clarity, defines speech as gesture and writing as an attempt to make such gesturing precise. "Speech cannot be divorced from subject matter, for a man speaking is a man speaking something, and the 'something' is what concerns him. Indeed, it is profitable to look upon the study of speech as the study of man as a gesturing creature. Sounds, words, movements, ideas, dreams, hopes — all are gestures by which man seeks to convey to those around him the secrets that must otherwise die within him. The function of the study of speech is to help men to gesture successfully. Written words are signs of gestures; they are symbols that seek to make gestures meaningful. Writing is often a preliminary to oral utterance, a way of trying to make the act of oral utterance more precise, more meaningful, by subjecting it to an ordering process through the formal organization of the gesture." Wallace A. Bacon, *The Art of Interpretation* (New York: Holt, Rinehart and Winston, 1972), p. 3.

matters most — to us, we would be hard pressed to notice anything significant in atypical speech. Apart from the standard referential quality of literal, everyday speech, heightened forms of figuration (e.g., oxymoron, metaphor) could hardly be assessed as either remarkable or simply odd.

The objective referent of literal speech in fact may be identical to the referent of more patently figurative speech, but often (though not necessarily always, as we shall see) the insight into that referent accorded by literal speech, while easily shared, may not be as abundant as the insight provided by less strictly conventional discourse. If literal speech is conservative, generally though not consistently intended to maintain the status quo, boldly figurative speech — we are not speaking here of merely decorative language or "purple prose," as must by now be clear — is radical and reformative. Still, heightened figuration is an unusual use of literal, more mundane speech. It stretches the limits of our common discourse, yet has as its referent what our common discourse also makes reference to, and so we can assess its aptness. Wendell Berry makes the point this way:

> A writer such as Shakespeare is of course distinguished by his language, which is certainly his gift and his love. But his language is, after all, the common tongue, to which his gift is uncommon grace and power. Without his commonness we could neither recognize nor value his distinction.[27]

Violet B. Ketels, in her essay on Václav Havel's understanding and use of language, has argued vigorously, and convincingly, how crucial it is to realize that speech, whether figurative or literal, is referential and not simply mystifying (and therefore not only polyvalent but finally indistinguishable from nonsense). She remarks:

> Tragically, the process by which anyone is led to abandon confidence in human communication blunts the moral sense and deadens the will to action. It is the obverse side of the same process which, in its positive aspect, laid the ground for the gradual social awakening that culminated in Czechoslovakia's Velvet Revolution.
>
> In Havel's essays, language, when it is used with candid regard for the integrity of every word to bear witness against lies and to cry out

27. Wendell Berry, *Standing By Words* (New York: Farrar, Straus and Giroux, 1983), p. 9.

truth, is repeatedly shown as the secret "power of the powerless" to
change history. Stubborn faith in that capacity of the word to mean
what it seems to mean and in its power to transform moral and social
consciousness underlies Havel's philosophical reflections and inevitably connects language to ethical action.[28]

Ketels goes on to demonstrate how literal speech, the speech of conventional figuration, when masterfully and faithfully used, can achieve star-
tlingly vivid, even overwhelmingly compelling, results. To do this she
discusses documents associated with the Czech dissident movement
known as "Charter 77."

> [T]he documents have an unnerving prosaic quality like similar ac-
> counts in Solzhenitzyn's *Gulag Archipelago,* their language chastely
> constrained, tone guarded, as if the slightest enthusiasm or impreci-
> sion might endanger the whole, as if the writers had yielded up the
> persuasiveness of passionate utterance to make meaning impeccably
> unambiguous. They persuade by their ordering of bleak detail. They
> prove the power of language when no shadow falls between the word
> and what it signifies.[29]

Such consummate and relentless use of literal speech in the service of
truth telling under conditions of oppression may reduce the polyvalence
of language, but it does not reduce the speaker's appeal to our imagination. Instead, it focuses our imaginative attention until we see what
needs to be seen.

In their use of heightened figures of speech, such as oxymoron
and metaphor, biblical authors, like other authors, are not simply
emoting. They are gesturing toward what is there, acting on the biblical
authors, causing them joy, anguish, hope, despair; and they are attempting to do so candidly.[30] Likewise, when they engage in what
seems to be much more prosaic talk, they are not referring to some-

---

28. Violet B. Ketels, "Václav Havel on Language," *Quinnipiac Schweitzer Journal*
1, no. 2 (Fall/Winter 1994-95): p. 20.

29. Ketels, p. 22.

30. Following the near-tragic nuclear accident at Three Mile Island, Wendell Berry
points out how language was used by the Nuclear Regulatory Commission to obfuscate,
even to hide the truth from the commissioners themselves. Candidness was eschewed.
Words pointed to what was not there instead of to what was there. Public responsibility
became public relations. Berry, pp. 37-42.

thing else, but to the same thing. Whatever the human position (socio-culturally defined) or condition (state of being) alluded to or inferred by the reader, God, and what God means to them, is at stake in all of it. As C. S. Lewis observed, the Scriptures are relentlessly religious.[31] To single out certain figures of speech as prototypically associated with divine self-disclosure, then, is not to say that no other speech is engaged in by those passing on to us from long ago their experience of the God who is one and the same yesterday, today, and forever. It is rather to say that even their literal (that is, more customary) speech must contend with God's radical otherness and freedom, including God's freedom to be with humanity where and as it seems fitting to Godself. Their literal speech must be understood to refer to the divine reality as it has made itself known to them and to others in mighty acts of self-definition, in *actio divina,* in divine self-performance. They cannot be understood to be referring only to the imaginations of their hearts. To paraphrase Wentzel van Huyssteen:

> The [figurative] nature of religious [speech] constitutes its essentially religious dimension. The [speech] of religion is the ordinary speech of [humankind], and its [figurative] nature does not reveal a supernaturalistic world; it opens up a limit — dimension for the benefit of this world, this experience, and this [speech]. This quality of religious [speech] eventually also points to its most essential characteristic, namely, that it never has a merely expressive function but rather a relational, reality-depicting or referential character.[32]

The God of whom the Bible speaks, and whom it addresses when it speaks, is present to the speaker in the text, and present with that speaker to us who read and hear what the biblical speaker says. Just so the human experience of the God of the Bible becomes our own. With startling clarity T. S. Eliot indicated what is going on in all of this when he remarked that it is the purpose of literature to turn blood into ink. William Brower was no less vivid and on target when he said that the

31. C. S. Lewis, "They Asked for a Paper: The Literary Influence of the Authorized Version," quoted in Amos N. Wilder, *Early Christian Rhetoric: The Language of the Gospels* (Cambridge, MA: Harvard University Press, 1971), p. xx.
32. Wentzel van Huyssteen, *Theology and the Justification of Faith: Constructing Theories in Systematic Theology* (Grand Rapids, MI: William B. Eerdmans Publishing Co., 1989), p. 133.

purpose of speaking literature is to turn the ink back into blood.[33] So
let it be with the Bible in the pulpit in our Lord's Day worship.

It *will* be so if we can get beyond treating the written text as if it
were an end in itself. It is not. The written text, insist Long and HopKins,
is an "arrested performance."[34] It is a happening about to happen again,
not as mere repetition of what has happened before, but as a fresh, new
happening, discernibly related to, but not completely determined by,
other, earlier performances of the work. It is a human experience about
to be lived and expressed in vocal and physical gesture. Robert Frost
said of poetry — and of prose too — that what was crucial to its success
as a work of art was "the speaking tone of voice somehow entangled in
the words." He continued: "That is all that can save poetry from sing-
song, all that can save prose from itself."[35] Like music, the text on the
page hardly can be considered in itself the work, the opus we are to
engage,[36] make sense of, be changed by. The text rather is the cue we
need (the indispensable cue, the cue we cannot do without) to realize
the work in space and time, in our neuromuscular systems, in flesh and
blood and muscle. As Louise Rosenblatt remarked:

> The literary work exists in the live circuit set up between reader and
> text: the reader infuses intellectual and emotional meanings into the
> pattern of verbal symbols, and those symbols channel his thoughts
> and feelings.[37]

We can compare it to music. Bach's *Magnificat* is not sitting there
on the page when the conductor opens the score. *Magnificat* is in the
music about to happen. It is in what musicians and singers, under the
conductor's direction, will disentangle from the notes; and it is in what
the rest of us will hear, feel, move with, at least covertly (rhythm, after
all, is kinesthetic), when the music is played and sung. Authors' and

33. Bartow, p. 15.

34. Beverly Whitaker Long and Mary Frances HopKins, *Performing Literature: An
Introduction to Oral Interpretation* (Englewood Cliffs, NJ: Prentice-Hall, 1982), p. 2.

35. Robert Frost, from the record sleeve, *Robert Frost Reads His Poetry,* Caedman
Records, 1956.

36. Arnold Berleant, *Art and Engagement* (Philadelphia: Temple University Press,
1991), pp. 121-23 and p. 231, n. 33.

37. Louise M. Rosenblatt, *Literature as Exploration* (New York: The Modern Language Association of America, 1983), p. 25.

composers' words and notes are important, crucial, as already has been mentioned. If we did not have them there in front of us, entangling the speaking tone of voice, precisely giving us the lines we need to realize *this* work as opposed to another, this human experience and not some different human experience, Bach's *Magnificat* or Beethoven's *Missa Solemnis*, exactly those works, and not others, our loss would be unbearable. S. S. Curry pointed out over a century ago that a text has power, a power granted it by authorial design, to constrain the human spirit and the human voice and body so that expression is not "born of impulse or random caprice."[38] Living playwrights in fact have been known to take umbrage (justifiably I think) when the texts they wrote got used to create performance works the playwrights themselves could not recognize as in any way seriously related to what they composed. So Sam Shepard complained to Richard Schechner and The Performance Group about their production of his play *The Tooth of Crime*:

> For me, the reason a play is written is because a writer receives a vision which can't be translated in any other way but a play. . . . It seems to me the reason someone wants to put that play together in a production is because they are pulled to its vision. If that's true then it seems they should respect the form that vision takes place in and not merely extrapolate its language and invent another form which isn't the play. It may be interesting theatre but it's not the play and it can never be the play. . . .[39]

Of course one may seek to do a performance that deconstructs the text, that adumbrates the socio-cultural-ideological sea out of which the text arose and into which it may again be sunk, thereby disestablishing the text, bringing into question its claim upon performers' options. That is not performance of the work, however. That is performance of one's critical assessment of the work. Here the text is not treated as a cue to performance of the work entangled in its words. Instead the text is treated as an impediment to be overcome in pursuit of the critic's own vision of the way things really are in the world. In a

---

38. S. S. Curry, *The Province of Expression* (Boston: School of Expression, 1891), p. 151.
39. Richard Schechner, *Performance Theory* (New York: Routledge, 1988), p. 76. It is of course to Schechner's credit that he published Shepard's remarks even as he took exception to them.

word, the text is made the ally of its own annihilation. Then too one may attempt to strip the text of its power to constrain performers' efforts at sense-making simply because the text, if left to exercise that power, might inhibit full self-realization. Why bother with Bach's *Magnificat* or Beethoven's *Missa Solemnis* when, with notes they have provided, one can compose one's own setting of Mary's song or one's own solemn mass? There is no reason to go to the effort to disentangle "the speaking tone of voice somehow entangled in the words" when it is one's own voice one seeks to disentangle from the texts that have choked it off. Here exegesis gives way to eisegesis, and freedom for interpretation becomes license to do what we please with what composers, authors, redactors, translators have left us. Texts now are neither inadequate nor false construals of reality that we need to expose any more than they are silent friends of ours to be appreciated. They are our slaves, exclusively bent to the service of what we would make of ourselves.

That use of texts is an option, and there are those who would celebrate our exercise of that option. But what about justice? What about giving voice to the voiceless? What about giving place to the marginalized? Is there a linguistically and socially constructed world more easily dismissed than one that has had all its blood drawn and turned into ink? Are there voices more easily silenced than the muted voices of literature? Are there human experiences of God more readily kept at the margins of consciousness than those entangled in words translated into living tongues from now dead languages and disputed manuscripts? In the church, the canon of Scripture can hardly be considered monolithic.[40] It speaks with many voices (some of them profoundly in conflict with each other); and, in the end, the church, and not simply individual members of it or parties within it, will decide which voices are ascendent and why. In other words, the church attends to the texts of its canon critically, "that is, according to the rule of Christ and with due consideration given to [the texts'] socio-cultural contexts."[41] But those varied texts, given the chance, can enable unique ways of being in the world to be known, and not just known about, to be seen, heard, felt (imaginatively even touched and smelled) as living speech. When that

40. Choon-Leong Seow, ed., *Homosexuality and Christian Community* (Louisville, KY: Westminster/John Knox Press, 1996), p. vii.
41. Charles L. Bartow, "Speaking the Text and Preaching the Gospel," in Seow, p. 87.

happens — and only when that happens — the church can understand itself at least to be attempting a faithful engagement of the word and the work of Scripture.

The voices of the canon are heard in the liturgy when the Scriptures are read (i.e., performed — which simply means "form coming through"[42] as opposed to form being inhibited or destroyed or imposed from without). The works the Scripture texts cue are wrought in those who speak those texts[43] and in those who see, hear, and respond to those texts as they are read.[44] Clearly in this transactional approach to the literary works[45] that compose the canon of Scripture, speaker's and congregant's experiences are tapped; and their persons — including the collective persona of the worshiping body — are made present to each other. The persons gathered for worship, attentive to each other and to Scripture, interact with and mutually influence each other, subtly, profoundly, and beyond calculation. Further, that mutual presence and influence involves more than sharing ideas about God and each other, for speech reveals "interiority."[46] Thus, within the transactional approach to speaking and hearing texts here being advocated, the word and work of Scripture is not enslaved to the will of the church as it conceives of itself and its God at any given moment. Nor is the church made the slave of its canonical texts (as if it could be, given the frailty of blood that has been turned into ink). Instead, through the speaking and hearing of biblical texts, the word and work of Scripture is offered to God, with our own souls and bodies, as "a reasonable, holy and living sacrifice,"[47] that God, in Christ, by the power of the Holy Spirit, and according to divine promise, may make of it, and of us, what God will.

42. Richard F. Ward, *Speaking from the Heart: Preaching with Passion* (Nashville, TN: Abingdon Press, 1992), p. 77.

43. Alla Bozarth-Campbell, *The Word's Body: An Incarnational Aesthetic of Interpretation* (Tuskaloosa, AL: The University of Alabama Press, 1979), pp. 51-114, esp. p. 51.

44. Charlotte I. Lee, *Oral Interpretation*, 4th ed. (Boston: Houghton Mifflin Co., 1971), pp. 67-70.

45. Louise M. Rosenblatt, *The Reader, the Text, the Poem: The Transactional Theory of Literary Work* (Carbondale, IL: Southern Illinois University Press, 1978).

46. Walter J. Ong, S.J., *The Presence of the Word: Some Prolegomena for Cultural and Religious History* (New York: Simon and Schuster, 1970), pp. 117-22.

47. *The Book of Common Worship* (Philadelphia: Presbyterian Church in the U.S.A., 1946), p. 173. See Romans 12:1. For a theological exposition see Donald M. Baillie, *The Theology of the Sacraments and Other Papers* (New York: Charles Scribner's Sons, 1957), pp. 108-24.

In other words, in our attempted faithful, public reading and hearing of Holy Scripture, God takes us as we are and presses us into the service of what God would have us be. The Bible does not sit upon the throne, nor do we. Instead, as the Bible itself persistently reminds us, Another sits upon the throne who is Alpha and Omega, beginning and end; and it is that One who makes all things new (Rev. 21:5-6).

Our task in this study is not to give technical "how to" information regarding the public reading of the Scriptures in divine worship. There are books currently available that do that.[48] Nevertheless it is important to discuss what needs to be done with texts if we are to take them seriously as cues to human experience generally, and as cues to human experience of God particularly. Turning ink into blood is nothing less than liturgical anamnesis, living memorialization of events of divine self-disclosure in which we participate with all that we have, are, and can hope to become. That being the case, responsible participation on our part requires precise delineation of what is expected of us. And the first thing that needs to be said in that connection is that scriptural texts will make sense if we bother to make sense with them. Sense making entails many things: knowing the originating historical context, if scholars have ferreted that out for us, knowing literary context, knowing redactional history (where possible and necessary), realizing the precise referents of allusive symbols (if that in fact can be determined), noting tradition history, theological trajectories, and canonical process, and recognizing evidences of what is called intertextuality. Even much more recent literature requires these things. For instance, Robert Frost once wrote a poem called "Choose Something Like a Star." Later he called it "Take Something Like a Star."[49] This is an instance of authorial redaction and not unimportant. To "choose something like a star to stay our minds on and be stayed" is subtly different from what we are doing when we "take something like a star to stay our minds on." "Choose" emphasizes

---

48. Four texts dealing with technical and personal discipline in interpretative speech and the ministry of the word are mentioned here: G. Robert Jacks, *Getting the Word Across* (Grand Rapids, MI: William B. Eerdmans Publishing Co., 1995); Charles L. Bartow, *Effective Speech Communication in Leading Worship* (Nashville, TN: Abingdon Press, 1988); Charles L. Bartow, *The Preaching Moment: A Guide to Sermon Delivery* (Dubuque, IA: Kendall/Hunt Publishing Co., 1995); Richard F. Ward, *Speaking from the Heart: Preaching with Passion* (Nashville, TN: Abingdon Press, 1992).

49. Robert Frost, "Take Something Like a Star," *The Poetry of Robert Frost*, Edward Connery Latham, ed. (New York: Holt, Rinehart and Winston, 1969), p. 403.

selection. "Take" emphasizes taking hold of, grasping, seizing. The former is more a matter of thoughtful calculation. The latter is more a matter of action in fulfillment of existential need. Frost changed one word and in so doing he came close to composing a substantially, though not entirely, different work.

Dorothy Thomas, in her poem "Far Echo," a poem in which a younger woman, with grief, assays the demented state of a beloved older woman who seems to be her mother, has this line: "The last of life was far from fair to you,/And not for it the first of life was made."[50] One can make good sense of the poem without recognizing the implicit critique of Robert Browning's famous reflection on old age in "Rabbi Ben Ezra." But one can make better sense of the poem if one does recognize the critique. Browning said:

> Grow old along with me!
> The best is yet to be,
> The last of life, for which the first was made.[51]

50. Dorothy Thomas, "Far Echo" (unpublished work, private collection). For the benefit of the reader, the poem is printed here in its entirety.

Far Echo

by Dorothy Thomas

Yours was a lovely voice when you were young,
A sweet contralto voice for hymn or round.
But at your work, or come to tie our bonnets on,
You'd whistle, like a mockingbird.

The last of life was far from fair to you,
And not for it the first of life was made.
The snuffer lowered on your shining mind
To bow and chill the twisting wick of it.

You called our names, saw others in our place.
You shook the clock to make it tell the time.
We thought that you had gone past all recall
And mourned your spirit, lifted from its shell.

And then one morning, handed you your cup;
You warmed your hands to it and smiled us past,
O'd up your lips and whistled five sweet notes —
As though a bird flew through a ruined house.

51. *Browning's Complete Poetical Works*, ed. Horace E. Scudder (Boston: Houghton Mifflin Co., 1895), p. 383.

Dorothy Thomas is not just commenting on a fact regarding old age. She is protesting a construal of it that contradicts her experience. Intertextuality counts for something, in other words. The way works are cited but not referenced in other works contributes to the careful delineation of human experience in those works. Performance of works, if it is to be "form coming through," will take note of that. And it will take note of historical allusion also. For instance, in reading "Three Floors" by Stanley Kunitz, it is important to realize that "doughboy" refers to an American soldier serving in Europe during World War I. It also helps to know that there were two songs entitled "Warum" composed by Schumann. Probably the more plaintive of the two is alluded to here. *Warum* in German of course means "why."

Three Floors

by Stanley Kunitz

Mother was a crack of light
And a gray eye peeping;
I made believe by breathing hard
That I was sleeping.

Sister's doughboy on last leave
Had robbed me of her hand;
Downstairs at intervals she played
Warum on the baby grand.

Under the roof of a wardrobe trunk
Whose lock a boy could pick
Contained a red Masonic hat
And a walking stick.

Bolt upright in my bed that night
I saw my father flying.
The wind was walking on my neck,
The window-panes were crying.[52]

Such intertextuality and historical and literary allusion occurs with great regularity throughout the Old Testament and the New Testament and,

---

52. Stanley Kunitz, "Three Floors" in Philip Dacey and David Jauss, eds., *Strong Measures; Contemporary American Poetry in Traditional Forms* (New York: Harper and Row, 1986), pp. 182-83.

obviously, in the New Testament's citation of the Old Testament. One of the most striking is Jesus' cry from the cross, "My God, my God, why have you forsaken me?" (Matt. 27:46). It is a quote from Psalm 22 and thus a prayer. Did Jesus pray the whole psalm? It is also a cry of dereliction, deity taking into itself the depths of human anguish, rejection, alienation. Is it a cry made on our behalf so that we might never have to utter it (though we do!), the presence of God in the thick of our feeling abandoned by God? Historical-critical study, form criticism, tradition history, theological trajectories, canonical process, redaction criticism, literary criticism, even performance as criticism (as we shall later see) can help us to make responsible, justifiable interpretative decisions, good readings if not demonstrably settled right readings,[53] and we doubtless would be foolish not to pay attention to all these sources of help, though finally privileging none over the text itself, the text as performed canonical work.

Sense making also requires careful attention to matters of phrasing (grouping of words into units of thought telling one thing at a time) and emphasis (giving prominence to what is most important in each phrase). W. J. Beeners has called this work vocal exegesis. Vocal exegesis needs to be done even if, as in poetry, the thought as it sits on the page, frozen in ink, or as it at last is spoken aloud, does not appear to make sense directly. For example, this poetic text by an eleven-year-old schoolgirl in San Anselmo, California, in the early 1980s:

Balloon

by Anna Jarrard

Once held fast
In the clammy hand
Of a three year old,
I now fly free,
A bright red speck
Against the gray sky
Of a midsummer storm
In Kansas.[54]

---

53. Monroe C. Beardsley, "Right Readings and Good Readings," *Literature in Performance* 1, no. 1 (Nov. 1980): pp. 10-22.

54. This unpublished child's poem is used with permission of the author, who is now a grown woman.

As prose we would think the text this way: "Once held fast in the clammy hand of a three year old, I now fly free: a bright red speck against the gray sky of a midsummer storm in Kansas." The form of the experience depicted by the poem, a coming together of images in sequence that shapes a unified thought only after the reader and listener have discerned the sense of the whole, works tensively (i.e., with creative tension)[55] in relation to ideational content in its strictly grammatical and logical construction. The experience as expressed in the voice and body of the speaker of the text and as covertly performed in the audience will need to manifest that tensiveness. Nevertheless, even in doing that, the grammar and logic of the whole, the sense the speaking voice in the poem at last comes to, will need to be kept in mind. The poem as experience — as opposed to mere cogitation upon experience — itself makes sense. It asserts something. We know that because we know how to make sense of it.

In principle it is no different from what we find in what may be nearly everybody's best loved psalm. In that psalm, and indeed in every psalm, sense, tensively related to experience, needs to be discerned, however the blood may have been turned into ink on the page.

Psalm 23:1-3a

The LORD is my shepherd, I shall not want.
He makes me lie down in green pastures;
he leads me beside still waters;
    he restores my soul.

As prose, we would write it out this way: "The LORD is my shepherd, I shall not want. He makes me lie down in green pastures; he leads me beside still waters; he restores my soul." But the psalm is not prose, it is poetic meditation; and it needs to be seen, heard, and felt that way by both readers and their congregants. We need to discern the sense of the text, yet we need to discern more than that too, or we will not have form coming through, but instead, form impeded, or deformed, or imposed.

The imagery of literature, for instance, is not added to texts — and to biblical texts — to enliven thought. It is there — as the world of

---

55. Bacon, *The Art of Interpretation*, pp. 37, 45, 95-99, 107, 134-35, 137-39, 140-42, 179-85, 197-98, 253-54, 259-60, 320-21, 323, 451.

sight, sound, smell, touch, and movement is there, here and everywhere
— to give rise to thought. Sensory experience is not a plus to thought,
it is the stuff of it. Docetism was a heresy doomed from the beginning,
for what we know we know though our bodies as well as our brains.
Cognitive science has made that clear. Mark Johnson, drawing on the
findings of cognitive science, has argued that even human beings' most
abstract concepts ultimately are grounded in image schemata impressed
upon the mind by bodily experiences that precede language acquisition
and the development of the power to think rationally, to categorize, and
to conceptualize. Metaphors of balance, to cite but one example, pervade
art, logic, mathematics, and ethics. However, the capacity to recognize
these metaphors and to assess their aptness develops through bodily
experiences of balance that have an impact upon the way our minds
actually work.

> The experience of balance is so pervasive and so absolutely basic for
> our coherent experience of our world, and for our survival in it, that
> we are seldom ever aware of its presence. . . .
>   It is important to see that balancing is an *activity we learn with our*
> *bodies* and not by grasping a set of rules or concepts. First and fore-
> most, balancing is something we do. . . . There are those few days
> [when a baby is learning to walk] when the synapse connections are
> being established and then, fairly suddenly, the baby becomes a little
> *homo erectus*. Balancing is a preconceptual bodily activity that cannot
> be described propositionally by rules. As Michael Polanyi has argued,
> you cannot tell another what steps to take to achieve the balanced
> riding of a bicycle. . . .
>   We also come to know the meaning of balance through the closely
> related experience of bodily equilibrium, or loss of equilibrium. We
> understand the notion of systemic balance in the most immediate,
> preconceptual fashion through our bodily experience. There is too
> much acid in the stomach, the hands are too cold, the head is too hot,
> the bladder is distended, the sinuses are swollen, the mouth is dry. In
> these and numerous other ways we learn the meaning of lack of
> balance or equilibrium. Things are felt as "out of balance." There is
> "too much" or "not enough." . . .
>   The . . . major point, then, is that the meaning of balance begins
> to emerge through our acts of balancing, and through our *experience*
> of systemic processes and states within our bodies. . . .
>   . . . the meaning of balance is tied to such experiences and, in

particular, to the image-schematic structures that make these experiences and activities coherent and significant for us (i.e., recognizable as present or absent, even if we have not yet formed concepts or learned words for them). . . . As I stressed earlier, the image schema is *not* an image. It is, instead, a means of structuring particular experiences schematically, so as to give order and connectedness to our perceptions and conceptions.[56]

Images in literature (this includes, of course, biblical literature), like raw sensory data in life, trigger these image schema so that we know, often more deeply than we can say, what is at stake for us in a passage of literature, a scriptural pericope, a prayer, a sermon, baptism and eucharist. Far from being less important than conceptual content, including theological conceptual content, these imagistically triggered experiences constitute the lived reality through which meaning is mediated to us and construed by us. Consequently, for would-be public readers of Scripture and preachers to work at developing imaginative, empathic, vocal, and physical gestural virtuosity is not to devote time to what is beside the point. Nor is it only to give attention to a matter of secondary importance, mere technical drill, that may help us to get across to others what we have, by other means, acquired for ourselves. It is, instead, to condition one's total self (not just one's mind through study, but also one's body through drill) as a site for the acquisition of knowledge. It is to hone the ways by which we come to experience and understand presence and The Presence.

In some literature, images, and the entire milieu of human bodily knowing, are depicted graphically. In other types of literature they need to be inferred. In either case, the speaker (and, through empathic response to the speaker's vocal and, especially, physical gesture, the audience)[57] needs to indwell the *mise-en-scène* in order to avoid conceptual reductionism. Don Geiger has observed that meaning is in solution in the communication process.[58] To extract it is to extract only part of it, not the whole of it. Connotation and denotation interact to form the gestalt of conceptual and felt knowing. Thus to "sum it all up

56. Mark Johnson, *The Body in the Mind: The Bodily Basis of Meaning, Imagination and Reason* (Chicago: University of Chicago Press, 1987), pp. 74-75.

57. Lee, *Oral Interpretation*, pp. 67-70.

58. Don Geiger, *The Sound, Sense and Performance of Literature* (Chicago: Scott, Foresman and Co., 1963), pp. 40-41, 65-70.

in a few words" is to give, perhaps, an impression of the work, or a particular insight into it; but it is not to engage the work itself. The following selection, for example, depicts the illegal slaughter of lambs. Yet to say only that is surely to miss much of what the work has to offer, human (but inhumane?) drama, echoes of sacrifice, the appalling precision of nearly dispassionate deadly action, the ineffable affect blends that body, mind, and soul can know, and that body (and to some extent tone of voice), but not words, can suggest. The text cues the work as our immediate human experience, and only performance (and not bloodless summations such as "depiction of the illegal slaughter of lambs") can approximate the full range of significations and effects of "Not for Sale."

Excerpt from "Not for Sale"

by Marie Thomas McNaughton

The big-armed man edged into the short-fenced pen. The sun warmed his back. To his right lay vast open pasture. To his left curious cows nudged the corral fencing. Grackles and finches flitted and chittered in the trees as he pulled a fatted lamb marked for slaughter out of the pen and away from the others. Holding her close, he paused as if in ritual, then shoved his short blade through her throat. With her jugular slashed and spinal cord severed, she jerked and her eyes rolled back. The butcher lay her heavily on the bright green grass. Her throat's crimson course splashed over emerald as her legs kicked reflexively against the turf. He turned to the pen to begin again.[59]

George Herbert's *The Agonie* also has to do with sacrifice, and more. The language is distant from us, obviously, but patient dealing with it will reveal a work cued by the text that is immediate, as much ours as Herbert's (if we would have it), as much now as then. One could sum it up as an early seventeenth-century traditionalist Church of England theology of communion set to verse. To say that something might be lost in such a summing up, however, certainly is to understate the case. To speak the text without at least an attempt at soul-deep, body-sure internalization of the full range of its significations and effects, to say the words without entering the world they figure, without being one

59. Marie Thomas McNaughton, "Not for Sale," *Meat and Poultry* 39, no. 9 (September 1993): pp. 28-30, 32, 36, 38.

"who would know Sinne" or "who knows not Love," also would be to miss the point. In fact it would be to miss the work entire, for Herbert (as we know him in his poem) is where he invites all who would hear him to be. The theological truth he asserts is of a piece with the human experience of God that gives rise to it. The word "pike," by the way, refers to a spear or lance. "Abroach" means to tap a flow of wine or liquor.

The Agonie

by George Herbert

> Philosophers have measur'd mountains,
> Fathom'd the depths of seas, of states, and kings,
> Walk'd with a staff to heav'n, and traced fountains:
>   But there are two vast, spacious things,
> The which to measure it doth more behove:
> Yet few there are that sound them; Sinne and Love.
>
> Who would know Sinne, let him repair
> Unto Mount Olivet; there shall he see
> A man so wrung with pains, that all his hair,
>   His skin, his garments bloody be.
> Sinne is that press and vice, which forceth pain
> To hunt his cruel food through ev're vein.
>
> Who knows not Love, let him assay
> And taste that juice, which on the cross a pike
> Did set again abroach; then let him say
>   If ever he did taste the like.
> Love is that liquour sweet and most divine,
> Which my God feels as blood; but I, as wine.[60]

A final thought on conceptual content in relationship to experiential content: In his senior year at Lincoln University, Langston Hughes conducted a statistical opinion survey of junior and senior class members. The survey covered food, living conditions, social life, academic standards, "and race relations between the Negro student body and the

---

60. *The Life and Works of George Herbert,* vol. 3, *Bemerton Poems,* edited and annotated by George Herbert Palmer (Boston: Houghton Mifflin & Co., 1905), p. 153.

white faculty. . . ."[61] He wrote a poetic prose foreword to the study. He said of the foreword, "This meant, I suppose, that where life is simple, truth and reality are one."[62] The "I suppose" suggests that even Hughes was uncertain that his text could be reduced to a single proposition. His uncertainty was warranted.

Foreword
(To a statistical research project for a course in sociology)

by Langston Hughes

In the primitive world, where people live closer to the earth and much nearer to the stars every inner and outer act combines to form the single harmony, life. Not just the tribal lore then, but every moment of life becomes a part of their education. They do not, as many civilized people do, neglect the truth of the physical for the sake of the mind. Nor do they teach with speech alone, but rather with all the acts of life. There are no books, so the barrier between words and reality is not so great as with us. The earth is right under their feet. The stars are never far away. The strength of the surest dream is the strength of the primitive world.[63]

We return now to Scripture and specifically to "the speaking tone of voice entangled in the words." In narrative material (material in the so-called epic mode)[64] the human experience of God that the biblical text cues features a narrator and various characters. The narrator stands outside the story and tells the story to the listeners. The narrator's attitude is shaped by the story itself, that is, its unfolding drama, and by his or her interest in telling the story. The story has an ideal audience,[65] an implied audience that will receive the story in a way suited to the narrator's interest in telling it, or in a way suited to implied authorial intent, if the narrating voice's credibility is called into question by the dramatic action. But the story also has an actual audience. The

---

61. Langston Hughes, *The Big Sea: An Autobiography* (New York: Hill and Wang, 1940), p. 306.

62. Hughes, p. 311.

63. Hughes, p. 311.

64. Judy E. Yordon, *Roles in Interpretation*, 3rd ed. (Madison, WI: W. B. Brown and Benchmark, 1993), pp. 101-8; 112-13.

65. Wayne C. Booth, *The Rhetoric of Fiction*, 2nd ed. (Chicago: University of Chicago Press, 1983), pp. 89-116.

object of story telling, then, is to do everything possible to match the actual audience to the ideal audience. The Bible story teller's primary focus thus is on the listener.

Narrative characters remain inside the story and focus on each other and on events as they develop according to the plot. The narrator, the person speaking the story, in giving the characters' lines, does what we all do when we share with each other accounts of incidents we have lived through. The narrator suggests the tone of voice and nonverbal behavior of the characters without necessarily trying to impersonate them or portray them fully. Depending on the kind of story being told and what the story is meant to accomplish, narrators' own tones of voice can vary greatly. So Ezekiel, talking about his encounter with God in the valley of the dry bones (Ezek. 37:1-14), speaking on his own behalf and saying what God told him as well, does not have the same attitude and tone of voice as Jesus telling a parable about the kingdom of heaven. Ezekiel is overcome with awe. Jesus, on the other hand, speaks as a rabbi using a story to instruct and challenge his listeners. Whatever the particular case may be, it is the Bible reader's responsibility to adopt the narrator's point of view, purpose, and motivation. She or he speaks as the narrator.

In poetic and epistolary material (material in the so-called lyric mode)[66] there is only one person speaking, a person (or persona) who seems to be the author of the work (though this is not actually the case in every instance). The task of the public reader of the text in corporate worship is to understand the situation, character, and motivation of this implied speaker and to internalize what is said so that the psalm or epistle reading has coherence and "rings true." The work the text cues must become one's own. Doing this is never easy; and, as is the case with all other aspects of interpretative performance — and to the extent possible — public readers of biblical psalms and epistolary texts will need to draw on historical-critical, form-critical, and literary critical scholarship. Their efforts as interpreters of Scripture via the spoken word, that is to say, will have to be woven into the history of interpretation of the text with which they are working, keeping in mind, above all, that Christ Jesus, crucified, risen, regnant, as attested by the Spirit in Scripture, is the Canon within the canon, the Norm of norms. Merely idiosyncratic and impressionistic readings

66. Yordon, pp. 105-13.

will not do. On the other hand, performance itself (and let us be reminded that we are speaking here of performance as form coming through, and not of performance as putting on an act) contributes to understanding the work the text cues. It provides distinctive contributions to critical understanding, and so may enhance, modify, or call into question the findings of other forms of scholarship. As Henri Bergson observed, performance of a work should not be thought of as an artistic accomplishment. He remarked:

> Instead of coming at the end of one's studies, like an ornament, it should be at the beginning and throughout as a support. Upon it we should place all the rest if we did not yield here again to the illusion that the main thing is to discourse on things and that one knows them sufficiently when one knows how to talk about them.[67]

Keeping that in mind, we conclude this chapter with an extended and detailed performative study of Psalm 27 in conversation with a number of biblical scholars. What we are trying to do is establish the persona or particular speaking voice of the text, the voice readers of the text in public, corporate worship will need to take up as their own. We are asking: Who says the psalm? Whose plea and praise do we need to internalize and express?

Psalm 27

1. The LORD is my light and my salvation;
     whom shall I fear?
   The LORD is the stronghold* of my life;
     of whom shall I be afraid?

2. When evildoers assail me
     to devour my flesh —
   my adversaries and foes —
     they shall stumble and fall.

*or *refuge*

67. Henri Bergson, *The Creative Mind*, trans. Mabelle L. Andison (New York: Philosophical Library, 1946), pp. 101-2. Quoted in Geiger, p. 17.

3. Though an army encamp against me,
      my heart shall not fear;
   though war rise up against me,
      yet will I be confident.

4. One thing I asked of the LORD,
      that will I seek after:
   to live in the house of the LORD
      all the days of my life,
   to behold the beauty of the LORD,
      and to inquire in his temple.

5. For he will hide me in his shelter
      in the day of trouble;
   he will conceal me under the cover of his tent;
      he will set me high on a rock.

6. Now my head is lifted up
      above my enemies all around me,
   and I will offer in his tent
      sacrifices with shouts of joy;
   I will sing and make melody to the LORD.

7. Hear, O LORD, when I cry aloud,
      be gracious to me and answer me!
8. "Come," my heart says, "seek his face!"
      Your face, LORD, do I seek.
9.   Do not hide your face from me.

   Do not turn your servant away in anger,
      you who have been my help.
   Do not cast me off, do not forsake me,
      O God of my salvation!
10. If my father and mother forsake me,
      the LORD will take me up.

11. Teach me your way, O LORD,
      and lead me on a level path
      because of my enemies.

12. Do not give me up to the will of my adversaries,
     for false witnesses have risen against me,
     and they are breathing out violence.

13. I believe that I shall see the goodness of the LORD
     in the land of the living.
14. Wait for the LORD;
     be strong, and let your heart take courage;
     wait for the LORD!

The recent history of scholarly interpretation of Psalm 27 has offered three primary options for the persona, or speaking voice, in the psalm. One option is that the persona of the psalm is actually three speaking voices and not one. Verses 1-6 have a voice of confidence at the center of them. Verses 7-13 feature a voice of lament. Verse 14 offers the voice of one reciting a liturgical formula "added later to the psalm in order to point the lesson to be drawn from it."[68] On the basis of form-critical criteria, that is to say, some scholars conclude that Psalm 27 actually is two psalms best understood as utterly distinct from each other, though complementary to each other, in that together they demonstrate the dialectic of plea and praise that is at the heart of the psalter.[69] Further, a liturgical coda has been added to the song of lament (vv. 7-13), and the voice of the coda (v. 14) is not praise or plea, but exhortation.

It is beyond our purpose now to specify all of the arguments used to justify the reading of Psalm 27 as two psalms plus a liturgical tag line. Nevertheless it is appropriate to indicate what appears to be the working assumption that underlies such a reading and that leads critics holding this view to select those textual features that give credence to their interpretation. The assumption underlying the two-voice, two-personae plus coda (featuring a third persona) view of Psalm 27 is that generic criteria, based on thematic content and poetic grammar, are to be privileged in reading any work. It is assumed, that is to say, that genre studies

68. William R. Taylor, "Commentary on Psalm 27," *The Interpreter's Bible*, vol. 4, ed. George Arthur Buttrick (Nashville, TN: Abingdon Press, 1955), p. 150.
69. Claus Westermann, *Praise and Lament in the Psalms*, trans. Keith R. Crim and Richard N. Soulen (Atlanta: John Knox Press, 1981), pp. 154-55.

do not simply provide insight into the discrete subject matters and compositional styles that typify certain psalmodic constructions that may appear apart or together in a variety of texts. Instead, they give readers of texts a way to categorize psalmodic works according to generic specifications. So, with regard to verses 1-6 of Psalm 27, a critic applying generic criteria can assert:

> Because of his experience of the divine guidance and protection in the course of his days, the psalmist can bid defiance to all who would menace his life. His prayer is that he may ever be permitted to enjoy access to God's presence in the temple. For under God's protection, in the shelter of the sacred dwelling place, no foe can touch him. The thought of what he owes for present and past deliverances leads him to vow hymns of praise and offerings of thanksgiving to God. *It is to be noted that in psalms of this type the Lord is spoken of in the third person.*[70]

The last sentence of the quoted paragraph makes it clear that Psalm 27:1-6 is being read as an instance of a certain type of psalm, which, expressing confidence in God, concludes with vows of praise and thank-offerings. A typical feature of this type of psalm, we are told, is that in it God is addressed in the third person. On the other hand, in Psalm 27:7-13, a lament, God is addressed in the second person. This approach to identifying the persona of Psalm 27, in addition to privileging generic considerations, also assumes that a psalmodic text will be univocal. It assumes, in other words, that the speaker in the text will pray or sing or speak in basically one mood, start to finish.[71] Further, it assumes that an inferred original, un-redacted version of the text, established according to generic criteria, constrains performance. Performances of the work, therefore, if one is to regard them as hermeneutically sound, are largely recreative. Nuances in connotation are possible, but, on the basis of textual details selected according to generic specifications, the three personae of Psalm 27 are delimited by arguments meant to establish original

---

70. Taylor, p. 145. Italics mine.
71. The strengths and weaknesses of the "one mood" approach to analysis of Psalm 27 are explored in detail by Gerstenberger. Erhard S. Gerstenberger, *Psalms Part I with an Introduction to Cultic Poetry* (Grand Rapids, MI: William B. Eerdmans Publishing Co., 1988), pp. 125-27.

authorial intents[72] or to clarify adumbrated authorial motives.[73] Performance as practical hermeneutics in this view does not seek to open up a future for the text. Instead, performance makes room in the present for people to see and hear "the past, happening over and over again."[74] Such performance is not merely the rehearsal of what used to be, however, for, as they speak the psalm, contemporary people appropriate the past. They enter it for a moment and live it as if it were their own present. In worship, such a speaking of the psalm occasions liturgical anamnesis, or living memorialization of a past event of praise and plea. To sum up, the personae of Psalm 27, in this view, are three in number, and they are discrete, univocal, and permanent.

A second approach to Psalm 27 sees it not as two totally independent psalms but as one psalm in two phases, with verse 14 being understood as an oracle from God uttered by a priest or temple servant in response to the petition spoken in verses 7-13. Most typically the one doing the speaking in both verses 1-6 and 7-13 is taken to be the king.[75] The occasion, it is conjectured, is the yearly celebration of the king's coronation. Verse 3 especially, with its allusion to a circumstance of war — "Though an army encamp against me, my heart shall not fear; though war rise up against me, yet will I be confident" — is taken to refer to the role of the king as "commander-in-chief of Israel's armies."[76] Also, the expression in verse 2, "When evildoers assail me to devour my flesh," is regarded as a sign of extreme military danger.[77] Hossfeld has asserted, "The entire section (vv. 1-3) thus is saturated with military metaphors."[78]

72. For a vigorous argument in defense of authorial intent as determinative for meaning in the reading and interpretation of texts, see E. D. Hirsch, Jr., *Validity in Interpretation* (New Haven: Yale University Press, 1967), esp. pp. 10-23.

73. The seminal studies in motives as a key to interpretation are: Kenneth Burke, *A Grammar of Motives* (Englewood Cliffs, NJ: Prentice-Hall, 1945); and Kenneth Burke, *A Rhetoric of Motives* (Berkeley: University of California Press, 1969).

74. Eugene O'Neill, *A Moon for the Misbegotten*, act 3 (New York: Random House, 1952), p. 128. Quoted in the preface to Leon Uris, *Trinity* (New York: Doubleday, 1976).

75. Peter C. Craigie, *Psalms 1–50*, vol. 19 of Word Biblical Commentary, ed. David A. Hubbard and Glenn W. Barker (Waco, TX: Word Books, 1983), pp. 228-35.

76. Craigie, p. 232.

77. F. L. Hossfeld and E. Zenger, *Die Psalmen I* (Würzburg: Echter Verlag, 1993), p. 274.

78. Hossfeld and Zenger ("Der ganze Abschnitt[1-3]ist gesättigt mit Kriegsmetaphern").

The second section of the psalm, verses 7-13, is not saturated with military metaphors. It consists, instead, of two petitions: A general petition in which the king humbly expresses his "determination to seek God's face,"[79] followed by a more specific petition in which "the king prays to be delivered from opponents."[80] The false witnesses breathing out violence (v. 12) are understood to be agents of foreign powers who could conceivably bring about the king's ruin and, with that, Israel's destruction. Craigie explains it this way:

> As a king in the context of international affairs, the king may have had imposed upon him treaties demanding his subservience to foreign powers; as a king in the covenant tradition of David, he could have allegiance only to God. The commitment to God in covenant could be perceived as a treacherous act by foreign nations, who sought to control the king as a vassal; thus, in poetic language, they are described as witnesses, giving evidence in court concerning the king's breach of treaty obligations.[81]

The reference to parental abandonment in verse 10, "If my father and mother forsake me, the LORD will take me up," also is given a monarchical twist: "The expression should not be interpreted literally, but should be understood in terms of the king's role as God's son" (see Psalm 2:7).[82] Craigie and others also refer to the common formulaic language of the psalm as an indication of its cultic rootedness and probable grounding in some sort of royal ritual. As argued by Craigie and others, then, Psalm 27 is a royal psalm; the principal persona is the persona of the king. A second persona is the persona of a temple official who pronounces a divine oracle in response to the king's petition in verses 7-13: "Wait for the LORD; be strong, and let your heart take courage; wait for the LORD!"

In the approach to Psalm 27 just described, generic criteria based

---

79. Craigie, p. 233.
80. Craigie, p. 234.
81. Craigie, p. 234.
82. Craigie, p. 233. Hossfeld offers rebuttal to this point of view. "Die Eltern haben den Beter verlassen, was hier bedeuten kann, dass sie verschieden sind und als natürliche Verbündete im Rechtsstreit ausfallen." (That the parents have forsaken the one praying here can mean that they are deceased and therefore cease to be his natural allies in his lawsuit or controversy.) Hossfeld and Zenger, p. 175.

on analyses of thematic content and poetic grammar again are given large place. However, the concern is not to slot parts of the psalm into already established generic categories, that is, psalms of confidence and psalms of lament. Instead, there is a recognition of features distinct to each section of the psalm: that is, the war metaphors of the first half of the psalm and the humble pleadings of the second half. Yet there also is a recognition of thematic congruity throughout the work as a whole, namely, the desire on the part of the principal speaker in the text to seek God's face. But this tension,[83] of similarity in difference and of difference in similarity, is ameliorated by imagining a possible liturgical setting for the psalm's original use. This setting, most likely a yearly coronation ceremony, is asserted cautiously though, for, as Craigie himself points out, "the evidence for the royal interpretation . . . is indirect . . . ," and "It is difficult to be precise in determining the setting for this liturgical psalm."[84]

In this view, the principal persona of the text is not limited primarily by reference to authorial intent or motive, though it is assumed that the psalm was composed for the king. Here the principal persona of the text is imagined within the context of a liturgical setting where the king speaks both as a military leader of his people and as their pious exemplar. The words of the second persona of the text, then, the words of the liturgical figure who responds to the king's petition with the divine oracle "Wait for the LORD . . . ," offer a word of exhortation applicable not only to the king, but also to all who identify with him in his acts of humility and piety. A window to the future of the psalm as a unified liturgical text for all the people of God thereby is thrown open.[85] Contemporary speakers of the text, whether individuals or a company of devout, can speak the first two movements of the text as their own hymn of confidence (vv. 1-6) and prayer of petition (vv. 7-13). The last movement of the text, however, the divine

83. A contrary reading of the text, instead of seeking to reduce tension, would seek to understand tension as significant for determining meaning. See Bacon, p. 37.

84. Craigie, p. 231.

85. Craigie, p. 231. Craigie indicates the psalm's contemporary liturgical use in Jewish worship: "In the later history of Judaism, and continuing into the present century, Ps. 27 has played a central role in the 'Days of Awe' (Yamim Noraim), being recited in the synagogue during each of the ten holy days. The psalm's substance, concerning God's compassion and love for his people, is most appropriate for the season in which judgment and deliverance are the central themes in the Jewish liturgy."

oracle "Wait for the LORD . . . ," must be spoken as to another, as public
proclamation. What was a personal word of direct admonition to the
king now becomes a word of exhortation to any and all who, in
confidence and trust, humility and awe, seek God's presence and God's
help.

In this approach to the psalm, the personae are only two in number. The first persona speaks both the hymn of confidence and the prayer
of petition. The second persona announces the divine oracle. But the
hymn of praise and the prayer of petition remain distinct and univocal,
the mood of the one substantially different from the mood of the other.
This is so because the liturgical movements to which they are related
remain discrete and sequential, even though thematic content (specifically, seeking God's presence) is carried over from the first half of the
psalm into the second half of the psalm. Performance of the psalm in
worship occasions anamnesis, as was the case with the earlier reading;
but added to that anamnesis there is spiritual and ethical mimesis, too,
as the people of God, "together or apart,"[86] follow the lead of the king
and appropriate royal piety as their own.

A third view of the text (the most plausible canonical reading
of it, in my view, and the reading most suited to our receiving the
text contemporaneously as sacred Scripture and as God's word to and
for us) sees it as a unity consisting of three movements.[87] The first
movement is a soliloquy of trust, praise, and aspiration in the midst
of danger. The persona, the speaker in the text, is facing up to immi-
nent dangers: "The stings of private enemies, the devices of political
oppressors, . . . the horrors of War."[88] Samuel Terrien has pointed out
that verses 1-6 need not be construed as featuring the voice of someone at ease and in possession of an all-undaunted confidence in God.
To the contrary, he insists: "Its undertones are vibrant with lurking
perils, and only its dominant melody is that of triumphant trust."[89]

86. Robert Frost, "The Tuft of Flowers," in *The Poetry of Robert Frost*, ed. Edward
Connery Latham (New York: Holt, Rinehart and Winston, 1969), pp. 22-23, lns. 10, 40.
87. This third approach to the psalm frankly is my own, though, in making my
case, I draw heavily on the work of Terrien and Mays. See Samuel Terrien, *The Psalms
and Their Meaning for Today* (New York: Bobbs-Merrill, 1952); and James L. Mays,
Psalms, Interpretation: A Bible Commentary for Teaching and Preaching (Louisville,
KY: John Knox Press, 1994).
88. Terrien, p. 216.
89. Terrien, p. 216.

Further, the persona need not be the king. Rather the persona may be thought of as a solitary, anonymous figure yearning to behold not God (for that would be to die) but "the beauty of the LORD" (v. 4). As Terrien puts it, the speaker in the text aspires to "gazing upon the delightfulness" or "the pleasantness of Yahweh" and to "contemplating."[90] Terrien defines the approach to contemplation in Psalm 27 this way:

> Contemplation is the sublime exercise of the devout spirit, the active concentration of all human energies toward a more penetrating knowledge of the purposeful goodness and graciousness of the divine toward the human. . . . It begins with the social participation of the individual in the aesthetic rehearsal of the Word which God has revealed of himself in the history of the nations and of the chosen people. It is rooted in corporate sharing in the drama of the liturgy, but it thrusts the individual forward and leads [that person] dynamically beyond the forms and limitations of the cult toward the most secret holy of holies, until the "thou and I" encounter is consummated and [the human being] is met by God alone.[91]

But such yearned-for moments of awful serenity are fleeting and rare. What enables the speaker in the text to survive long absence of signs of the divine presence and the lurking dangers that haunt life, making it as much a terror as a solemn joy, is obstinate trust. God does not always hide the devout soul in the precincts of the temple, but in the divine "hut," "booth," "pavilion," the "secret of his tent" and the security of a "high rock." The plurality and inconsistency of the images make it clear that the persona of Psalm 27 has no expectation of dwelling forever secure in a literal sanctuary space.[92] True sanctuary, and the firm ground of obstinate trust, is afforded those from whom the divine face has not been turned away in forgetfulness or wrath.

So the speaker in the text prays, "Hear, O LORD, when I cry aloud" (v. 7) and "Do not hide your face from me" (v. 9). Here begins the second movement. The speaker turns from soliloquy to prayer. Yet elements of soliloquy remain: " 'Come,' my heart says, 'seek his face!' " (v. 8), and "If my father and mother forsake me, the LORD will take me up" (v. 10). In

90. Terrien, p. 217.
91. Terrien, p. 217.
92. Terrien, p. 218.

fact, the lament or plea of the persona of Psalm 27 alternates regularly between prayer and soliloquy. The two modes of speech are so bound together that no sharp distinction between them finally can be made. They belong together in the same moment of utterance: prayer (v. 7), soliloquy and prayer (v. 8), prayer (v. 9), soliloquy (v. 10), and prayer (vv. 11-12). Also, contrary to the expectation that the prayer of lament feature speech to God in the second person, there is an instance when the persona of Psalm 27:7-12 speaks of God in the third person, "If my father and mother forsake me, the LORD will take me up" (v. 10). Further, verses 7-14 pick up motifs established in verses 1-6: "salvation" (vv. 1, 9); "adversary" (vv. 2, 12); "heart" (vv. 3, 8, 14); "rise" (vv. 3, 12); and "seek" (vv. 4, 8).[93]

The anonymous speaker in Psalm 27 pleads with God, "Do not cast me off" (v. 9), "Do not give me up to the will of my adversaries" (v. 12), and beseeches God for ethical guidance so that life may be both safe from error and safe from enemies: "Teach me your way, O LORD, and lead me on a level path because of my enemies" (v. 11). The "level path" is the path of moral duty, uprightness, and godliness. It is the way God "knows" (see Psalm 1). It is not merely the smooth, easy, comfortable way of the untroubled spirit. Said Calvin: "[Those] who thus desire to commit [themselves] to the safeguard and protection of God, must first renounce crafty and wicked devices."[94] Finally, since it is to the eyes of faith alone that God can be seen as succor in the midst of trial and danger, the persona of Psalm 27 leaves off praying (or finishes praying, if one chooses to link v. 13, contra NRSV, to vv. 7-12) with a desperate credo: "I believe that I shall see the goodness of the LORD in the land of the living" (v. 13). The NRSV and RSV translation here is emotionally weak compared to the KJV: "I had fainted, unless I had believed to see the goodness of the LORD in the land of the living." And the KJV itself is weaker than the translation proposed by Terrien: "If I did not believe to see the goodness of the Lord in the land of the living . . . !"[95] The sentence is left incomplete because the "prospect is too horrible for verbal formulation."[96]

---

93. Mays, p. 130.

94. Quoted in Terrien, p. 219.

95. Terrien, p. 220. See also H. J. Krause: "Alas, if I did not have the assurance to behold the goodness of Yahweh in the land of the living — !" Hans-Joachim Krause, *Psalms 1–59: A Commentary*, trans. Hilton C. Oswald (Minneapolis: Augsburg Publishing House, 1988), p. 331.

96. Terrien, p. 220.

With lament and credo thus completed, the persona (continuing in soliloquy) speaks the third, final, brief movement of the psalm: "Wait for the LORD; be strong and let your heart take courage; wait for the LORD!" (v. 14). Is this statement directed to the self, as Terrien would have it?[97] Or is the exhortation, as Mays prefers, "a concluding commendation of the stance of trust expressed in the psalm addressed to whoever uses it and to a personified congregation"?[98] Both are possibilities, it would seem. Already it has been noted that the psalm moves from soliloquy to prayer (with moments of soliloquy interspersed throughout the prayer itself) and back again to soliloquy. With the Terrien option, the soliloquy all along hints at an unspoken invitation to others to join with the persona of Psalm 27 in this act of praise and plea. With the Mays option, the invitation becomes overtly public and direct (a considerable, though not implausible, shift in attitude and perspective on the part of the speaker in the text). The function of soliloquy, in any case, is precisely to invite others into what one is working through oneself. In it there is yearning for human companionship and solidarity. Soliloquy is speech overheard and meant to be overheard. At the same time, whether one chooses to address the words "Wait for the LORD . . ." to oneself or to others, the words can be understood as a divine oracle. But now the oracle comes to the speaker in the text as insight, direct from God. It is not mediated to the supplicant by a temple official. The stance of the persona of Psalm 27, which from start to finish has been a stance of faithful waiting, is confirmed by God. The face of Yahweh has turned to the supplicant, the eternal "thou" to the temporal "I." Here faith sees "the goodness of the LORD in the land of the living" not as deliverance from all danger and ambiguity, but as encouragement to see them through.

This reading of the text can be seen as emerging from the previous readings, in which case those readings are not simply superseded, but enriched and transformed. The previous readings of the text take us behind the canonical psalm to its possible antecedents in psalmodic history, its arguably authentic authorial shape, and its liturgical use at some point, perhaps, as royal ritual. The third reading receives the psalm in its present, canonical shape,[99] and seeks its future, not

97. Terrien, p. 220.
98. Mays, p. 132.
99. R. Coote and M. Coote trace the shaping of the canon from a perspective

through imaginative appropriation of the psalmist's experience only, or through identification with the ethos of the king, but through anonymous and varied contextualized performances.[100] Performance here is not a recreative art, but a creative art. Furthermore, performance is not just an act of technical virtuosity following upon scholarly analyses of the work and totally dependent upon them. Instead, it is a type of public criticism that brings fresh understanding to the work, and so contributes to the body of knowledge concerning it. Even the work called Psalm 27 itself can be seen as that to which the text points instead of that which the text is.[101] In fact, the text can be seen as an "arrested performance"[102] (as indeed all texts can, as already has been discussed), a stilled word waiting to be spoken, in much the same way that a musical score can be understood as stilled music waiting to be played and sung. Performance of a work, that is to say, is a way of coming to know it in oneself, and with and for others. In the case of Psalm 27, performance is a way of bringing to expression the persona of the text while not fixing that persona as a particular historical figure, author or king. The persona is protean. The persona is other than the performer, clearly, though who the performer is, his or her resources of experience, influences the realization of the persona. Yet, because

---

of "social realism" and show how that shaping was hardly a disinterested, spiritual endeavor. Yet the canon can triumph even over the forces, humanly speaking, that gave rise to it and subvert the powers that would use canonical texts to protect vested interests and the prerogatives of religious elites. So, in the present instance, Psalm 27 may accrue meanings beyond those related to authorial intents, and an anonymous persona at prayer may displace the king as moral exemplar. See Robert B. Coote and Mary P. Coote, *Power, Politics and the Making of the Bible* (Minneapolis, MN: Fortress Press, 1990).

100. So Christians use psalms as hymns of praise, petition, and lament, as texts for sermons, as words of comfort for mourners, as words of encouragement for the sick and persecuted, as vehicles of public, corporate prayer, and as a resource for private and familial devotional life. The use of psalms in Judaism also is richly varied: "The regular reading of Psalms was not confined to services. The recital of the whole Book of Psalms is widespread, whether as an act of piety by saintly individuals, or by groups of unlearned people. For this purpose 'societies of reciters of psalms' *(hevrot tehillim)* were formed in Jerusalem whereby two separate groups recite the whole Book of Psalms daily at the Western Wall." *Encyclopedia Judaica*, vol. 13 (New York: Macmillan, 1971), p. 1325.

101. Louise M. Rosenblatt, "Act 1, Scene 1: Enter the Reader," *Literature in Performance* 1, no. 2 (April 1981): p. 13.

102. Long and HopKins, p. 2.

that persona can speak only through a succession of performances in which people take upon themselves that persona's ubiquitous anonymity, the persona of Psalm 27 receives only the "name of the nameless."[103] It is, so to speak, a persona with nowhere to lay its head.[104]

A final thought: as has been noted previously, in the third reading of the text of Psalm 27, categories of performance analysis are brought into play not only upon completion of one's preparation of the text for public reading, but as part of that preparation. Performance analyses are undertaken along with, and not just after, historical-critical, form-critical, generic, stylistic, and thematic analyses. Already the function of soliloquy has been discussed. Two other matters should be mentioned as well. First, working with the text in its canonical form allows the performer-critic to observe three elements of lyric progression defined by Charlotte Lee: fulcrum, climax, and denouement.[105] The fulcrum of the text is that point where the emotional weight of the passage is balanced: One half of the emotional weight of the lyric precedes the fulcrum. The other half of the lyric's emotional weight comes after the fulcrum. The fulcrum of Psalm 27 is reached where the persona says, "Hear, O LORD, when I cry aloud . . ." (v. 7). This point of balance, or fulcrum, also marks the transition in the text from soliloquy to prayer. The climax of the lyric, the point where the tensional forces of praise and plea, confidence and lament, reach their peak, occurs in verse 13, perhaps best translated as, "If I did not believe to see the goodness of the LORD in the land of the living. . . ." The denouement, then, consists of one verse, "Wait for the LORD; be strong, and let your heart take courage; wait for the LORD!" (v. 14). Here the persona of Psalm 27 receives as spiritual insight the word from Yahweh needed to "keep on keepin' on" in the midst of a precarious (literally, full of prayers) situation.

Second, performance of the text in its canonical form allows the performer-critic to experience and express what Wallace Bacon has

103. George Arthur Buttrick, "The Name of the Nameless," in *Sermons Preached in a University Church* (Nashville, TN: Abingdon Press, 1959), pp. 164-71.

104. See Matthew 8:20; Luke 9:58.

105. Lee, *Oral Interpretation*, pp. 27-28. Also see Charlotte I. Lee, *Oral Reading of the Scriptures* (New York: Houghton Mifflin Co., 1974), p. 146. Finally, See Charles L. Bartow, *The Preaching Moment*, pp. 21-31.

called the *tensiveness* of the work.[106] Tensiveness, briefly defined, is that creative tension of oppositional forces that lets a poem sing. The oppositional forces of Psalm 27 are drawn taut, like cello strings, in the performer's heart, soul, mind, will, voice, and body.[107] Knowing those tensive elements, deeply feeling them, and not seeking their amelioration, is to know the psalm and the psalm's singer, its persona. For the persona of Psalm 27 is not engaged first in a song of confidence, then in a song of lament. Instead, the persona is engaged in both from start to finish.[108] The subtext of the soliloquy of confidence is the prayer of lament, and the subtext of the lament is trust in God. The waiting is like the waiting of Milton in "On His Blindness."[109] It is waiting filled

106. See note 55.

107. Charles L. Bartow, *Effective Speech Communication in Leading Worship* (Nashville, TN: Abingdon Press, 1988), pp. 20-22.

108. W. Brueggemann states: "This psalm is difficult to categorize under any rubric, for it seems to contain two different and unrelated elements. Verses 1-6 are indeed an expression of confidence, but verses 7-14 sound more like a complaint. Thus to treat the whole as 'confidence' is uncertain. I do so, however, under the impression that this motif is overriding, even in lament. Confidence wins out over trouble." Walter Brueggemann, *The Message of the Psalms: A Theological Commentary* (Minneapolis, MN: Augsburg Publishing House, 1984), p. 152. But with Terrien and Mays, this writer is inclined to view the psalm as an unresolved tension between plea and praise, a steady, if disturbed, waiting that requires both.

109. John Milton, "On His Blindness," in *Milton's Minor Poems*, ed. Mary A. Jordan (New York: American Book Co., 1904), p. 31. The waiting of Milton is even more clearly reminiscent of the waiting expressed in Psalm 27 when one considers Milton's historical moment, his political and ecclesiastical commitments, and his existential situation. He believed the cause of Cromwell was the cause of liberty, and God's cause. And he wished with all his powers to be involved in it. He was thus opposed to monarchy, to much established religious authority, and to the papacy. He lost his sight precisely at the time he wished to have it for his work. Yet the sonnet "On His Blindness" hovers between lament and a credo of confidence, and concludes, "They also serve who only stand and wait." One can share his plight, of course, without necessarily sharing his conviction. Interestingly, contrary to Psalm 27, the persona of "On His Blindness" is very hard to wrench free from the person of the author. The text of "On His Blindness" is as follows:

On His Blindness

by John Milton

When I consider how my light is spent
Ere half my days in this dark world and wide,
And that one talent which is death to hide

with chastened expectancy. It is waiting in prayerfulness and in dreadful awareness that life at last comes to God or comes to nothing. Note that it is precisely the canonical form of the text that liberates Psalm 27 from any past history that might keep it a psalm of royalty and privilege. The canon presents the psalm as the psalm of common folk and of folk decidedly uncommon in their weakness and isolation. The canon of Scripture here truly is a means of grace, a means by which God draws near to the neediest of the needy, to the "third world" of "the third world." To be in solidarity with the persona of this psalm is to be in solidarity with the voiceless. And to speak this psalm is to make their voice heard in our services of worship, whatever our own social location.

Lodged with me useless, though my soul more bent
To serve therewith my Maker, and present
My true account, lest he returning chide,
"Doth God exact day-labor, light denied?"
I fondly ask. But Patience, to prevent
That murmur, soon replies, "God doth not need
Either man's work or his own gifts. Who best
Bear his mild yoke, they serve him best. His state
Is kingly: thousands at his bidding speed,
And post o'er land and ocean without rest;
They also serve who only stand and wait."

4. A Conflagration of Love

THE GOSPEL FOR "INTERESTING TIMES," the kerygmatic expectation, which provides the frame of reference for speaking and hearing the Scriptures, also provides the frame of reference for composing and preaching sermons. We come to the biblical witness "in Christ Jesus." We take account of that witness in him. In him we frame our response to it. With our sermons we bear witness to what we have seen, heard, tasted, felt, and been led to understand of God, as God has made the divine self known to us in Jesus Christ, through the agency of the Holy Spirit, and with the words of Scripture. Jesus Christ therefore is not only the definitive locus of *actio divina*. He is also the locus of *homo performans*. True humanity is found in him. We are baptized into Christ, Saint Paul observes:

> Therefore we have been buried with him by baptism into his death, so that, just as Christ was raised from the dead by the glory of the Father, so we too might walk in newness of life.
> . . . The death he died, he died to sin, once for all; but the life he lives, he lives to God. So you also must consider yourselves dead to sin and alive to God in Christ Jesus. (Rom. 6:4, 10-11)

That is what we need to keep in mind about our common humanity and our individual lives as we approach the task of preaching. As the eternal Son of the Father was incarnate "by the Holy Spirit of the Virgin Mary, and was made [human],"[1] so, through baptism, each of us is

---

1. "The Nicene Creed," *The Book of Confessions* (Louisville, KY: Presbyterian Church [U.S.A.], 1994), C.1.2, p. 3.

incarnated into Christ. We are joined to his body. His standing before the Father is our standing, not according to our merit, of course, but according to God's free choice. Calvin observed that God may be known and feared in nature. But in Christ Jesus God may be known and loved,[2] for "while we were yet sinners, Christ died for us" (Rom. 5:8). No one need approach the task of preaching with awe and dread only, then, but with faith and hope as well; for the promise is this: that in Christ Jesus, God takes us as we are — *as we are* — and presses us into the service of what he would have us be. Our social location, our public and private moral track record,[3] our ethnic identity, our gender roles, these are not the things that define us ultimately. What defines us ultimately is holy love, kindled love, love that burns away even our virtues, as Flannery O'Connor once put it,[4] until there is nothing left of us but what God wants of us forever. Where *homo performans* meets *actio divina* there is a conflagration of love. We call it preaching.

Already we have seen that as spoken text, as performed work, the Bible cues realization of human experience of God. The text itself is a material object, but the work entangled in its words is not a material object. It is a human drama played out in acts of interpretative speech. The text has something to say, and the meaning of the text never can be less or other than what is asserted in it. Its asserted meaning is its conceptual content. Yet the text's significations and effects go beyond what can be said. Denotation is enriched by connotation. Therefore scriptural texts, particularly in their canonical form, accrue meanings that, though not inconsistent with meanings inherent in their originating contexts, nevertheless go beyond them. Publicly defensible constru-

2. Edward A. Dowey, Jr., *The Knowledge of God in Calvin's Theology* (Grand Rapids, MI: William B. Eerdmans Publishing Co., 1994), pp. 41-49. Also see Benjamin A. Reist, *A Reading of Calvin's Institutes* (Louisville, KY: Westminster/John Knox Press, 1991), pp. 28-30.

3. Said Fosdick, "We may have secret infidelities that seep through our cleverest concealments and poison the springs from which other folks must drink." Harry Emerson Fosdick, "Forgiveness of Sins," in *Riverside Sermons* (New York: Harper & Bros., 1958), p. 297.

4. Flannery O'Connor, "Revelation," in *The Complete Stories* (New York: Farrar, Straus and Giroux, 1982), p. 508. See also E. Johnson's etymological definition of the word "God" itself as meaning ". . . to take care of and cherish all things, burning all malice like a consuming fire." Elizabeth A. Johnson, *She Who Is: The Mystery of God in Feminist Theological Discourse* (New York: Crossroad Publishing Co., 1994), p. 44.

als of authorial intent, to the extent that textual and extratextual evidence makes them possible, are mandatory. Not to make them assumes that authors, redactors, and textual commentators have nothing to say to us, an absurdity considering the quantity and quality of their efforts![5] Indeed, if they have nothing to say to us, how can we logically assume that we have anything to say to each other with what they have left us? As was indicated in the previous chapter, texts make sense as we make sense with them. But conceptual content, originating historical circumstance, authorial intents, and redactional developments set the trajectory for textual meaning. They do not delimit it. Meaning is always more than what was meant. Through performance, scriptural texts evoke worlds of human being "real enough for people to enter, to believe in, and to be changed by."[6]

The text as sound frozen in ink is an object capable of manipulation. It is related to its preacher-interpreter as things are related to him or her. The text, in fact, is precisely an "it" in Buber's sense of the term.[7] Within the given limits of its semantic structure, which includes its thematic structure (the structure of its subjects and concrete referents) and its dramatic structure (the structure of its attitudes, actions, and events), and within the given limits of its sound structure, which includes its meter or verse-by-verse count of syllables or stress in poetry (or its dramatic pacing in the case of prose)[8] and its "orchestration,"[9] that is, its patterns of rhyme, alliteration, assonance, syntactic patterns, pause patterns, phonetic juxtapositions, and the like, a text is as predictable as the would-be speaker of it is competent to read it. It cannot surprise or discomfit him or her. It simply is what it is and what the preacher-interpreter has the training and skill to make of it. Receiving the text as cue to the realization of the work entangled in its words, however, can surprise and discomfit, for as soon as preacher-interpreters embody and sound the text, they realize, through the very choices they

5. L. D. Hurst in his foreword to G. B. Caird, *New Testament Theology* (New York: Oxford University Press, 1994), p. xi.

6. Charles L. Bartow, *The Preaching Moment: A Guide to Sermon Delivery* (Dubuque, IA: Kendall/Hunt Publishing Co., 1995), p. 14.

7. Martin Buber, *I and Thou* (New York: Charles Scribner's Sons, 1937), p. 3.

8. For a superb and accessible discussion of prose rhythm see Charlotte I. Lee, *Oral Interpretation*, 4th ed. (Boston: Houghton Mifflin Co., 1974), pp. 146-48.

9. Don Geiger, *The Sound, Sense and Performance of Literature* (Chicago: Scott, Foresman and Co., 1963), p. 30.

make (and *must* make), that they can never fully embody and sound the text's life and world, the complete range of its significations and effects. That in fact would require the satisfactory completion of all the possible performances of all the possible preacher-interpreters and hearers of the text. When one speaks of the text as cue to the work entangled in its words, one is speaking of a nearly infinite range of significations and effects. One is speaking of a textual life and meaning beyond the full comprehension of the preacher-interpreter. One is speaking in fact of a life and meaning that comprehends him or her. Just as *Hamlet* is more than any Olivier can make him, and just as Bach's *Magnificat* and Beethoven's *Missa Solemnis* outlive all their performances, so texts of Scripture, viewed as "arrested performances," as cues to works entangled in words, resist full comprehension, and continue to conscript, into the service of the worlds of human being they would evoke, all who would listen to them, speak them, or preach and read about them. When one is dealing with the world of a text, and not just with the text as literary object, one is dealing at the level of intersubjectivity, or what Buber calls "I-thou relations."[10]

Further, the world of human being evoked in performance of texts is a world of human being with God. Not only has the text something to say that must be taken seriously, not only does the work of the text entangled in its words articulate meanings rich with connotation as well as denotation, but the God of or to whom the text speaks also speaks in the speaking of the text, laying claim to human life in the here and now. When Jesus came preaching, he came preaching the kingdom of God (Mark 1:14-15),[11] that is, the realm and *rule* of God, and what he was and what he did were fully commensurable with what he preached. There was no separation of the medium from the message, of the man from his work. So likewise there can be no separation of preachers and their congregants from what is preached in the church. Whatever rule of God preachers preach will be God's rule in them and not just among those to whom they preach. Whatever challenge they speak will be a challenge to the conduct of their own affairs and to the affairs of their congregants, and not just a challenge to the conduct of affairs in the

10. Buber, pp. 105-6.
11. The importance of preaching not only Jesus but the kingdom Jesus preached was forcefully argued by D. Buttrick. See David Buttrick, "Who Hears the Sermon on the Mount?" *Studia Homiletica* 1 (1995): pp. 38-48, esp. pp. 42-44.

world "out there." Likewise, whatever consolations God's presence and rule bring will be consolations thankfully received by preachers themselves, with and on behalf of all sorts and conditions of humanity.

In fact, since all creation "waits with eager longing for the revealing of the children of God" (Rom. 8:19), among whom there is a celebration of God's just rule and an exercise of human dominion in *life* instead of in waste, destruction, and death (Rom. 5:17), the claim, consolation, challenge, and succor preachers and congregants come to know in the preaching moment is claim, consolation, challenge, and succor experienced with and on behalf of the entire created order. What it means in Christ Jesus to be taken as we are and pressed into the service of what God would have us be thus is redefined in every preaching event, on the basis of the particular witness of the text in question, its denotation, its connotation, and its construal of the presence of God. No status quo of personal morality, public ethics, ecological governance, or even comprehension of the gospel — what it is and what significance it has for human and cosmic life[12] — is left unquestioned. So if our gospel for "interesting times," or kerygmatic expectation, orients us in our approach to Scripture, our encounter with Scripture's God and Christ disorients us and reorients us[13] with that sovereign freedom that belongs to the One who says, "I am that I am, I will be what I will be, I will be there."

Sermons bearing faithful witness to the encounter of the worlds of text and preacher in Christ thus will feature, at their core, narrative testimony to God's redefinition of the terms of human existence in the divine presence. They will not feature dispassionate consideration of ideas concerning deity. Still less will they feature inspiration for human aspiration. They will not be given on Sunday to get everybody from

---

12. So Long observes: "The word of God we encounter in scripture does not attack idolatry in general; it dethrones *our* idols, severs the bonds of *our* old and crippling loyalties. It is not the word of God in abstract but of God who is for us, of God who is against us in order to be truly for us." Thomas G. Long, *The Witness of Preaching* (Louisville, KY: Westminster/John Knox Press, 1989), p. 55.

13. Walter Brueggemann uses the pattern of orientation, disorientation, and reorientation to link human experience to psalmodic literature. He uses the categories to identify psalms according to the genre of orientation, disorientation, and reorientation, however, while I am using the pattern to identify not types of psalms but experiential possibilities in reading *any* psalm. See Walter Brueggemann, *Praying the Psalms* (Winona, MN: St. Mary's Press, 1982), pp. 15-24.

Monday to Friday. Perhaps their form and function will be governed by the form and function of the text,[14] doxological passages yielding sermons that lead into praise, lament psalms yielding sermons that "rage, rage against the dying of the light,"[15] proverbial passages yielding sermons full of wise, situationally apt insights regarding the ways of humanity with God, self, and neighbor and the ways of God in Christ with everybody and everything. However that may be, sermons, above all, through all, and in all, will narrate, give account of, the rule of God in Christ in the life of the church and world in the light of what a biblical text, as performed work, says and does, asserts and signifies. They will trace trajectories of meaning given by God in Christ, through the agency of the Holy Spirit and with the words of Scripture. Pursuing neither praise nor blame, but rather fidelity, preachers, with their sermons, will bear witness to that to which the Scriptures themselves bear witness, for, as with all evidential rhetoric, including judicial testimony, what is required is integrity of life and word.[16] Said Schleiermacher of his preaching: "it is the pure necessity of my nature; it is divine call; it is that which determines my position in the world and makes me what I am."[17] Exactly.

Preaching, then, is first of all narrative discourse. It is a performance of story. Preachers bear witness to what a biblical text says and evokes. And they bear witness to the encounter of the biblical world with their own world. Their own world of course includes the daily round of congregational, family, and civic life. But it ranges farther afield too. It includes culture, in its broadest definition, and even cosmos, for the God who speaks in the speaking of the Scriptures, while addressing us as individuals and as a church, addresses us also in the full range of our associations with

14. Thomas G. Long, *Preaching and the Literary Forms of the Bible* (Philadelphia: Fortress Press, 1989), esp. pp. 43-65. Sermons, of course, should also be governed by the theological and ethical trajectory of the text and by the world of human being with God the text evokes when spoken with full attention to connotative and denotative meaning.

15. Dylan Thomas, "Do Not Go Gentle into that Good Night," in *The Collected Poems of Dylan Thomas* (New York: New Directions Publishers, 1957), p. 128.

16. Paul Ricoeur, "The Hermeneutics of Testimony," *Essays on Biblical Interpretation*, ed. Lewis S. Mudge (Philadelphia: Fortress Press, 1980), p. 129 and pp. 140-42.

17. Friedrich Schleiermacher, *Servant of the Word: Selected Sermons of Friedrich Schleiermacher*, trans. with an introduction by Dawn DeVries (Philadelphia: Fortress Press, 1987), p. 8.

all created things. More surely than is true of even the greatest literature, the Word of God incarnate in Christ and attested in Scripture

> speaks to our capacity for delight, for wonder, to the sense of mystery surrounding our lives; to our sense of pity, and beauty, and pain; to the latent feeling of fellowship with all creation — and to the subtle but invincible conviction of solidarity that knits together the loneliness of innumerable hearts; to the solidarity in dreams, in joy, in sorrow, in aspirations, in illusions, in hope, in fear, which binds [persons] to each other, which binds together all humanity — the dead to the living and the living to the unborn.[18]

The word of God speaks to those things not simply to leave them as they are, but to strengthen them, stretch them, challenge them, break them, mend them; for God seeks not only a holy people but a hallowed cosmos, and a temporality blessed with eternity.

Yet there is resistance to the scope of the divine self-disclosure and claim in the Word made flesh, and to sound that resistance is to sound the depths of human fascination with the self. Joseph Sittler put it starkly:

> The reality is this: that we incline to define ourselves, take the measure of our actuality, admit as educative and civilizing, acknowledge as relevant and powerful — only that in experience or reflection which is authenticated by its occurrence within the biographical brackets of the self's existence.[19]

So the memory of the church in Bible, creed, confession, and liturgy is thought "forever amber,"[20] sealed away like fossil remains in translucent gold, suitable for arcane scholarship and beautiful to behold, certainly, but hardly troublesome or delightful, alarmingly or encouragingly immediate. When the performance of the self is all, it is not surprising to find preaching that is self-absorbed, strictly local, folksy, moralistic, and therapeutic; hardly a conflagration of love. Under the tyranny of the self, said Sittler:

18. Joseph Conrad, *A Conrad Argosy*, ed. William McFee (Garden City, NY: Doubleday, Doran & Co., 1942), p. viii.

19. Joseph Sittler, *The Ecology of Faith: The New Situation in Preaching* (Philadelphia: Muhlenberg Press, 1961), p. 12.

20. Michael D. Leonick, "Forever Amber," *Time*, Feb. 12, 1996, pp. 66-68.

Preaching becomes primarily personal, the history of the church becomes an anecdotal arsenal useful for its supply of supportive items.
The "mighty deeds of God" are transformed into such interior "patterns of sensibility" as are readily marketable, and the mighty TE
DEUM of the people of God becomes trivialized into a "worship
experience."[21]

Sittler further sees the tyranny of the self allied with the "tyranny
of the boundless," with the sense that human potential is illimitable,
and that possibilities for self-definition, self-realization, and self-expression are endless.[22] The most ancient — yet current — sense of the illimitable self is articulated in the doctrine of the immortality of the
soul, which, according to Shirley Guthrie, is profoundly at odds with
the Christian doctrine of the resurrection; for "the Christian hope is
not in the indestructibility of [the human being], but in the creative
power of God, who by the power of his word can call life into being
out of nothing and make dead [people] live."[23] The plural particularity
of *actio divina,* discussed in previous chapters, likewise offends confidence in the illimitable character of *homo performans.* For example, this
observation from the mid-1950s:

> When the theme of the second assembly of the World Council of
> Churches was announced, and more acutely when the preliminary
> study document was made available to the churches in North Amer-
> ica, there was a curious reaction. The reaction was compounded of
> bafflement, annoyance, and impatience. Some were baffled by the
> declaration that nothing less than Jesus Christ was the hope of the
> world, for were there not broader, more generally "religious" and less
> radical sources of hope? Others were annoyed because they regarded
> this blunt statement as a frantic oversimplification of Christian the-
> ology, a retreat into pre-enlightenment piety. Others were impatient
> because they believed themselves allied with redemptive powers and
> possibilities whose adequacy was threatened by this identification of
> hope with so scandalous a historical particularity.[24]

21. Sittler, p. 14.
22. Sittler, pp. 14-25.
23. Shirley C. Guthrie, *Christian Doctrine* (Atlanta: John Knox Press, 1968), pp.
382-83.
24. Sittler, p. 14.

Preaching as a conflagration of love, however, preaching that testifies to the encounter of *actio divina* with *homo performans,* the world of the Bible with the world of the preacher, will not indulge this tyranny of the boundless, but will resist it and overcome it. It will strive to be inclusive. In content and style it will seek to deal with all kinds and conditions of human life caringly. But it will not spare preachers, their congregants, or their cultures the eschatological judgment of God in Christ, the discernment and appraisal of the "beyond time" in time, divinity's own witness to its future in the appointed prophetic and apostolic testimony of the past. In the opening lines of his review of a production of Harold Pinter's *Old Times,* Richard Schickel had this to say:

> Memory is the personal journalism of the soul. From eyewitness accounts of yesterday's melodramas and mundanities, it fashions plausible self-serving reports that it passes off as truth. Indeed, polished by repetition, they become the truth.[25]

But preaching as a conflagration of love places self alone, culture alone, and the polished truth of self-serving memory alone into the crucible of *sola scriptura,* where they are heated up (yet not necessarily burned up) and purified.[26] *Sola scriptura* has never meant that the only thing we are to study or learn from is the Bible (since the Bible itself evidences anything but so limited an interest). What it has always meant is that the God who has spoken in Scripture, and who speaks in it still, there takes the measure of us, judging us to save us, even if "only as through fire" (1 Cor. 3:15). Said Sittler:

> [A] central affirmation of the Scriptures [is] that [humanity's] life, in solitude and in history is found and held within the hand of God. That operating within history, and dramatically at the consummation of history, is the judging and restoring activity of history's God. There is a limit which stands not only at the end of human life as death,

25. Richard Schickel, review of *Old Times,* by Harold Pinter, *Time,* Jan. 23, 1984, p. 63.

26. For a convincing statement concerning the significance of *sola scriptura* in relation to *lex orandi, lex credendi,* particularly in the Reformed tradition, see Donald M. Baillie, *The Theology of the Sacraments and Other Papers* (New York: Charles Scribner's Sons, 1957), pp. 142-43.

but which is built into the structure of human life by virtue of its creaturely character. All birth and development, all unfolding and enterprise, all moral vision and achievement are not only enfolded within this limit but receive their urgent character from it. Here is a "given" time, a "given" space, a "given" possibility. Within the boundary of this "given" there are, to be sure, vast and absolutely crucial possibilities for affirmation or denial, hearing or deafness, decision or stasis — but no elaboration of these possibilities can avoid the limit of sin and of death.[27]

While preaching is, in the first instance, narrative discourse, a form of discourse uniquely suited to kerygmatic statement (since Christ crucified and risen is the definitive moment of *actio divina* and *homo performans*), it also is, at the same time, discursive and expository. The story told is a story interpreted, explained, made sense of, with reference to the church's corporate and historic memory articulated in creed and confession. *Kerygma* and *didache* are joined; they are, in fact, the two sides of the single coin of the gospel. They are joined in the canon of Scripture, and they cannot be disjoined in preaching that bears witness to that to which the Scriptures themselves bear witness. Form and content are one; therefore preachers bear witness to *actio divina* and *homo performans* in Christ *as* the Scriptures do so. This means that preachers inevitably are teachers. Their work has a catechetical dimension. This does not mean that preachers only have to attend to the theology of the past any more than *sola scriptura* means that the only thing one needs to read to make sense of God and life is the Bible. Familiarity with contemporary theological reflection from various schools of thought is indispensable if one's work is to be other than sectarian or even entirely idiosyncratic.

Feminists, for instance, have something to say to all. When they indicate, as they do, that the divine name "Father of our Lord Jesus Christ" has been wrongly understood in the church for most of its life, and that that wrongheaded understanding has for too long led to the silencing of women, making them subject in almost all things ecclesiastical to domination by men, they are clearly correct. Any witness that denies that observation would be hard-pressed to defend itself by means of a scriptural critique of the creeds and confessions of the church; for

27. Sittler, p. 23.

Scripture argues with itself on this matter,[28] and Scripture's argument at last has been adjudicated in the favor of women in the official doctrinal affirmations of at least certain church traditions. So, for example, in "A Brief Statement of Faith" of the Presbyterian Church (U.S.A.), where it speaks of the work of the Holy Spirit, we read:

> The same Spirit who inspired the prophets and apostles rules our faith and life in Christ through Scripture, engages us through the Word proclaimed, claims us in the waters of Baptism, feeds us with the bread of life and the cup of salvation, and calls women and men to all ministries of the church.[29]

Of course, a wrong "read" of the implications of the divine name means that a more adequate and faithful "read" can be achieved, and that there are scriptural and doctrinal warrants for a corrected "read."[30] Further, the naming of God, which has been done by God in and through the Son, bears with it richly plural images of how the Father fathers, mothers, and befriends those who, in Christ, have been called to be the Father's own. This rich imaging of the Father's work on our behalf frees us to identify our *experience* of God in ways that clearly challenge patriarchal hegemony. So again, with regard to God's providential oversight of human life, "A Brief Statement of Faith" notes:

> Like a mother who will not forsake her nursing child,
> like a father who runs to welcome the prodigal home,
>   God is faithful still.[31]

---

28. Letty M. Russell, *Church in the Round: Feminist Interpretation of the Church* (Louisville, KY: Westminster John Knox Press, 1993), p. 161. (See chapter 3, n. 49.) For a recent study of feminist hermeneutics in relation to homiletics, emphasizing the relationship of feminist thought to other liberation theologies and the tradition of critical theological scholarship, see Annett Noller, *Feministische Hermeneutik: Wege einer neuen Scriftauslegung* (Neukirchen-Vluyn: Neukirchener, 1995).

29. "A Brief Statement of Faith," *The Book of Confessions,* C.10.4, p. 276.

30. Garrett Green, "The Gender of God and the Theology of Metaphor," in Alvin F. Kimel, Jr., ed., *Speaking the Christian God: The Holy Trinity and the Challenge of Feminism* (Grand Rapids, MI: William B. Eerdmans Publishing Co., 1992), pp. 34-63, esp. pp. 56-63.

31. "A Brief Statement of Faith," C.10.3, p. 276. Further, for discussion of humanity's freedom to be truly human as grounded in God's own freedom to be human, see Cynthia L. Rigby, "Freedom to Be Human: Limits, Possibilities and the Sovereignty of God," *Theology Today* 53, no. 1 (April 1996): pp. 47-62.

In Jesus Christ, as he is attested in Scripture, and as he is known in the encounter of Scripture's world with the world of the preacher, the divine reality names itself and interprets the divine name with such a rich variety of tropes that not only what "God the Father" means needs to be understood in terms other than maleness (to attribute sex to God, of course, was heretical from the start, since God is uncreated Spirit), but human fatherhood likewise needs to be understood in fresh ways. The apparently given, socially constructed gender roles that have tended to determine explication of fatherhood in Western culture, and indeed in nearly all cultures, not only *may* be challenged; a fresh read of *sola scriptura* in fact mandates that they *be* challenged. To come up against the scriptural witness to eschatological limit, then, is not to suffer diminution of the self, but enhancement of it. Christ, as *homo performans,* is immeasurably richer in hope for us women and men than any privileging of our own experience over it. Rather, our experience gathered up into it is experience vouchsafed to the community of faith that belongs to Christ. Our little measure of life and insight then has significance for others whom we may never know, in ways we could never guess. To preach and to teach the gospel in attempted fidelity to the scriptural witness, and in a way informed by plural, critical, and responsible readings of the creedal and confessional tradition, is to catechize congregations so that they not only may come to grips with the content of the faith, but may learn to read themselves "the Christian message as expressed in its classical documents."[32] The preacher-teachers who proclaim the gospel are servants of the Word and servants of those to whom (along with the preacher-teachers themselves) the Word is addressed. And just so they are servants of congregants' empowerment as theologians in their own right. Since the office to which they are called by God through the voice of the church is an office of vocation and not of status, preacher-teachers serve the one who has called them and not their own advancement or the advancement of their purely personal opinions and commitments. P. T. Forsyth got it right. He said:

> [Preachers] are not invited into a pulpit just to say how things strike [them] at [their] angle, anymore than [they are] expected to lay bare to the public the private recesses of [their souls].[33]

32. Baillie, p. 148.
33. P. T. Forsyth, *Positive Preaching and the Modern Mind* (Grand Rapids, MI: Baker Book House, 1980 [from the 1907 Beecher Lectures]), p. 103.

The preacher-teacher's learning is linked to service; and to bear faithful witness to the gospel (or to attempt to do so), and to explicate one's witness responsibly and not selfishly, is to know and to tell something quite beyond one's own experience. The teaching in preaching is ecclesial, not individual.

Further, as Paul Scott Wilson has pointed out, the teaching in preaching is pastoral. It does not regard "the congregation as the opposition;"[34] and it is cognizant of consequences. When it comes to assessing what is at stake in Christian doctrine for Christian faith and life at its untutored best, among the simplest folk whom preachers or their Lord have ever known, it knows how to call a spade a shovel. Donald Baillie brings home the point in this anecdote from his own pastoral and professional experience in Scotland decades ago.

> Some years [past] a very able student of our College suddenly fell ill and died. He was the only son of parents who had lost their only other child while very young. They were poor and simple folk. The father was a half-blind ex-service man, and they were making a living by keeping a small poultry-farm. Their son was the joy and crown of their lives, and they did all they could for him. He was dux [that is, leader] of his school, then distinguished himself in his Arts course at the University, came to St. Mary's College, was suddenly taken ill and died. A few days after the funeral I mounted a bus to go out to the country and visit his parents. There happened to come into the bus an old acquaintance, a layman, whom I hadn't seen for years — a quite untheological, even unintellectual man. He sat beside me, and presently asked me where I was going. I told him, and gave him an outline of the sad story. Suddenly he said to me: "Now, was it God who did that, or was it the Devil?" What is the answer? There is no short and easy answer. The question can't be answered in one word. For that question, coming straight from life, and asked quite spontaneously by a plain man, plumbs the very depths, the mysterious paradoxical depths, of the Christian doctrine of providence. It just shows how real even the deepest theological questions can be to [plain people] when they confront [them] in practice. . . .

> I believe that what first led or drove [people] to the full, rich, high Christian doctrine of providence was the episode of Calvary, the

---

34. Paul Scott Wilson, *The Practice of Preaching* (Nashville, TN: Abingdon Press, 1995), p. 86.

crucifixion of Jesus Christ. Was it God that did that dreadful thing? Or was it the Devil? The New Testament is quite realistic in saying that it was the forces of evil that did it — the mob that cried "Crucify Him," and the . . . leaders who incited them, and Pontius Pilate, and Judas Iscariot, and behind all that the Devil, who put it into the heart of Judas, and indeed the mysterious cosmic powers of darkness, the "princes of this age" who "crucified the Lord of glory." And yet somehow behind *all* was the "determinate counsel and foreknowledge of God," His infinitely gracious purpose of redemption. So that they could say with a lyrical note of joy: "God commendeth His own love toward us, in that, while we were yet sinners, Christ died for us." That is where the doctrine of providence passes into the doctrine of reconciliation and redemption. But even these mysteries are not too high to be declared and explained to our people from the pulpit. And how can we preach the gospel without them?[35]

If preaching is narrational (bearing witness to the encounter of the world of the text and the world of the preacher) and discursive and expository (offering an interpretation of the significance of that encounter in light of what a scriptural text says and connotes, and in light of the confessional and creedal tradition of the church as well as contemporary theological "readings" of Scripture and tradition), it also is dialogical. It sustains awareness throughout of the presence of God in Christ, in the power of the Holy Spirit, with preachers and their congregants. The prayer of the psalmist, adapted to the context of proclamation, has warrant:

> Let the words of my mouth and the meditation of [our hearts]
>   be acceptable to you,
> O LORD, [our] rock and [our] redeemer. (Ps. 19:14)

For God truly is present in preaching, whether preachers and their congregants in fact take cognizance of God's presence or not. Indeed, as Bultmann averred, the Christ who is preached himself preaches,[36] addresses preachers and their congregants, assesses the fidelity of what is spoken and heard concerning him, and, by his Spirit, instances faith,

---

35. Baillie, pp. 152-58; 154-55. Italics Baillie's.

36. James F. Kay, *Christus Praesens: A Reconsideration of Rudolf Bultmann's Christology* (Grand Rapids, MI: William B. Eerdmans Publishing Co., 1994), p. 114.

thereby forming and reforming the church. "So faith comes from what is heard, and what is heard comes through the word of Christ" (Rom. 10:17). Preaching is an "I-Thou" dialogue where "deep calls to deep" (Ps. 42:7). It is not dialogue reduced to the level of coffee-klatsch chat. As a matter of fact, the dialogue of preaching begins in silence.[37] It begins in the silence of God.

Typically we are inclined to think of God's word, presence, and power as speech and action, *actio divina* as not just standing there but doing something. Bernhard Anderson makes the point:

> God's sovereignty is manifest in effortless creation by the word:
>
>> "Let all the earth fear the Lord,
>>   let all the inhabitants of the world stand in awe of him.
>> For he spoke, and it came to be,
>>   he commanded, and it stood firm" (Ps. 33:8-9).
>
> This divine sovereignty, the poet continues to say, is manifest in God's overruling of the counsel of the nations and frustrating the plans of the peoples (Ps. 33:10-17).[38]

Anderson further indicates that God "pushes back the watery chaos and interposes a separating barrier. . . . If God did not sustain this fragile cosmic structure, the earth would be threatened with a return to pre-creation chaos."[39] Also, God's power is manifest in holiness. Holiness, however, is not simply the *mysterium tremendum,* but the " 'saving Presence' of the exodus and the 'commanding Presence' of Sinai."[40] However, "God's power does not crush human freedom but 'addresses' it; it does not prompt despair over human weakness but summons to action and covenant relationship."[41] Still, in all that, God's sovereignty and power, the word and deed we have been calling *actio divina,* "is often hidden except to the eye of faith. This note is struck in some of the psalms of

---

37. Buber. For Buber any spoken "I-Thou" encounter implies and arises from a solidarity with the Thou that is the very condition of speech. See Steven M. Panko, *Martin Buber* (Waco, TX: Word Books, 1976), p. 64.

38. Bernhard W. Anderson, "The Kingdom, The Power, and the Glory: The Sovereignty of God in the Bible," *Theology Today* 53, no. 1 (April 1996): p. 6.

39. Anderson, pp. 6-7.

40. Anderson, p. 7.

41. Anderson, p. 7.

lament, which raise the cry, 'how long?' (Ps. 6:3; 13:1-2), and especially in the prophecy of Habakkuk."[42]

> Your eyes are too pure to behold evil,
> and you cannot look on wrong doing;
> why do you look on the treacherous
> and are silent when the wicked swallow
> those more righteous than they? (Hab. 1:13)

Apparently there are times when God does just stand there, when *actio divina* holds its peace, as with Jesus before Pilate:

> Now Jesus stood before the governor; and the governor asked him, "Are you the King of the Jews?" Jesus said, "You say so." But when he was accused by the chief priests and elders, he did not answer. Then Pilate said to him, "Do you not hear how many accusations they make against you?" But he gave him no answer, not even to a single charge, so that the governor was greatly amazed. (Matt. 27:11-14)

And there is the terrifying silence of Calvary when everybody except God seems to have something to say:

> Those who passed by derided him, shaking their heads and saying, "Aha! You who would destroy the temple and build it in three days, save yourself, and come down from the cross!" In the same way the chief priests, along with the scribes, were also mocking him among themselves and saying, "He saved others; he cannot save himself. Let the Messiah, the King of Israel, come down from the cross now, so that we may see and believe." Those who were crucified with him also taunted him. (Mark 15:29-34)

"Vulnerability," says Patrick D. Miller, "may be the most popular new attribute of God, but it is in fact as old as Scripture, if vulnerability involves the pathos of God, the openness of the divine decision to human intercession, and the execution of God's anointed."[43]

In other words, God is powerful not only in words and deeds but in silence, not only in speech but in listening. Could it be that God's silence is God's attending to us, even in the midst of our inattention to

---

42. Anderson, p. 12.
    43. Patrick D. Miller, "Editorial," *Theology Today* 53, no. 1 (April 1996): p. 3.

those of our own human family who are threatened with injustice as was Christ before Pilate? Could it be that God's silence sometimes is God's way of addressing — and taking the measure of — power? Could it be that God's silence is God's waiting to see what humanity will do with its divine commission to exercise dominion over the earth, for the earth's own sake, in order that, properly cared for and not despoiled, it, with humanity, might be "to the praise of [God's] glory" (Eph. 1:14)? Could it be that God's silence is the pause before God speaks, as Christ's tomb was stillness and death without a hint of resurrection? Cynthia L. Rigby remarks:

> In the person of Jesus Christ, we discover not only that the sovereign God is transcendent to the creaturely community, distinct from it and in dialogue with it. We discover not only that God is immanently present in the world, supplying spiritual gifts and relational power to the dynamics of creaturely existence. God's freedom in the event of Jesus Christ demonstrates that God is actually an active member of the community, a human member in whom we encounter both what it is for God to be sovereign and what it is for us to live as human subjects. Our subjectivity is discovered in Jesus Christ both insofar as he reveals (as the incarnate God relating to other human beings) the nature of the divine interaction with the human subject and as he embodies (as a human being fully united with God) the reality that human beings and God exist in relation.[44]

Where *actio divina* and *homo performans* meet in Christ, where the worlds of text and preacher encounter one another in the preaching moment, where narrative discourse bears witness to how, with the scriptural word, God takes us as we are and presses us into the service of what God would have us be, and where discursive expository rhetoric interprets the significance of that narrative with considered reference to the creedal and confessional tradition of the church, *there* there is silence as well as talk; for God's human speech involves pause, listening on God's part and on our part, and not just speech. Bluntly put, the talk never is all.[45]

Dialogue in preaching consequently requires not a multiplication

44. Rigby, "Freedom to Be Human," p. 54.
45. Bartow, pp. 13-14.

of speakers but a multiplication of listeners. Preachers themselves are listeners who speak to facilitate other people's listening. Narrative discourse and discursive commentary issue from deep silence, the silence of God, wherein God, in sovereign freedom, with us instead of only as one above us, bears with what may appear to us to be unbearable: the poignant, that is painful and piercing, questions that trouble all our answers. There, and only there, in ineffable prayer, where it seems perhaps that "nothing" lurks behind us — and perhaps before us too — can we take heart in the insight of Pascal: "We would not seek thee, O God, if thou hadst not already found us."[46] The rule of God present in preaching, as previously discussed, thus is not to be thought of as an exercise in indifferent almightiness; for God's almightiness, as the creed attests, is yoked to divine vulnerability, as the three persons of the Trinity constitute the one and only true God and not three different kinds of God. So also the power of the resurrection cannot be preached apart from the stark reality of the crucifixion, wherein God's strength to endure suffering — with and on behalf of suffering humanity and, precisely in that, to forge a more godly and humane future — is manifest. Suffering humanity, after all, is humanity no less in the image of God than humanity full of itself and "on top of the world." And if we cannot see, touch, and honor God there, it is quite unlikely that we can see, touch, and honor God anywhere. Elizabeth A. Johnson, C.S.J., has expressed it graphically:

> Is the raped and murdered concubine from Bethlehem *imago Dei?* Are the young and old women killed as so-called witches [300,000 between the years 1484 and 1782][47] images of God? Are the victims of state torture in the likeness of God? Do these . . . offer yet another symbol of the suffering God? I think they do. *Ecce homo:* in an unspeakable way they are images of the crucified.[48]

So is the mouth of divine holiness and justice wide open, silent and appalled before it roars. Dialogue in the conflagration of love we call preaching begins, ends, and is permeated throughout with that

46. Helmut Thielicke, *Nihilism: Its Origin and Nature — With a Christian Answer,* trans. John W. Doberstein (New York: Harper & Bros. Publishers, 1961), p. 178.
47. John Mulholland, "Witchcraft," *The World Book Encylopedia,* vol. 20 (Chicago: Field Enterprise Educational Corporation, 1966), p. 311.
48. Johnson, p. 263.

appalling silence even as it roars the kerygmatic truth that he who has been crucified has been raised "to the right hand of power" (Matt. 26:64), and with him all who have died in him. Resurrection is not felt now simply in dreams of a happier hereafter. It is felt now especially as power to look steadily at what most frightens us, and, never blinking, to speak and sing hope straight into the face of that fear. It is to hear requiem and to shout: "Hallelujah! For the Lord our God the Almighty reigns" (Rev. 19:6b). Hear Paul Scherer:

> We are not living in a world which is being lifted inch by inch out of its poor estate. We are living in a world where there is something that is incorrigible; so vast and demonic that [very God] . . . had to get into it and die before anything could be done about it; until out of despair is born not cynicism, but courage. Not defeat, or absolute conflict, or paradox, so much as tension. Not idealism; realism — which is idealism in the process of becoming incarnate on my street: a gallant facing of the dark with a faith that is not subservient to facts, but creates them. *Credo in unum Deum, Patrem Omnipotentem.*[49]

There is the end toward which the dialogue of preaching urges us: not into merely facing the facts, but into creating them in faith.

We have noted that sermons narrate, bear witness to the encounter of the biblical world with the world of the preacher. They offer a confessionally responsible explication of that encounter, and they sustain awareness of the living God's dialogical engagement of preachers and congregants in and through Jesus Christ as he is attested in Scripture for us through the agency of the Holy Spirit. Still further, sermons are designed with sensitivity to congregations and contexts. As we have been told often enough, sermons are not stones thrown into a lake of listeners. Listeners contribute to the shaping of sermons by who they are and by what they expect. Who listeners are has to do with people's identity in Christ. "Who am I?" Bonhoeffer asked from his prison cell. And the answer he sought came to him: "Whoever I am, thou knowest, O God, I am Thine."[50] Those gathered before

---

49. Paul E. Scherer, *For We Have This Treasure* (Grand Rapids, MI: Baker Book House, 1979), p. 110.

50. Dietrich Bonhoeffer, "Who Am I?" in *Letters and Papers from Prison,* ed. Eberhard Bethge, trans. Reginald H. Fuller (New York: Macmillan Co., 1953), pp. 221-22.

preachers to hear the word of God already belong to God. They are not anonymous in God's sight, even if their names are not known to the preacher or if their faces seem unfamiliar. They also belong to each other because they belong to God. When Paul says to the Galatians, for example, "My friends" (Gal. 6:1), literally *Adelphoi*, brothers, or, as we would now say, "brothers and sisters," he is not in some preachery fashion seeking to ingratiate himself with the congregation at Galatia. He is recognizing who his listeners really are in relation to him and to each other. They are his friends because Christ has made them — and Paul — *his* friends at cost. True friends, of course, do not fail to let each other know where they stand on matters of importance. Instead they speak candidly, sometimes even boldly, urgently, and with a measure of severity. Paul with the Galatians managed all those moods. But above all friends speak as friends, held together by iron bonds of affection they do not forge and cannot break.

In Jesus' parable of the prodigal son, the elder brother speaks to his father about his younger brother in terms of derision: "this son of yours" (Luke 15:30), he calls him. But the father replies, "this brother of yours was dead and has come to life; he was lost and has been found" (Luke 15:32b). Brothers and sisters, friends in Christ, sons and daughters of the living God do not berate each other but seek each other's good. And no preaching can be truly prophetic (even in the most sharply critical sense of that term) that is not thus pastoral, personal, and profoundly filial. Preachers do not only speak *to* their congregants, they speak *with* them, on their behalf, and as one of them. The dialogue of preaching is carried on person to person in Christ. It is carried on among people chosen by God in Christ to be saints of God, *hágioi* (Rom. 1:7). The preeminent fact of faith that preachers and congregants must contend with is the fact of the church. Is the church rarely, if ever, all that it is supposed to be? Is it too often not only in the world but of it? Does it seem at times hardly worth the effort expended to keep it going? Does it pray, "Thy kingdom come," and then get in the way of its own prayers? Is it too much like its preachers for its own good and its preachers' comfort? How then shall it be changed if its preachers will not be changed? And how shall the world "out there" be affected for the better if the world "in here" is ignored, belittled, or inappropriately condoned and celebrated?

The transforming word of our gospel for "interesting times" is a word on target because it is aimed straight at congregants as at friends and at friends as at preachers. With regard to the gospel as personal address, Paul Scherer had this to say:

> The sweep of revelation in history is not from it but toward it. Here is the polestar of our voyage; and none of us may come to salute our captain, reporting with the novice on the old sailing vessel, "Sir, I have passed that star; give me another!" One may have little sympathy with the religion which in so many of our hymns, for instance, to say nothing of our churches, turns out to be an end in itself, taking its satisfactions wherever it may find them, and looking on an evil order with complacency or resignation. But one can have equally little sympathy with a religion which is blindly determined to start with the transformation of human society, breaking one egg after another . . . in an effort to provide that ultimate omelet which we hope sometime to enjoy.
>
> In Jesus' day the air was full of political, social, economic, ecclesiastical, international questions. There were slavery and tyranny and war and intemperance. Two-thirds of the world were slaves, if you like figures, three-quarters drunkards, and nine-tenths adulterers. So it is reported. Yet there is not a word from Jesus' lips that has not to do with human hearts. There for him was the center that fixed the circle. And it must be the center for us.[51]

Yet the center is not the circumference; and the preached gospel is not truly personal address unless it is, at the same time, address to people in their relationships to each other in the church and in the world.[52] The gospel is personal, but it is not individualistic. Already we have discussed at some length the need for preachers to be in solidarity with all sorts and conditions of humanity. But what that means for speaking to the gathered people of God as a gathered people of God — that is, as a church — we have not yet discussed. A recently published work by Nora Tubbs Tisdale, *Preaching as Local Theology and Folk Art,* delineates helpfully and in considerable detail how preachers may go about "exegeting" their congregational contexts.[53] Tisdale's work pro-

51. Scherer, pp. 116-17.

52. H. H. Farmer, *The Servant of the Word* (Philadelphia: Fortress Press, 1964), pp. 21-36.

53. Nora Tubbs Tisdale, *Preaching as Local Theology and Folk Art* (Minneapolis, MN: Fortress Press, 1996).

vides needed correction for contemporary homiletical thought. Recent homiletics texts, while not neglecting the congregation as context for preaching and as party to the homiletical transaction, have not focused on how, theoretically and practically, the congregation's role might be defined. It is beyond the scope of this study to give a thorough exposition of Tisdale's probing and nuanced discussion. Still, a few observations inspired by her work may be made. We begin with this: the gospel itself as *actio divina*, as God's self-performance in accommodation of divine reality to human experiential and reflective capacity, is at the very heart of proclamation. What we preach and teach is the gospel of the incarnation. The gospel of Jesus Christ as a Word fitly spoken, of course, is not a word that reconciles God to humanity. It is instead a word that reconciles humanity to God (2 Cor. 5:18-20). Such reconciliation nevertheless entails God's reaching us human beings in and through our mundane life and thought. William J. Bouwsma has made that point clear in his monograph "Calvinism as Theologica Rhetorica." Quoting from one of Calvin's sermons, Bouwsma remarks that, for Calvin, "Preaching, like consolation, is medicinal":

> It is as if one went to a doctor and asked him for a remedy for an illness, and he discoursed of his art in general and argued about it, and the poor sick man meanwhile died. . . . It is necessary to adapt the medicine to those who need it.[54]

To accommodate one's preaching to one's congregants therefore is not a betrayal of the gospel. It is instead a mark of fidelity to the gospel. Sermon design, diction, and delivery are undertaken to facilitate congregants' hearing of God's word. Consequently they cannot be undertaken without sensitivity to how congregants actually listen.

Since congregations are a subculture of some broader culture that influences all of its parts — yet no doubt is more than the sum of its parts — congregants, in large measure, listen as all others listen. They share a common language with their particular broader culture. And they share certain common habits of communication. They exercise what communication theorists have taught us to call "selective percep-

54. William J. Bouwsma, "Calvinism as *Theologia Rhetorica*," in *Protocol Colloquy 54*, ed. Wilhelm Wuellner (Berkeley, CA: Center for Hermeneutical Studies in Hellenistic and Modern Culture [Graduate Theological Union and The University of California at Berkeley], 1958), p. 13. Also see p. 21, n. 142, for the reference in Calvin's sermons.

tion"[55] and what, more recently, performance theorists have called "selective inattention."[56] They incline to hold fast to those things said that are consonant with their previous experiences and understandings of the gospel. And, when they are preached to, their minds now and then may drift, picking up an idea or image and "running with it" as we say, while the preacher moves ahead in the direction set in advance by the sermon as composed. Later the congregant is drawn back into the narrative, expository, and dialogical discourse of the preacher, catching up to what is going on as she or he is able, thereby getting reestablished in the unfolding drama of the sermon as preached. Appropriate sermon delivery can aid and abet that reestablishment so that congregants "hang in there" from initiating action or thought, to climax, to resolution.[57] Also, since the sermon is suasory but not manipulative, directing attention but not dictating response, congregants finally will assess what preachers have to say on the basis of their own "insight and sense of the truth."[58] Congregants have some idea of what the gospel is all about. They are not hearing it from the preacher for the first time; and, as Fred Craddock has pointed out, the preacher should not intend to preach "another gospel" (Gal. 1:8). Rather she or he should attempt to give a fresh account of the gospel given in Scripture, creed, and ecclesial experience.[59]

Congregants also attend to preaching as a congregation. All "audiences" have this corporate identity, even casually constructed audiences such as theater, concert, sports events, and movie audiences. Humor and pathos are intensified when shared in a corporate setting. My teenage laughter at *Teahouse of the August Moon* while reading the play in the library at Michigan State University back in the 1950s was one thing. Seeing it "staged" on film and rocking with the guffaws of the movie "congregation" was quite another. Hearing in your head "God of Our Life, Through All the Circling Years" by H. T. Kerr, Sr., is enough to stir up all the scenes of a lifetime and to fill them with faith. To stand with a congregation and to sing that hymn through grief in a memorial

55. Jon Eisenson, J. Jeffry Auer, and John V. Irwin, *The Psychology of Communication* (New York: Appleton Century-Crofts, 1963), pp. 247-48.

56. Richard Schechner, *Performance Theory* (New York: Routledge, 1988), p. 197.

57. Bartow, pp. 21-31.

58. Farmer, p. 49.

59. Fred B. Craddock, *Preaching* (Nashville, TN: Abingdon Press, 1985), pp. 159-62.

service for a loved one is to know the "solemn joy" of the church's faith praying for you more than you know how to ask for yourself. Yet more profoundly, since congregations have their own unique Christian subcultural experiences, corporate attention is more than enriched in the gathering of the people who attend to sermons. It is to some extent determined by it. Congregants who have fought over budgets together, lived through times of extremity together, cried together over untimely deaths, and celebrated together the gathering to the ancestors of "old-timers," brothers and sisters, mothers and fathers full of years, have more than a notion of what Christ means to them, have more than a little idea of what Scripture has said of Christ to them, have better than a vague apprehension of what God expects of them together and apart.

Congregations have their own kerygmatic expectation, their own gospel for interesting or not so interesting times, and woe betide the preacher who pays no attention to that. Whether or not preachers ever get around to doing detailed cultural-anthropological "thick descriptions"[60] of their congregations, they will need to become "participant observers" in the lives of their congregations — and more. They will need to live into their congregants' lives and to love them, as Christ loves them, in all their grandness and despite their pettiness. They will need actually to *be* friends, be brothers and sisters in Christ to their congregants, as their congregants are those things to them. They will not just sprinkle a few casual "my dear friends" or "my dear sisters and brothers" into their sermons. Such code words can never make up for a real absence of friendly, siblinglike caring. And if the friendly, siblinglike caring is there, the code words probably are not needed. As I have elsewhere noted:

> Preaching . . . does not take place in a vacuum. It happens within the context of a specific community that possesses tradition, that is presently alive, and that continually is choosing new directions and purposes. Preaching seeks the transformation of the life of that community, and at the same time, it is continuous with that life. It envisions new possibilities for its people. Yet it does so with the facts and images, the resources of the past and present of those people. The act of preaching employs memory and stimulates forethought. It involves analysis and prescription, and those who engage in it, preachers and

60. Tisdale, ch. 3.

listeners alike, therefore are required to exercise their capacity for empathy (reading themselves into actual or imaginary events of the past or present) and imagination (projecting future possibilities — extrapolation). Preachers who would listen carefully to what is happening in their sermons and who would have others do so with them, consequently must have one ear cocked in the direction of the Scriptures [and the creedal-confessional tradition] and the life represented therein, and the other in the direction of their peoples' developing history and present life and the various possibilities for grappling creatively with them.[61]

The congregation has its own role in preaching. It also has its peculiar responsibility. H. H. Farmer spoke about that responsibility over fifty years ago. And he spoke so vividly and pointedly that his remarks stir and sting yet.

Every minister knows how some congregations seem to give power to the preacher, whereas others seem to inhibit it in greater or less degree. An intrinsically poor address can become a strong word of God when it is part of, and expresses a strong and deep fellowship of God's people. . . . On the other hand an intrinsically good sermon may be ineffective, or at least nothing like so effective as it might be, if the congregation is not a fellowship [of the Spirit], but only a crowd . . . , wanting above all things else not that God's word should have free course among them . . . , but that they should be interested for twenty minutes or so. Ready, if they have been bored, to grumble . . . as though they had been cheated out of something they had bought and paid for. And it is not only lovelessness on the part of the preacher that turns him [or her] into a sounding brass and a tinkling cymbal. It is lovelessness in the church, for preaching is an act of the church. "I cannot hear what you say, because what the congregation is shouts so loud."[62]

Farmer went on to say, "Yet, even so, it would be a mean thing for us preachers to blame our congregations for our ineffectiveness."[63] It would be more than mean. It would be foolish and theologically irresponsible. Preachers, after all, do not possess their congregations any more than

61. Bartow, pp. 18-19.
62. Farmer, p. 70.
63. Farmer, p. 71.

their congregations possess them. They also do not possess the preaching office. That belongs to Christ and to the church, which is his body; and preachers are called to service in that office by God through the voice of the church. The primary accountability of preachers is to God in Christ as the prophetic and apostolic witness attests him. And "effectiveness" is to be judged first and foremost in terms of that accountability. In short, fidelity is more important than acclaim. Therefore, preachers are not dependent upon the eager or sluggish, affirmative, negative, or indifferent response of their congregants. The congregation's own comportment in the preaching event in fact is to be measured against that same standard of fidelity to apostolic testimony; for, in all its parts, the body is accountable to its head.

> The "Ministry of the Word and Sacraments" belongs to no [person]; all believers belong to it. And among these some are acknowledged as having been given a charism, undergone preparation, and announced their intention to serve the gospel in this particular ministry. In the full gravity of this gift, task, and intention a [person] is ordained to this ministry, charged in specific terms drawn from the dominical imperative faithfully to fulfill it. The self-image of the minister is then more than a self-image; it is an image of the vocation and task of the self gathered up into a gift and a task that was before the self came to be, having a reality that transcends while it involves the whole self, and which will be bestowed upon the church by her Lord when this particular self is no longer of the church in history.[64]

To recapitulate: sermons narrate the encounter of the biblical world with the world of the preacher. Sermons also explicate or interpret that encounter, taking into account the creedal and confessional tradition of the church. Sermons sustain awareness of God's dialogical engagement of preachers and congregants through Jesus Christ as the Holy Spirit attests him in sacred Scripture and in the hearts of those who receive the scriptural word as God's own human speech to them. And, in their design, composition, and delivery, sermons show evidence of preachers having taken seriously congregational-cultural contexts. That is, sermons are crafted to speak a word on target; and they are spoken to facilitate, not to impede, congregational attentiveness to kerygmatic content. Last, but not least, sermons, like texts of Scripture, need to be

64. Sittler, pp. 82-83.

understood as "arrested performances," as blood turned into ink. They are rich in connotation as well as denotation, and so they mean more, but not less or other, than they say. It is impossible to overstate the significance of this. Too often the sermon manuscript or outline is thought of as the sermon itself, when in reality the sermon as a work, as an artistic human accomplishment and divine act, is a happening about to happen again. It is a world of meaning entangled in words waiting to be disentangled. It is blood turned into ink that, through speech, may be turned back into blood. It is not like milk bottled and ready to be delivered to market. From exegesis to speech to hearing — and to liturgical, ethical, and missional enactment — it is performance, form coming through. It is witness as event, as felt claim and succor. According to Dawn DeVries, Schleiermacher understood this early and well:

> As speech or conversation, language is enhanced by non-verbal messages from the speakers. This non-verbal part of spoken language is essential in religious discourse. "Religion . . . withdraws itself from too wide circles to the more familiar conversation of friendship or the dialogue of love, where glance and action are clearer than words, and where a solemn silence is also understood." Unlike "dead letters" on a page of printed text, speech has life. It can speed up or slow down. It can be pronounced forcefully or delicately. In short, it carries within it in a nearly literal way the breath of the speaker — the very symbol of life. As living word, then, the sermon, or any kind of spoken communication [e.g., speaking the Scriptures], is the primary form of religious language. . . . The atmosphere of the moment — the glances, gestures, and "solemn silences" of the gathered congregation — is essential, not only for the form, but also for the content of the sermon.[65]

To realize something approximating the full range of significations and effects of a sermon requires the connotative input not only of preachers but of their congregants, for the world of the sermon unfolds through the collaborative effort of author (that is, preacher), text (sermon manuscript or outline), and audience (congregation). Like the performance of any work, the performance of the sermon is risky business. The work can get mangled, subverted, turned into an excuse for

65. Schleiermacher, p. 9.

the performance of something other than itself. Preachers can subvert the sermonic work by accommodating it to their own expectations of themselves. They can confine it within the margins of a comfortable self more given to dishing out conclusions than to reliving scriptural and contemporaneous human experience of God. And congregants can put on liturgical asbestos and walk through the conflagration of love called preaching unsinged. They can do that — failing to recall that asbestos kills — and they do. Scripture has a name for it: "hardness of heart." Yet preachers can take the lead in stripping off the asbestos and softening congregants' hearts by taking those congregants more seriously than they may take themselves or their proclamatory duty. Preachers, even in their research for and in their writing of sermons, can engage the world of the text and the world of creed and confession as congregants, as those to whom God speaks. Just so, before pen has been put to paper, they are listeners speaking to facilitate other people's listening. They are actors, too, in the ethical, not simply theatrical, sense of that term, taking action to facilitate other people's enacted obedience. For God's word heard means that you do not just stand there; you *do* something. The goal is "every thought captive to obey Christ" (2 Cor. 10:5). Preaching for congregants as well as for preachers is not a status but a calling. "You will give your life for something," Paul Scherer once proclaimed in this writer's hearing. "The only question is for what?!"

Listening, said Richard Ward, "is . . . a performance in which projections come forth from the listener's most intimate self."[66] It must be added, though, that those projections of the self come face to face with the self-disclosure of the divine. *Homo performans* as the self-performance of preachers and congregants comes up against the Word God sent, the *actio-divina/homo-performans* that is Christ. In that meeting what we would be is transformed into what God would have us be. "God's freedom to be human affirms human existence and enables human beings to live as relational, responsible, and passionate subjects."[67] The eternal in the temporal, the beyond time in time, the eschatological judgment of a God who is merciful in judgment yet just in divine compassion, burns away the illimitable self as with flames that cannot be quenched. But, at the same time, it restores and refines the

66. Richard F. Ward, *Speaking from the Heart: Preaching with Passion* (Nashville, TN: Abingdon Press, 1992), p. 126.
67. Rigby, p. 57.

finite self till it burns with a radiance beyond its ken. The poet speaks
for the preacher:

> The dove descending breaks the air
> With flame of incandescent terror
> Of which the tongues declare
> The one discharge from sin and error
> The only hope, or else despair
>> Lies in the choice of pyre or pyre
>> To be redeemed from fire by fire
>
> Who then devised the torment? Love.
> Love is the unfamiliar Name
> Behind the hands that wove
> The intolerable shirt of flame
> Which human power cannot remove.
>> We only live, only suspire
>> Consumed by either fire or fire.[68]

68. T. S. Eliot, "Four Quartets," IV, in *The Complete Poems and Plays, 1909–1950*
(New York: Harcourt, Brace & World, Inc., 1952), pp. 143-44. ("Suspire" means to sigh,
to long, to yearn, and to breathe.)

5. What to Make of Sunday's Sermon

SOMEHOW — IT IS ALWAYS A MIRACLE — we survive the conflagration of love called preaching. In the context of that survival, and in anticipation of it, the question becomes: What do we make of it all? The "we" includes preachers themselves, their congregants, and those vocationally responsible for taking account of the church's proclamation. Since the concern of this particular text is focused on preachers' responsibilities in proclamation through the public reading of the Scriptures and the speaking of God's word, the approach to homiletical criticism undertaken in the following pages centers on what preachers need to keep in mind in preparation for, during, and after the preaching moment. What are preachers to make of their attempts at proclamation of the gospel? How are they to take stock of them? Well, they are to take stock of them by articulating criteria appropriate to their preaching duties. Then they must assess their homiletical efforts under the guidance of those criteria. The criteria themselves, of course, may be freshly understood in the light of successive critiques of sermons, and those criteria from time to time may need to be modified, subtly or substantially changed. All preachers are responsible for developing and preaching a "sound theology,"[1] said H. H. Farmer. Yet, he said, all preaching must have an appropriate

---

1. H. H. Farmer, *The Servant of the Word* (Philadelphia: Fortress Press, 1964), p. 2.

125

note of humility;[2] it cannot pretend to more comprehension of divine self-disclosure than is granted it.

> The paradox is this: Christianity affirms that, while God has bestowed upon us a real community of being with himself, in that he has made us to be persons and has personal relationships with us, nevertheless it is also true that he is "wholly other" than we are; he is "wholly other" because he is God, and we are not God, we are [human beings].[3]

Actio divina, the plural particularity of God's self-disclosure in history and, most especially, in Jesus Christ, God's definitive Word to humanity, preserves the tension of immanence and transcendence in real presence. Any speech concerning *actio divina*, if it is to be true to what occasions it, therefore must preserve that same tension.

> [T]he awareness of the transcendent otherness of God is never submerged by the awareness of his personal nature and approach, nor is the awareness of his personal nature and approach submerged by the awareness of his transcendent otherness. Both elements are held together, and reciprocally pervade one another, in a single unitary apprehension of, and encounter with, God.[4]

Preachers' assessments of their sermonic efforts must do the same. They must keep the note of humility, for theologies of and for preaching cannot be both sound and absolutely settled. And they must not seek, in explaining and evaluating sermons, to explain away the mystery of God with us even in the most humble and broken discourse. The question is not, Have we heard the Word of God with these words, these vocal and physical gestures? By God's grace we have! The question instead is, Have we heard from the preacher words suitable to the Word, vocal and physical gestures attempted in faithfulness to Christ as he has made himself known in the apostolic witness? We make reasoned judgments, for God's self-disclosure, while not a product of human reason,

2. Farmer, *Servant*, pp. 61-63.

3. H. H. Farmer, *God and Men* (New York: Abingdon-Cokesbury Press, 1947), p. 53.

4. H. H. Farmer, *Revelation and Religion* (New York: Harper and Bros., 1954), p. 60.

is not unreasonable; and sermonic efforts that attempt to bear witness to God's self-disclosure are not beyond reasonable appraisal.

> If we believe in God at all, it is absurd and impious to imagine that we can find him out by our own reason, without his being first active in revealing himself to us. Therefore all our discovery of him is his self-manifestation, and all rational theology is revealed theology. And . . . if God does reveal himself to us, we cannot acknowledge . . . what he reveals without the use of reason. Therefore, all his self-manifestation is also our discovery of him, and all revealed theology is rational theology.[5]

Preachers, as homileticians and practical theologians,[6] are servants of the Word, and academic specialists in preaching and speech communication in ministry are servants of the servants of the Word.[7] The purpose here, then, is to stipulate and further explore criteria for homiletical criticism that emerged in the discussion of the nature and purpose of preaching presented in chapter 4. It also will be necessary to indicate in further detail how those criteria may serve preachers (their congregants and academic colleagues too) in taking the measure of their work.[8]

5. Austin Farrer, *The Glass of Vision* (Westminster, England: Dacre Press, 1948), pp. 1-2.

6. John S. McClure makes the point that academic homiletics as practical theology is in service to the pastor-preacher as practical theologian. The preacher herself or himself takes what is offered in books like McClure's and this one and gives an account of her or his own work. No one can make those descriptive, constructive, and critical moves on the preacher's behalf. The best the academician can do is provide resources for the preacher as a practical theologian. See John S. McClure, *The Four Codes of Preaching: Rhetorical Strategies* (Minneapolis, MN: Fortress Press, 1991), esp. p. 14.

7. Charles L. Bartow, "In Service to the Servants of the Word: Teaching Speech at Princeton Seminary," *Princeton Seminary Bulletin* 13, no. 3 (1992): pp. 274-86.

8. Precedent for this approach to homiletical criticism can be found in two doctoral dissertations, one from the early 1970s, the other from the early 1990s. See Charles L. Bartow, "An Evaluation of Student Preaching in the Basic Homiletics Courses at Princeton Theological Seminary: A Farmerian Approach to Homiletical Criticism" (unpublished Ph.D. dissertation, New York University, 1971). See also Jana Lynn Childers, "A Critical Analysis of the Homiletical Theory and Practice of Browne Barr: First Congregational Church, Berkeley, 1960-1977" (unpublished Ph.D. dissertation, The Graduate Theological Union, Berkeley, CA, 1992). See also Charles L. Bartow, *The Preaching Moment: A Guide to Sermon Delivery* (Dubuque. IA: Kendall/Hunt Publishers, 1995), esp. pp. 103-12. (My concern in *The Preaching Moment* was exclusively with

It is not claimed that these criteria are the only criteria imaginable. But it is claimed that these criteria are reasonable, consistent with what so far has been said in these pages about the proclamation of the gospel. They, therefore, are responsible to theory and relevant to practice. They are sound if not incontrovertible and settled.

Preaching as a conflagration of love possesses the following characteristics:

1. Preaching has a *present-tense tone:*
   It acknowledges that proclamation begins with the public reading of the Scriptures. It comes to grips with the Bible's denotative and connotative meanings, dealing with texts of Scripture not merely as documents to be reconstructed as history, but as worlds of meaning evoked and engaged in living speech;

2. Preaching emphasizes the *divine initiative:*
   It bears witness to the encounter of the biblical world with the world of the preacher, providing a balanced narrative of that en-

---

sermon delivery.) Besides the Bartow and Childers approaches to homiletical criticism, which stress biblical/theological grounds and feature performance studies as the predominant cognate discipline, there are the following: Prakash's approach stresses exegetical, theological-thematic, and stylistic analysis of sermons in the context of a detailed biographical account of the preacher's life. See Perumala Surya Prakash, *The Preaching of Sadhu Sundar Singh: A Homiletic Analysis of Independent Preaching and Personal Christianity* (Bangalore, India: Wordmakers, 1991). Schmit brings preaching theory into conversation with the aesthetic theory of Susanne K. Langer, arguing that preaching can be evaluated as an art form featuring, as does poetry, the illusion of life. In preaching there is "virtual life" but "real presence." See Clayton J. Schmit, "Feeling and Form in Worship" (unpublished Ph.D. dissertation, The Graduate Theological Union, Berkeley, CA, 1994), pp. 48-90. Kennedy makes a case for preaching as sacred rhetoric, a rhetoric of folly grounded in a theory of metaphor that sees figuration as normative for the construction of knowledge. See Rodney Kennedy, *The Creative Power of Metaphor: A Rhetorical Homiletics* (Lanham, MD: University Press of America, 1993).

All of these approaches attempt to take seriously postmodernity's so-called hermeneutical, rhetorical, and performance turns. Throughout this book we have been discussing proclamation, and now homiletical criticism, in performance modes of thought. But the content of our discussions has been, and continues to be, governed by the biblical, creedal, liturgical witness to *actio divina* and *homo performans* in Jesus Christ. Since preaching gives an account of that, the criticism of preaching, above all, focuses on kerygmatic content. Criteria for sermon evaluation thus are valid only as they help critics to keep their attention where it belongs: on the sermon's witness to that to which the Scriptures themselves bear witness.

counter (i.e., a narrative with an aesthetically satisfying beginning, middle, and end), revealing how, with a particular biblical text, and in Christ Jesus, God takes us as we are and presses us into the service of what he would have us be;

3. Preaching offers a *Christian interpretation of life:*
   Implicitly or explicitly it offers a confessionally responsible explication of the encounter of the worlds of text and preacher; that is, it teaches as it preaches so that congregants may be empowered to do their own critical and faithful theological reflection on life under the authority of Scripture and guided by the creedal-confessional tradition of the church;

4. Preaching is in the *indicative mood:*
   It sustains awareness of the living God's dialogic engagement of preachers and congregants (God's speech and silence, God's claim and succor) in Jesus Christ — crucified, risen, regnant — as he is attested for us in Scripture through the agency of the Holy Spirit;

5. Preaching features a *dexterous use of a variety of sermon strategies, and its diction (word choice) aims at cause, not at effect.* To aim at cause is to depict the scenes that stir up what connotative responses congregants may make. To aim at effect is to tell congregants what connotative responses, in the preacher's opinion, they ought to make. In preaching, however, diction, design, and delivery demonstrate a concern for speaking to all sorts and conditions of humanity personally and corporately, and with such respect for the integrity of listeners that they are left free to respond on the basis of their own insight and sense of the truth.

Having identified the criteria for homiletical criticism, it is necessary now to explore their implementation. Let us be reminded that the criteria not only can be used to check up on sermonic efforts after the fact. They also can be used as a guide in the preparation of sermons. Preachers are self-critical, that is to say, throughout the homiletical process, in the preparation and delivery of sermons, and, afterwards, when the preaching moment is revisited.[9] This does not mean that preachers are "uptight," forever second-guessing themselves. But it does mean that they are self-aware, conscious of what they are doing, not just before and after, but also while they are doing it.

9. Bartow, *Preaching Moment,* pp. 103-12.

In preparation for preaching (for example, composing the manuscript) the criteria function as traffic lights, flashing green, red, and
amber for "go," "stop," and "proceed with caution." While preaching they
are more felt than brought to mind. Internalized they become a guide
to intuition. Somehow we know that something just said needs modi-
fication, amplification, correction. Somehow we sense our involvement
or lack of it, our believability or unbelievability. We sense the involvement or lack of it of our congregants too. And we take action as needed
on the basis of our tutored (by our criteria) instincts. Somehow God
may be enabling the church to hear the divine word with us or despite
us. Yet we may perceive some incongruity between the divine word and
our words, *actio divina* and our vocal and physical gesture. When our
preaching is done, over time, with determination, persistence, and
patience (with ourselves, with our work, with our congregants), we can
very deliberately and rigorously subject our homiletic efforts to systematic scrutiny. And others — especially, but not only, academic homileticians — can do the same.

The goals of homiletical criticism are constructive, not destructive.
Homiletical criticism has nothing to do with mere carping, creating
victims, ourselves among them. Instead it has to do with encouraging
further attempts at faithful witness to that to which the Scriptures
themselves bear witness. It has to do with vocational integrity and
growth in preaching competence. It has to do with honing insight into
what preaching is all about, acting on that insight, and sharing it. Not
all critics will come to the same conclusions about a particular sermonic
effort. Not even the same critic — or the preacher herself or himself —
will hear a given sermon always as she or he has heard it before. People
do change even if the words they speak or listen to remain the same. In
any case, the goal of criticism is not uniform verdicts, but *just* verdicts,
reasoned judgments that can guide further practice.

Marie Hochmuth Nichols, in her book *Rhetoric and Criticism*,
defined humane studies as those studies concerned with the formulation
of judgment and choice, and rhetoric as "the theory and practice of the
verbal mode of presenting judgment and choice, knowledge and feeling."[10] Homiletical criticism, it is suggested here, involves the presenta-
tion of theologically informed judgment and choice, knowledge and

10. Marie H. Nichols, *Rhetoric and Criticism* (Baton Rouge, LA: Louisiana State
University Press, 1967), p. 7.

feeling, by a critic (including oneself as critic of one's own work) of an attempt at preaching. However, if the critic's exercise of judgment and choice, knowledge and feeling, is to be valid (honing insight into homiletical theory and practice), and reliable (demonstrably guided by publicly articulated standards), the criteria for criticism must be suitable to the phenomenon under observation. As Carter and Fife have pointed out with regard to critics' criteria of judgment in all evaluative studies:

> They may be personal, they may be adapted from . . . the ancients, they may be derived from more recent [sources]; but, regardless of the source of our criteria, they should be appropriate to the specific problem under investigation [that is, what, as practical theologians and homileticians, we want to know about our preaching] even if they must be tailor made.[11]

That is why, following a trajectory set in homiletical scholarship by Conrad H. Massa,[12] we have identified the work of homiletical theory, practice, and criticism as practical theology (local, performative, interdisciplinary theological reflection), grounding our criteria for the criticism of sermons in a detailed discussion of the nature and purpose of preaching.

What preachers and homileticians need to look for with reference to the implementation of criterion number one in the analysis of preaching is what may be called the *present-tense tone* of the sermon. If the Scriptures are understood not only denotatively, but also connotatively, not only as dated documents, but as a living speech intended to evoke worlds of alternative human being with God on the turf of contemporaneous life, there is no need for what has been called "ping-pong" speech, exposition followed by application: "This is what the text meant then, here is what the text means now." Whatever the exegetical method behind the sermon, in it, with texts of Scripture, God speaks to us in the present. *Now* God bids us turn from preoccupation with self-definition to a consideration of what God would have us be and do. *Now* God takes "every thought captive to obey Christ" (2 Cor. 10:5). *Now* God

---

11. Elton S. Carter and Iline Fife, "The Critical Approach," in *An Introduction to Graduate Study in Speech and Theatre*, ed. Clyde W. Dow (East Lansing, MI: Michigan State University Press, 1961), p. 83.

12. Conrad H. Massa, "Toward a Contemporary Theology of Preaching" (unpublished Ph.D. dissertation, Princeton Theological Seminary, 1960), esp. p. 5.

. . . has shown strength with his arm;
he has scattered the proud in the thoughts of their hearts.
He has brought down the powerful from their thrones,
    and lifted up the lowly;
he has filled the hungry with good things,
    and sent the rich away empty.
He has helped his servant Israel,
    in remembrance of his mercy,
according to the promise he made to our ancestors,
    to Abraham and to his descendants forever. (Luke 1:51-55)

Has the sermon to do with the temptation of Jesus in the wilderness? Then the challenge of the Devil is the Devil's challenge right now, spoken with our lips: "If you are the Son of God . . ." (Matt. 4:3, 6). Has the sermon to do with the mob shouting, "Crucify him" (Mark 15:13, 14)? It is the shout of people today who, as so many in days gone by, "have no king but Caesar" (John 19:15). Has the sermon to do with an enigmatic remark such as Jesus' comment about stones on the occasion of his "triumphal entry" into Jerusalem as recorded in the Gospel according to Luke: "I tell you, if these were silent, the stones would shout out" (Luke 19:40)? The sermon still can address us in the present even as the preacher reaches into the past to make sense of the text. Jana Childers manages it this way:

> "If these [disciples] fall silent, the very stones will cry out" has always gone by me as a way of saying that songs of praise could be raised from stone if God wanted to do that. . . .
> But a wider look at biblical usage points us in a different direction. For the Bible often speaks of the *accusing cry* of lifeless objects . . . objects that turn, as it were, against their human owners, invoking divine retribution. The blood of murdered Abel cries out, for example, in Genesis 4:10. So does the plundered field in Job 31 and the withheld reward of the workers in James 5.
> AND — SO DO THE STONES — THE STONES — AS INVOL-UNTARY WITNESSES OF VIOLENCE AND IDOLATRY — cry out in Habakkuk 2.

> > Woe to the one who gets evil gain for his or her house —
> > For the stones will cry out from the wall —
> > Woe to the one who says to a wooden (idol): Awake —
> > To a dumb stone: Arise!

So, construed along these lines Jesus' cryptic remark can be read to imply that if the disciples withheld their acclaim the stones would cry out, not in praise, *but in accusation!* And the second reference to stones — Jesus prophesying the destruction of Jerusalem, saying, "One stone will not be left upon another" — strengthens this imagery. . . . Jesus is saying (between the lines and for those who have ears to hear) to us as well as to Jerusalem, that the stones — those very stones you raise in violence and idolatry — those stones that you so carefully pile up in self-tribute — those stones in which you trust — by which you oppress and exploit laborers — with which you wall each other out — those very stones you pile up — one upon another — in the building of your "city" — in the foolhardy pursuit of "peace" apart-from-God — those stones . . . will in the end cry out against you *and* share your destruction.[13]

Preaching that acknowledges the public reading of Scripture as critical to the liturgy of proclamation; preaching that comes to grips with the Bible's denotative and connotative meanings; preaching that deals with texts of Scripture not merely as documents to be reconstructed as history, but as worlds of meaning evoked and engaged in living speech, is *present-tense* preaching. It may deal with the past. It may look to the future. But its stance from beginning to end is in the here and now. *Now* God speaks in the speaking of the Scriptures, in the preaching of sermons. *Now* God takes us as we are and presses us into the service of what God would have us be.

Criterion number two, then, has to do with assessing the narrative of the *divine initiative* and human response in preaching. The tendency is to focus on the human response, to make preaching more our thing than God's thing, so to speak. Who has not heard it time and again: "We do this" and "We do that"? Paul Scherer mocked this preachery proclivity, calling it "We, we, we all the way home." But it is the task of preaching much more to add verbs to the Bible's vast noun than to speak about what *we* do. Whether the sermon literally takes the form of a story or the much beleaguered — and underrated — "three points and a poem," in, with, and under all that is said God is to be seen, felt, heard. Begin with this: that God forgives our "attempts" at preaching

---

13. Jana Lynn Childers, "One Stone Upon Another," in *And Blessed Is She: Sermons by Women,* ed. David Albert Farmer and Edwina Hunter (San Francisco: Harper & Row, 1990), pp. 132-33. Italics for emphasis by Childers.

before we offer them. So God is an active source of hope for what we say even before we get around to saying it. *Simul justus et peccator* (At once justified and sinners)! It is true of the church, true of the world, true of the sermons preached in the church for the sake of the world.

So too the Bible. In the worlds of meaning cued by its texts, God speaks and is spoken to, God acts and is responded to; God forgives and would have us be forgiving, God justifies sinners and, in doing so, condemns all self-righteousness. The initiative in human affairs and in all creation is God's initiative. The difference between the poet and the prophet, said Austin Farrer, is that "the poet is a maker, the prophet is a mouthpiece."[14] And God is the maker, the doer, the speaker, calling up from the prophet what perhaps the prophet would prefer not to hear. Typically prophetic utterance *(ne'um Yahweh)* takes the form of poetry (or of poetic prose), but the poetic images, instanced by God, remain plastic to the will of God. Prophets *bear* the word, they do not invent it, and their intentions do not limit what the word can accomplish. The prophets' speech is *God's* human speech, and the images of prophetic poetry are made to serve purposes of God beyond human ken.

> The prophets do not know that the images are changing their natures — they do not know that the true temple will have to be no temple, but the flesh of the Virgin's Child.
> . . . it is the process of the incarnation of God preparing its own way and casting its shadow before.[15]

If preaching today seems rather tepid as compared to the preaching of the prophets of old, it may not be so because preachers have failed to match the entertainment value of televised discourse. Perhaps it is because they have succeeded! If "sound bite" preaching is "in," perhaps what is "out" is the long narrative of God's jealousy, perduring across millennia, striving against the odds to get back what belongs to it. There is nothing "aesthetically satisfying" in a truncated narrative, in a narrative that is all endings (dishing out conclusions, it has been called). If, in preaching, God in Christ takes us as we are and presses us into the service of what God would have us be, there can be no short cut to what *we* do or need to do that steps past what God has done and is doing.

14. Farrer, p. 129.
15. Farrer, p. 135.

The beginning, middle, and end of the narrative of the encounter of the world of Scripture with the world of the preacher is filled with the Bible's vast noun: God standing there *and* doing something, God listening, God speaking, God redefining the terms by which we live, turning our troubled endings into unexpected beginnings, as was the case with the preaching of the evangelist Mark.

The Gospel according to Mark *is* preaching, and Mark's sermon ends (see p. 43) with these words:

> So they [Mary Magdalene, Mary the mother of James, and Salome] went out and fled from the tomb, for terror and amazement had seized them; and they said nothing to anyone, for they were afraid. (Mark 16:8)

Is this not a sermon ending any sensible preacher would choose? Maybe, then, it is an ending chosen by God, inevitable given the aesthetic sensibility that belongs to *actio divina:*

> Now walks Barabbas free, and Christ is bound.
> The sun is up: our hope is underground.
> Come, Mary Magdalene, Salome, come,
> With funeral odours grace the guarded tomb.
> Seeking immortal Act among the dead,
> They heard his angel, trembled, turned, and fled.

> Now if you say to me "Go on: give us another pair of rhymes to tell us what happened after that," I shall break all the strings of my lyre, and hang myself upon a willow tree. . . .
> The act of God always overthrows human expectation: the cross defeats our hope; the Resurrection terrifies our despair.[16]

Preaching not only has an immediate, or *present-tense,* quality; preaching not only provides a *narrative account of God's initiative* and human response in the encounter of the world of the Bible with the world of the preacher; preaching also proffers what H. H. Farmer has called a *"Christian interpretation of life."*[17] In their sermons, preachers trace — directly and explicitly or by indirection and suggestion — the

16. Farrer, p. 139.
17. Farmer, *Servant,* p. 89.

implications arising from the fact that, in Christ Jesus and with the words of Scripture, God takes us as we are and presses us into the service of what God would have us be. They do this guided by the creedal and confessional tradition of the church, which throughout insists that Christian faith and life are to be pursued in accordance with the apostolic testimony given in canonical texts. The church is one, holy, catholic, *and apostolic.* From its earliest days the members of the church have "devoted themselves to the apostles' teaching and fellowship, to the breaking of bread and the prayers" (Acts 2:42).

There can be no doubt that preachers teach, and that what they teach is given them, not invented by them. Preachers in their sermons do not stretch "this way and that the elastic possibilities of human nature,"[18] for preaching is not a response to human urgings. It is a response "to the demands of the eternal will . . . as they make themselves heard in the determinate situation"[19] where preachers and their congregants stand. A *Christian interpretation of life,* therefore, is not an exploration into the relevance of the gospel to the exigencies of the moment. It is, instead, a "read" of those exigencies in terms of their relevance to the gospel of Christ as the prophetic and apostolic witness attests him. In presenting a Christian interpretation of life, preachers do have an apologetic task, but it is not to make sense of God to God's "cultured despisers" in the face of all life throws up at them. It is to make sense of all life throws up at them in the face of the plural particularity of *actio divina* as the Scriptures speak of it. Central to the apologetic task in the preacher's offering of a *Christian interpretation of life* is the need to help people see that neither faith nor life makes sense so long as it is humanity that sits in the center of it all, putting the questions and demanding answers.

Back in the sixties, when this writer was a bachelor of divinity student at Princeton Theological Seminary, the slogan that rallied the troops was this: "The world sets the agenda for the church!" No doubt the world would have it that way if it could get it that way. But the truth then as now is that God sets the agenda for the world *and* for the church. Both exist for the glory of God or they exist for no reason at all. And both make sense, have relevance and significance, only as people "strive first for the kingdom of God and his righteousness" (Matt. 6:33). There are practical advantages — blessings — to believing in God, but no one will come

18. Farrer, p. 126.
19. Farrer, p. 126.

upon them who sets out after them. There are rewards to be had in service to Jesus Christ, but no one receives them who makes them the object of his or her serving. And life is worthwhile — even in its extremities. But it is not worthwhile because of its length or quality as measured in human terms. What makes life worthwhile is not possessions, rhymes and reasons. It is Presence, God in the midst of it, at the start of it, at the end of it, as the creator of it, as the redeemer of it, as the Alpha and the Omega of it.

Perhaps a rather personal recollection will press home the point. My wife Paula's Aunt Eirene once was a tough and tender teacher. She also was a member of First Presbyterian Church, Ramsey, New Jersey, for well over seventy of her now ninety-five years. She loved her students, and she loved teaching them. She loved her church, and her pastor too; and she loved her Lord. Today, however, Aunt Eirene lies nearly mindless, but well cared for, in a Christian nursing home in Wyckoff, New Jersey. Not too long ago, Paula and I went to visit Aunt Eirene. Nothing about her life seemed worth the effort her heart was making to keep it going. Aunt Eirene lay there and mumbled incoherently, now and then calling out, "Teacher! Teacher!"

"Why doesn't God end it?" I thought. And I do not believe I was alone in what I thought. "And if God doesn't end it, should somebody else end it, for Aunt Eirene's sake, for God's sake?" Paula found a palm frond on Aunt Eirene's bulletin board, a little cork board of pictures, notes, and cards Aunt Eirene could make sense of no longer. Paula waved the palm frond, caught Aunt Eirene's attention, and said, "This is from church, from the Palm Sunday service. People waved the palms to welcome Jesus, Aunt Eirene." Aunt Eirene replied with the only intelligible remark she made in the twenty or so minutes we were with her. "I don't know him," she said. "I don't know any of that — Teacher! Teacher!" But Paula said to her, "Jesus remembers *you*, Aunt Eirene." On our way out the door I said to Paula, "It's come down to this: she can't even remember Jesus." But Paula repeated what she said to her aunt: "No, she can't. But Jesus remembers *her*." Jesus remembers *her*! Precisely! "What is your only comfort, in life and death?" the catechism asks. And it answers: "That I belong — body and soul, in life and death — not to myself but to my faithful Savior, Jesus Christ. . . ."[20]

The fourth criterion for sermon evaluation has to do with the living God's dialogic engagement of preachers and congregants (God's

---

20. "The Heidelberg Catechism," *The Book of Confessions* (Louisville, KY: Presbyterian Church [U.S.A.], 1994), C.4.001, p. 29.

speech and silence, God's claim and succor) in Jesus Christ — crucified, risen, regnant — as he is attested for us in Scripture through the agency of the Holy Spirit. Already we have seen that the initiative in the dialogic encounter of the world of the Bible and the world of the preacher is with God. Now it is time to point out that human response to that divine initiative is instigated by God for us and with us in Jesus Christ. This reality is expressed in the *indicative mood* of the sermon. This is not to say that there is no imperative, that there is no "must" or "should" or "ought" to faith. Rather it is to say that the "must," "should," and "ought" are implicit in the "is" of the faith we preach. The imperative rises out of the indicative as praise rises from a grateful heart. To proclaim that fact is not to proclaim "cheap grace" either. Quite to the contrary, it is to proclaim costly grace. Hearts are not made grateful for nothing; they are made grateful for something. And the thankful praise of God is not a mood of the moment; it is the risk of a lifetime.

The "something" that makes for gratitude is Jesus Christ, crucified, risen, reigning in power among the strong and among the weak, among the "haves" and among the "have nots," among the God-fearing and among the God-hating, with never so much as a "by your leave." In Christ the realm of God is opened up to humankind. In him the rule of God is exercised as of old, among peoples and nations. Caiaphas and Pilate in their day wielded power. And the confluence of religious commitment and political establishment still is a potent force. But the power of the crucified is stronger than the power of death — the most dreaded weapon of entrenched privilege — and cannot be intimidated by it. "The cross is not and cannot be loved," said Jürgen Moltmann:

> Yet only the crucified Christ can bring the freedom which changes the world because it is no longer afraid of death. In his time the crucified Christ was regarded as a scandal and as foolishness. Today, too, it is considered old-fashioned to put him in the centre of Christian faith and of theology [and of preaching, let us hasten to add]. Yet only when people are reminded of him, however untimely this may be, can they be set free from the power of the facts of the present time, and from the laws and compulsions of history, and be offered a future which will never grow dark again.[21]

21. Jürgen Moltmann, *The Crucified God: The Cross of Christ as the Foundation and Criticism of Christian Theology* (San Francisco: Harper and Row, 1974), p. 1.

In Christian worship, in response to the proclamation of the word, there is the offertory, and, with it, in many church traditions, the singing of the *Doxology:*

> Praise God from whom all blessings flow;
> Praise him, all creatures here below;
> Praise him above, ye heavenly host:
> Praise Father, Son, and Holy Ghost.[22]

Such praise springs from the word of the cross *received,* from hearts filled with gratitude and stirred to faith: stirred to commitment to Christ, and to the way he would have it, instead of to commitment to "the way it is." Praise him Caiaphas! Praise him Pilate! Praise him Caesar! Praise him in Jerusalem! Praise him in Rome! Praise him in Washington and Beirut, in Nicaragua and Somalia! Praise him wherever, whatever the cost. And now here and now there it could cost you as much as your life. "Praise Father, Son, and Holy Ghost." Praise *that* God, and no other, for there is no other. Praise the Father of the blessed Mary's blessed Child, the God who would be as a mother to us, as a friend to us, as a neighbor to us as to our enemies. Praise *that* God, who, out of love for the world, draws near to women and men *of* the world in him who is *not* of the world, and whom the world hates, that "the world might be saved through him" (John 3:17).

It is not a "warm fuzzy" love, this love of God. It is a "two edged sword" (Rev. 1:16) kind of love, in the mouth of "one like the Son of Man" (Rev. 1:13). Nothing is as it was, or can continue as it is, in the face of such love; for such love is fierce as it is tender, and it will have "the way it is" pressed into the service of what God would have it be. The *indicative mood* of the sermon implies all that. So is the praise that arises from it the praise of souls entering the kingdom of God. Such praise is subversive. As Jon Sobrino, S.J., points out:

> Our term "Kingdom of God" may tend to support a static situation which has no place in the original Hebrew expression *(Malkuth Yahweh).* The latter suggests two basic notions: (1) God reigns with acts of power, (2) in order to establish or modify the order of things.[23]

---

22. *Doxology* by Bishop Thomas Ken, 1695, 1709. See, for example, *The Presbyterian Hymnal* (Louisville, KY: Westminster/John Knox Press, 1990), Hymn No. 592.

23. Jon Sobrino, S.J., *Christology at the Crossroads: A Latin American Approach,* trans. John Drury (Maryknoll, NY: Orbis Books, 1976), pp. 42-43.

To be trapped in "the order of things" is what is meant in Ephesians where it says:

> You were dead through the trespasses and sins in which you once lived, following the course of this world, following the ruler of the power of the air, the spirit that is now at work among those who are disobedient. (Eph. 2:1-2)

Yet, said Calvin, preaching "revivifies the dead."[24] Such is the sermon's *indicative word*. It does more than demand human praise. It enables it.

The fifth and last criterion for homiletical criticism has to do with the surface shape (as opposed to deep narrative structure) of the sermon, the wording of it, and the manner of speaking it. David S. Cunningham would have us understand all that in rhetorical terms. Christian theology, he insists — and there can be little doubt that he would include preaching as a form of theological work — is inherently rhetorical. It is faithful persuasion. It aims "to speak the word that theology must speak, in ways that are faithful to the God of Jesus Christ *and persuasive to the world that God has always loved.*"[25] There can be no denying that there is a good deal of truth in what Cunningham asserts. There *is* a rhetorical, suasory dimension to all communication. One cannot even speak of the weather or the time of day without at least hoping someone will get the message. To win or to hold attention — and preachers surely attempt to do the latter — is to influence somebody, to affect somebody's behavior. It is to persuade.

Ever since the so-called "rhetorical turn," scholars have not only spoken of the various rhetorics (and public performances, for that matter) attendant to dealing with certain kinds of problems (for example, ethical, legal, aesthetic, and theological problems). They also have argued that knowledge itself is rhetorical, socially constructed, not given and received — except in the sense that all cultures pass on to succeeding generations cultural wisdom and bias — but invented.[26] Some have

24. Quoted in Jane Dempsey Douglass, *Women, Freedom and Calvin* (Philadelphia: Westminster Press, 1985), p. 41.

25. David S. Cunningham, *Faithful Persuasion: In Aid of a Rhetoric of Christian Theology* (Notre Dame, IN: University of Notre Dame Press, 1991), p. 5. Italics mine.

26. See John S. Nelson, Allan Megill, and Donald N. McClosky, eds., *The Rhetoric of the Human Sciences: Language and Argument in Scholarship and Public Affairs* (Madison, WI: University of Wisconsin Press, 1987). See also Herbert W. Simons, ed., *The*

attempted to make the case that what theologians do — especially theologians whose work is regarded as seminal — is create a new suasory language for theological discourse, a language that sets the terms for theological study and debate. This theological rhetoric then is susceptible to rhetorical critique aimed at determining how successful it might be in terms of its own objectives, and at winning adherents in given times and places.[27]

It is not questioned here that knowledge is socially constructed, that it is invented, made, even at times made up "out of whole cloth." But it is questioned here whether or not the only agent making up what people come to know (and to believe as trustworthy and true) is people themselves. In fact it has been asserted throughout this study that God is the Agent of agents, the Creator of creators, the Rhetor of rhetors, the Performer of performers, and that what Christian preachers are called to do is to interpret responsibly — that is, under the direction of the Holy Spirit speaking in the Scriptures — the *actio divina/homo performans* that is Jesus Christ. The limit of situationally apt suasory discourse concerning God, including that practical theological discourse called preaching, is Jesus Christ as he is attested for us in Holy Scripture and confessed in the creeds of the church that is in discipleship to him, that is seeking to follow him — albeit often at a scandalous distance and with considerable ambivalence. Jana Childers put it bluntly and succinctly:

> Rhetoric . . . is about discovering the available means of persuasion in a given situation. Homiletics is about the discovery of the proper means of interpretation of an authoritative text and its appropriate proclamation for a situation. Rhetoric is not, or not necessarily, about flying under somebody else's banner, speaking under orders or being a "herald" for somebody else's news. Preaching is.[28]

Rhetorical Turn: Invention and Persuasion in the Conduct of Inquiry (Chicago: University of Chicago Press, 1990). Also see John Bender and David E. Wellbery, "Rhetoricality: On the Modernist Return of Rhetoric," in *The Ends of Rhetoric: History, Theory, Practice,* ed. John Bender and David E. Wellbery (Stanford, CA: Stanford University Press, 1990), pp. 3-39.

27. See for example Stephen H. Webb, *Re-Figuring Theology: The Rhetoric of Karl Barth* (Albany, NY: State University of New York Press, 1991).

28. Childers, "Critical Analysis," pp. 27-28.

The preacher's design and composition of the sermon and, most importantly, the preacher's *delivery* of the sermon is, or ought to be, a design, composition, and delivery that takes seriously who is listening, where, when, how, and why. This means that "canned" outlines are out, that a personality-of-the-preacher-determined single approach to all occasions is out; and that *dexterous use of a variety of possible sermon strategies* is in. There is solid, traditional support for such flexibility too. For example, Jane Dempsey Douglass, speaking of Calvin, remarked:

> Calvin . . . learned from his Renaissance humanist studies that one must always inquire into the particular historical setting in which writing [and preaching too] takes shape in order to understand its life setting. He is extremely conscious of the cultural changes evident over time within the Bible itself, and of the cultural difference between biblical times and his own. And so he makes use of the principle of "accommodation," that *God in the incarnation and the Scriptures accommodates his message to the changing human capacity for understanding. . . .*[29]

Note that with Calvin, as with the Christian tradition generally, it is *God* who takes the initiative to accommodate the gospel to specific audiences and contexts. Even in accommodation, therefore, preachers follow God's lead, not their own whims. Further, if, in Cunningham's terms, it comes to a choice between "the word that theology must speak, in ways that are faithful to Jesus Christ" and what may seem more likely to be "persuasive to the world that God always loved," the preacher must bear the word — as Jeremiah bore it to a cistern, as Christ bore it to a cross — sans concern for rhetorical effectiveness. Fidelity is more important than success (to understate the case), and homiletics never can be reduced to finding the available means of persuasion.

One more thing remains to be said about this fifth and final criterion for homiletical criticism. Preachers are to attempt to speak in such a way that congregants are left free to respond on the basis of their own insight and sense of the truth. Preachers, of course, as already has been noted, will strive to hold and direct the attention congregants give them; but they will not seek to manipulate response. What happens with the word in people's hearts is the work of the Spirit and the worry of

29. Douglass, pp. 32-33. Italics mine.

the auditor. It is not the business of the preacher. So the preacher's diction, *the preacher's wording of the sermon, must aim for cause, not for effect.* The effect of a sermon may be that someone feels guilt, but that does not mean the preacher must have appealed to people's sense of guilt. The effect of a sermon may be that someone feels empowered to live beyond his or her means, to do for others, for example, what apparently cannot be done, loving one's enemies for instance. But that does not mean that the preacher must have appealed to that person's want to be wanted, or need to be needed. In any case, how can preachers actually know what somebody else is or ought to be feeling, say at a wedding, or at a funeral, or at an Advent or Eastertide service? And how can preachers know what others should be feeling about arms merchandizing, the savaging of the environment, the maneuvering for power and privilege that goes on in the affairs of states, homes, churches, academies, play yards?

Paint people into the scenes of the encounter of the biblical world with the world of the preacher, and there let people discover for themselves how they feel and what, if anything, they feel they must do. People listening to Jesus preach his parables realized quickly enough "that he was speaking about them," and some decided on the spot what to do. They plotted to get rid of him (Matt. 21:45). The word of God "kills as well as makes alive; it hardens as well as renews."[30] And there is no need for preachers to tell it what it ought to be doing with this person or that, in one case or another. Until they themselves have heard God's word, preachers cannot be sure what the word will do with *them*, or they with it. Much less does it make any sense for preachers to try to determine in advance how their congregants will respond to the word. Let people respond to God's word *with* if not *as* their preachers, that is, *after*, and *not before* the word has entered their hearts. Congregants, after all, do not invent what they hear any more than preachers invent what they say. The word of God is not a work of inscrutable art people must do their best to make of what they will.[31] Yet neither is it all denotation

---

30. John H. Leith, *The Reformed Imperative* (Philadelphia: Westminster Press, 1988), p. 29.

31. Long, drawing on Craddock, compares the hearing of sermons to the contemplation of impressionist art, a not inscrutable, yet not simply representational, style of painting. Even so, to compare is not to identify. Clearly the preached word invites personal, even ineffably personal, appropriations. And since, I take it, that is what Long means by

and no connotation, all raw assertion without any room for personalized appropriation. The Spirit inspires the speaking *and the hearing* of the word, through the apostolic testimony, and with the words of preachers. The rule of *sola scriptura*, that is to say, is exercised among the people who listen to preaching, not only among those who preach; and "the test of the validity of a witness is finally the approval of the people of God, the priesthood of all believers, over a period of time."[32]

At the start of this study in Scripture reading and preaching as a practical theology of the spoken word, we explored together the nature of God's human speech as oxymoronic, metaphoric, and metonymic. Oxymoronic figures of speech focus on the discontinuities experienced in divine self-disclosure. Metaphoric tropes focus on the account given those discontinuities in terms of the familiar; they signal difference in sameness, reorientation in the midst of disorientation. Metonyms signal transcendence in immanence, real presence in the face of felt absence;

---

insisting that preaching invites congregants' meanings, the comparison to art is helpful. If, on the other hand, someone were to take Long's comparison to mean that the word of God preached lacks all clarity and precision, all weight of divine intention, that it is all connotation and no denotation, then the comparison could not hold. See Thomas G. Long, "And How Shall They Hear? The Listener in Contemporary Preaching," in *Listening to the Word: Studies in Honor of Fred B. Craddock*, ed. Gail R. O'Day and Thomas G. Long (Nashville, TN: Abingdon Press, 1993), pp. 167-88, esp. p. 169. In this connection of denotation and connotation, manifest authorial intent and the listener's contribution to meaning (the coming together of which always is a matter of sense *and* significance, not merely one or the other), mention often is made of the so-called intentional fallacy, a concept developed by Beardsley and Wimsatt. It is sometimes argued that we cannot know authorial intent, that there are virtually no limits to meaning, and that therefore one contextualized "read" of a text (or shall we say, a sermon) is axiomatically as valid as any other. Wimsatt and Beardsley — pardon the pun — *intended* no such extravagant claim. Wimsatt himself stated as follows: "What we meant . . . [in "The Intentional Fallacy"] . . . and what in effect I think we managed to say, was that the closest one could ever get to the artist's intending or meaning mind outside his work would still be short of his *effective* intention or *operative* mind as it appears in the work itself and can be read from the work." (Italics Wimsatt). The authors of "The Intentional Fallacy" also apparently meant that not only authorial intention, but even authorial presence, could be, and should be, discerned in a work. See Colin Lyas, "Personal Qualities and the Intentional Fallacy," in *Aesthetics: A Critical Anthology*, ed. George Dickie, Richard Sclafani, and Ronald Roblin (New York: St. Martin's Press, 1989), pp. 442-54, esp. p. 448. The relevance of this for preaching is clear: The preacher is to attempt to say what the text asserts, interpreted in the light of Christ; and that likewise must be what congregants attempt to hear in, with, and under whatever connotative meanings they bring to the preaching moment.

32. Leith, p. 31.

and they can be transposed from the world of words to the world of action and concrete symbol. So the bread and wine of the eucharist, broken and shared, at least in Reformed thought, signal the real presence of Christ among the people of God. Likewise, preaching, the speaking *and hearing* of God's word in sermonic form, undertaken in attempted fidelity to the apostolic witness, signals the authority, person, presence, and rule of God in Christ, through the agency of the Holy Spirit, in the church which is Christ's body. In preaching we are reminded that it is precisely the crucified Christ who reigns in power and who is coming again as eschatological judge. Cross and scepter are held together, not torn apart as if the one could have nothing to do with the other. The priestly, prophetic, and monarchic offices of Christ belong to the whole church, and not only to those set aside for peculiar service in those offices. Therefore the preaching of the word cannot merely be a statement of the personal faith story of the preacher. Instead it must be, or attempt to be, a statement of the faith story of the church, which the church itself, the people of God, assesses in light of the church's canon: Jesus Christ as he is attested for us by the Holy Spirit in sacred Scripture.

In his just-completed dissertation on the royal psalms, Scott R. A. Starbuck makes the case that the emerging, liturgically shaped theological anthropology depicted in that literature points to a democratizing of the divine regal office. That is, God's rule is exercised at last not in the person of the king, but, so to speak, in the person of the community of God's people.[33] So we note that the reign of God in preaching is exercised not simply in the speaking of sermons, but in the hearing of them, among preachers and their congregants, and among preachers *as* their congregants. Like the sacred liturgy, in the context of which preaching most regularly takes place, preaching, as a practical theology of the spoken word — that is, of proclamation — is "communitarian, even proletarian . . . long term and dialectical; and . . . its agents are more likely to be charwomen and shopkeepers than pontiffs and professors."[34] God's human speech is speech among the people of God, and *for* them, and for the world into which the divine Word has been sent.

33. Scott R. A. Starbuck, "And What Had Kings? The Reappropriation of Court Oracles Among the Royal Psalms of the Hebrew Psalter" (unpublished Ph.D. dissertation, Princeton Theological Seminary, 1996), esp. pp. 246-56.

34. Aidan Kavanaugh, *On Liturgical Theology* (New York: Pueblo, 1981), pp. 74-75.

6. The Love God Does: Sermons

THIS CHAPTER CONSISTS ENTIRELY of sermon manuscripts, "arrested performances" of earlier homiletical "attempts." Each sermon is intended to assert what its biblical text asserts concerning the ways of God with humanity and the ways of humanity with God. Yet each sermon also draws on those connotations (the factors of human impact and emotional content) evoked in the preacher (that is, this writer) in the encounter of his world with the world of the text. The preacher himself at least aspires to be a faithful listener who speaks to facilitate other people's listening. So he prays that God will speak with his words, or in spite of them, and with, or in spite of, the vocal and physical gestures implicit in those words. Then, let those with ears to hear, hear.

To some extent (one hopes not entirely) these sermons may fail to measure up to the criteria for homiletical criticism explicated in the preceding chapter. On the other hand, to some extent, the theory may fail to measure up to the practice. In other words, there is always the chance that the practice of preaching — itself being theory laden — will reform constructive homiletical thought and criticism. Also, though each of these sermons has its origination in a particular ecclesial context, each also has a future home with those who read these sermon manuscripts, whoever they may be, wherever they may be. Since sermon manuscripts are "arrested performances," they, like the Scripture lessons they seek to interpret, must be spoken and heard to be rightly understood and assessed. Therefore the reader is encouraged to read the following Scripture lessons and sermon manuscripts aloud, to bring them to living speech. Just so God may take the sermons as they are and press them into the service of what God would have them be. The divine initiative is there, no less than at the beginning of the homiletical process, *there,* where the ink stains on the page are again turned into blood.

One last introductory thought concerning the following sermons: "Wilhelmina's House Is Clean" is an attempt at a contemporary parable inspired by a scriptural anecdote — the story of Mary and Martha. Such attempts need the context of regular, more directly expository preaching in order to be rightly heard; for the contemporary teller of the parable (unlike the teller of biblical parables) is not Jesus (to state the obvious). And congregants would see *him.* It is the prayers preceding and following Wilhelmina's story that direct our attention to him. Apart from the prayers, therefore, the story (the would-be parable) is not a sermon. The story cries out for the divine intervention in the person of Christ the prayers seek and affirm.

The Love God Does

Text: 1 John 4:7-12

Though we cannot see you, O God, nevertheless grant that we may know you as Eternal Love in him who is your Word of Love made flesh; and so enable us to love one another that we may see your love perfected in us, through him who is the atoning sacrifice for our lovelessness, even Jesus Christ, your Son, our Savior. Amen.

"God is Love." The church believes it. You and I believe it. Everybody I know who believes in God believes it. Yet the once extraordinarily popular Irish dramatist, poet, and wit, Oscar Wilde, said there was enough suffering in any London lane to show God's love is fancy, not fact.[1] Could he be right and we wrong? When times are good it is easy enough to say it: "God is love." When times are tough, though — and times are tough right now for many — the words may stick in our throats and nearly choke us. Say it — "God is love" — when a loved one dies, after "the muffled drum's sad roll has beat the soldier's last tattoo."[2] Say it after "the snuffer [has lowered on some] shining mind to bow and chill the twisting wick of it,"[3] after Alzheimer's, that is.

How can it be true that God is love when, in so many places in our world today, "famine, sword, and fire crouch for employment"?[4] How can it be true that God is love when in a land that used to love to sing, "give me your tired, your poor, your huddled masses yearning to breathe free,"[5] refugees from famine, sword, and fire are often neglected

---

1. Cited in Paul E. Scherer, "The Gospel According to St. Luke: Exposition," in *The Interpreter's Bible*, ed. George Arthur Buttrick, vol. 8 (Nashville, TN: Abingdon Press, 1952), p. 385.

2. Theodore O'Hara, "The Bivouac of the Dead."

3. Dorothy Thomas, "Far Echo."

4. Shakespeare, *The Life of King Henry the Fifth*, prologue, lns. 7-8.

5. Emma Lazarus, "The New Colossus."

or harassed now instead of helped, sent back to the places of terror and deprivation from which they have fled? No love for them? Shakespeare put it in a stark and chilling phrase when he said, "all our yesterdays have lighted fools the way to dusty death."[6] Life, good Lord, we pray, if there is no sense in it, there can be no love in it. First God must be sane, only then can God be love.

So it is possible to sit in the center of one's own universe daring God to explain the divine self, like the poet, Robert Frost, speaking to a distant star: "use language we can comprehend, tell us what elements you blend,"[7] and like Frost's star, God may seem to give us "strangely little aid,"[8] no clear answers to our hardest questions, no settled way of salvation. And out there somewhere, far away from heaven's white light, "a grave for all [our] bright hopes with the heavy earth falling."[9] Is that it? And, if that is it, no wonder we wonder why, why anything? Why has this marriage soured? Why has learning lost its thrill? Why has love lost its value? Now we're at the bottom line, aren't we? If God is love there ought to be some payoff for those of us who believe that he is.

Could it be that God will not define divine love in ways that suit us, in words and actions that appeal to our native instincts? Back in the sixties and seventies love was a "warm fuzzy." Now that's not much, but it does have some value. It's better than a "cold prickly." In the eighties love was romantic again; it was roses and candlelight, tuxedos and evening gowns, a limousine to take you to the prom. In the nineties love has to be made of sterner stuff. We all know that.

Love has to work hard to keep people from harm's way. In Florida, just four years ago, people prayed that love would send them deliverance from wind and rain. Do you remember? Then the hurricane came, bringing with it destruction such as never before had been seen in this country except, perhaps, during the human havoc of the Civil War nearly a century and a half ago. Then came the Nicaraguan tidal wave, the Hawaiian hurricane, the earthquakes of Egypt, and, through it all, starvation in Somalia and the Sudan, ethnic war in Bosnia-Herzegovina —

6. Shakespeare, *The Tragedy of Macbeth,* act 5, sc. 5, lns. 22-23.

7. Robert Frost, "Take Something Like a Star," in *The Poetry of Robert Frost,* ed. Edward Connery Latham (New York: Holt, Rinehart and Winston, 1969), p. 403.

8. Frost, "Take Something Like a Star," p. 403.

9. Paul E. Scherer, "Let God Be God," in *The Word God Sent* (Grand Rapids, MI: Baker Book House, 1977), p. 151.

we are still trying to mop up after that — and our own living and dying seemingly beyond our means.[10] No heaven-sent deliverance from harm.

We plead for a logic to love, yet God fills love with the illogic of sacrifice, suffering, forgiveness, and death. Like the homeless and the dispossessed, it has nowhere to lay its head. "In this is love, not that we loved God, but that God loved us." How? With a Christ and a cross, that's how, with a death wretched as any anyone has died, with a silence deep and lonely as human grief — deeper. *God* is love. *God* is love. And God loves us. That is the heart and soul of the gospel. God loves us, not on our terms but on his own, not according to our wants but according to our needs, and not according to the measure of our demand but according to the measure of divine grace.

Often people ask for far less than God wants to give. They want an answer to the riddle of life. Instead they get life. They want deliverance from death, though there is no deliverance from it. Yet God brings people through death into the divine presence. So death, though inevitable, is not loveless. People want ease, God gives them adventure. They want the homeless housed and the hungry fed, refugees cared for at last and victims of human and natural disasters guarded from further harm. God gives them the chance to do it. They want things to make them happy. God gives them himself and each other. A great Presbyterian preacher of a generation ago, George Arthur Buttrick, expressed it memorably. He said: "We ask, 'what's the use of religion?' [But] God does not 'use' us, and we may not 'use' [God]. The 'use' is to save us from the utilitarian blasphemy of asking, 'What's the use of religion.'"[11] And religion saves us from asking, "What's love's bottom line?"

In other words, love, as men and women often think of it today, and as you and I perhaps would have it if we could have our druthers, is not God. Instead, God made known to us in Jesus, the Christ, is love. God defines love. Our varied understandings of love do not define God. Love is something God does to us, among us, with us, for us. With love God makes us a divine possession — each of us and all of us together. Do you want to see God's love in action? Look around you. It is what has brought us all together and made us a church. God's love is not the

10. Paraphrase of Oscar Wilde's words, "I am dying beyond my means." See Hesketh Pearson, *Oscar Wilde: His Life and Wit* (New York: Harper and Bros., 1946), p. 331.

11. George Arthur Buttrick, *Sermons Preached in a University Church* (Nashville, TN: Abingdon Press, 1959), pp. 185-86.

private possession of any of us. It is God's public possession of all of us. For better or worse, for richer or poorer, in sickness and in health, though death do us part, God loves us.

Therefore we may love one another, not as well as God loves us, of course, for we are not God. We are very human beings and our affections run hot and cold. Shakespeare said that "love is not love which alters when it alteration finds."[12] Our love does alter, however, doesn't it? Our caring for one another is not definitive. Now and then men and women have been known to take up their lives for their friends. They even have laid them down for their friends and enemies. But, when faced with such challenges, they also have been tempted to pray, "not thy will, but mine be done." Was that really the last temptation of Christ? Who has not prayed and acted that way one time or another, wishing to know love, yet hoping to duck what love requires in order to be known: life-long, life-deep devotion to the other's well-being?

Yet, despite it all, now and then, even when we have encased ourselves in a shell of self-concern, fearing to risk love, there seeps in a need that somehow cannot be neglected, a claim that cannot be refused, an offer of friendship that, for pity's sake, cannot be turned down, something that, instead of making life bearable, makes it inescapable,[13] and God has us, for God's own glory and our neighbor's good, however vacillating our affections. "If we love one another," even if we love one another just a little bit, "God lives in us, and [God's] love is perfected in us." Think of it: God perfects — or brings to completion — the circle of divine caring in you and in me, in the fellowship of the church, in the midst of the world, in flesh and blood and muscle, in what a poet somewhere has called "the clash and scratch of dirt." God's love is as close as the heartbeat of the person sitting next to you in that pew. It is as hearty as a handshake and the passing of the peace. It is as tight and tender as an embrace.

Tucked away in the hills of North Central New Jersey there is a town called Liberty Corner. I love the place. Why? Because on television in the 1950s I saw it photographed and mentioned in a movie melodrama from the 1930s or 40s? Not likely. Then why? Because one of my favorite students, Linda Owens, at whose service of installation I

---

12. Sonnet 116.

13. Peter S. Hawkins, *The Language of Grace: Flannery O'Connor, Walker Percy and Iris Murdoch* (Cambridge: Cowley Publications, 1983), p. 98.

preached, serves on the ministerial staff of the Liberty Corner Presbyterian Church? Well, yes, in part. But most of all I love the place, and
will love it, because my late mother spent her earliest days on earth
there, and because, from her, in my earliest days, I learned that God is
love. And I learned to sing the truth: "Praise him, praise him, all ye little
children. God is love, God is love." Actually I thought it was "Raisin,
raisin, all ye little children." I was into food at an early age.

At the start of this sermon, you will recall, I indicated that Oscar
Wilde once said there was enough suffering in any London lane to show
that God's love is fancy, not fact. Yet toward that fancy Oscar Wilde
himself came at last to stretch out his arms. In a poem, he wrote: "Come
down, O Christ, and help me, reach thy hand, for I am drowning in a
stormier sea than Simon on thy Lake of Galilee."[14] So Christ came down,
we may dare to believe, not this time to calm the storm, but to steady
the man in the midst of it, for Oscar Wilde was left to die in Paris, under
an assumed name, in poverty and disrepute. No longer was he the
extraordinarily popular Irish dramatist, poet, and wit.

So Christ comes down to where the most neglected, or abused, or
disreputable, or grief-stricken hurt today, down to the streets of cities
and towns like Sarajevo, Miami, Los Angeles, Princeton, and Liberty
Corner, down to places where people cry, "Why?" He comes to our
sanctuaries and pulpits, too, to speak to you and me with the rugged,
wonderful words of Scripture, and with the sometimes clumsy, sometimes eloquent words of us preachers. He comes in unspeakable joy, for
he loves us, and in pain, for he loves us as we are. He comes with a
peace that passes understanding. "In this is love, not that we loved God,
but that God loved us." And "if we love one another, God lives in us,
and [God's] love is perfected in us."

> O God, you are love, and you love us perfectly even as we love
> each other now and then in fits and starts. Grant us to know
> your love more fully, that, as individuals and as a church, we
> may grow in love continually, until we attain to the measure
> of the stature of the fullness of Christ and are mature in love.
> This we ask in Jesus' name and for his sake. Amen.

14. Oscar Wilde, "E Tenebris."

God Trusts You

Text: Matthew 25:14-30

Eternal and ever-blessed God, whose glory is humanity set free from enslavement to false and friendless masters, by your word preached and heard, free us to be a true people of God, friends of Christ, women and men determined to do justice, and to love kindness, and to walk humbly with you, our God — whatever the risks. So in all things, and even now in this sermon, let us be to the praise of your glory, through Jesus Christ our Lord. Amen.

The parable of the talents is preached somewhere every fall when the leadership of the local church gets after the membership for money. Tithe your time. Tithe your talents. Tithe your cash. That is the conventional wisdom, and there is nothing wrong with it. It is wisdom that has stood the test of time and circumstance. That is precisely why we call it conventional wisdom. It may be tried and trite, but it is also true. We do expect members of the church to turn over a portion of their assets to the church's care. We look for quarter tithes, half tithes, full tithes, and we do not look in vain. Many members of the church are exceedingly generous in their support of it and of its mission.

There is more to the parable of the talents than that, however. There is this: There is a master who turns over to his slaves enough of his own wealth to scare half to death even the most confident Wall Street money manager. Do you know how much one talent is? It is 10,000 denarii. It is 10,000 times a day's wage. That makes two talents 20,000 times a day's wage and five talents 50,000 times a day's wage. If the master of this parable did give to his slaves according to their ability, they were extraordinarily able workers and managers, or he was very wide of the mark in his estimate of them. In any case, if somebody entrusted me with that much of his or her cash or personal property, I'd play it conservative, wouldn't you? I'd squirrel it away. As a radio financial advisor used to recommend, I'd find a way to keep it safe from "the government, the IRS, and relatives with long, sticky fingers."

That is exactly what the one-talent servant in Jesus' parable did. Please don't blame him. He did neither more nor less than what was expected of him according to rabbinic law. The law reads that "whoever immediately buries property entrusted to him is no longer liable because he has taken the safest course conceivable."[15] The one-talent slave followed the letter of the law. He obeyed the conventional wisdom. Yet he suffered terrible abuse for his rectitude. Perhaps his master was "a harsh man, reaping where [he] did not sow, and gathering where [he] did not scatter seed" (Matt. 25:24). What that means is that the master earned his bread by the sweat of others, caring not a whit what happened to them. People were the means to his "bottom line" end. The master did not deny the allegation either. Instead, almost as if to confirm it, he insisted that his anxious, cautious, dutiful one-talent slave should have sweated his way through the markets or at least placed his master's money in a bank account on the merest chance that he might have turned a profit. Given the temper of the times, according to rabbinic law, that expectation apparently could be considered utterly unrealistic and unjust. The startling success of the five- and two-talent servants, in other words, was the exception, not the rule. In fact, such success was beyond improbable; it was inconceivable.

The master's temerity did not end with his excoriating his one-talent slave for failing to invest his funds profitably, however. No, risking further proof of just how hard-nosed he could be, he took what had been kept safe for him by the one-talent slave and gave it to the slave who had increased his five talents to ten. One can only guess the measure of that poor fellow's timorous gratitude. "For to all those who have will more be given, and they will have an abundance; but from those who have nothing even what they have will be taken away" (Matt. 25:29). So cold justice is sealed with epigrammatic eloquence. Finally, the master called his one-talent slave names: "Wicked, lazy, worthless." Not much there for improving the self-image of the walking wounded. And he cast the poor fellow out into the streets without benefit of pension, to weep and gnash his teeth with the rest of the homeless and dispossessed. So the poor we have with us, always, a pitiful, if common, sight.

15. Eduard Schweizer, *The Good News According to Matthew* (Atlanta: John Knox Press, 1975), p. 471.

Now what can we learn from this perplexing and disturbing parable? Well, considering who told it, we cannot learn from it that God is like a reckless at best — or at worst cruel — master who expects people to do more for him than he will do for himself. God does not earn divine bread, so to speak, by the sweat of our human brow. Milton got it right in his poem, "On His Blindness" where he said God "doth not need either man's work or his own gifts."[16] We cannot learn from the parable of the talents any little lesson in what might be called "possibility theology" either. If you tithe to the church — and God grant you do — there is no certainty at all that the other 90 percent of your time, talent, and cash will increase geometrically. Frankly, you could lose it all, for the rain falls alike "on the righteous and on the unrighteous" (Matt. 5:45), the generous and the tight-fisted. Time runs out. Talents fail. Savings shrink. Nothing human lasts. "Matter it is" that we are made of, said the poet, Eli Siegal, "and matter dies and dies."[17]

Even the church can fail for all the time, talent, and cash poured into it. Especially the church can fail if it tries too hard to succeed. What was it Jesus told his disciples? "If any want to be my followers, let them deny themselves, take up their cross and follow me. For those who want to save their life will lose it, and those who lose their life for my sake will find it" (Matt. 16:24-25). Now there is something we can learn from the parable of the talents. Life with God in the world is a terrible risk, and there is no safe way to heaven. "For [the kingdom of heaven] is as if a man, going on a journey, summoned his slaves and entrusted his property to them" (Matt. 25:14).

There it is: God trusts you and me to care for what belongs to God. Now what might that be? The kingdoms of this world know what belongs to them, or at least they think they do. Do you remember when the Pharisees (who had come to detest Herod) and the Herodians (King Herod's supporters) — politics makes strange bedfellows — put Jesus to the test, saying, "Is it lawful to pay taxes to [Caesar] or not?" (Matt. 22:17)? Jesus replied, "'Show me the coin used for the tax.' And they brought him a denarius. And [Jesus] said to them, 'Whose head is this

16. John Milton, "On His Blindness," in *Milton's Minor Poems,* ed. Mary A. Jordan (New York: American Book Co., 1904), p. 31.

17. Eli Siegal, "Ralph Isham, 1753 and later," in *Hot Afternoons Have Been in Montana* (New York: Definition Press, 1957), p. 8.

and whose title is this?' They answered, '[Caesar's].' Then he said to them, 'Give therefore to [Caesar] the things that are [Caesar's], and to God the things that are God's'" (Matt. 22:19-21). Coins minted by Caesar, Caesar could have, but lives, minted by God, belonged to God. Your heart, your soul, your hopes, your dreams, and those of neighbors, strangers, friends, enemies, belong to God. That is what Jesus meant. Never was Caesar to get hold of them.

Caesar did want them, you know. From time to time he sought to purchase them, if he could, with imperial favors. (And where have we heard of that kind of thing before?) By the way, it was Augustus Caesar, a Roman god, whose image was engraved on the coin handed to Jesus. The Roman Senate had voted divine honors to the emperor. So if Caesar's coin came your way, could his idolatry be far behind? Give Caesar his denarius. Get rid of it. For what profit is there in gaining a day's wage and losing your soul? Matthew's version of *The Sermon on the Mount* records it: "You cannot serve God and wealth" (Matt. 6:24).

Can you manage more risk than that in dealing with what belongs to God? You will risk more, for life with God is life on the edge. That is the context for Jesus' telling of the parable of the talents. Already Jesus had gone to the heart of Jerusalem and inveighed against it. Hear him: "Woe to you, Scribes and Pharisees, hypocrites! For you build the tombs of the prophets and decorate the graves of the righteous, and you say, 'If we had lived in the days of our ancestors, we would not have taken part with them in shedding the blood of the prophets.' Thus you testify against yourselves that you are descendants of those who murdered the prophets. Fill up, then, the measure of your ancestors. . . . Jerusalem, Jerusalem!" (Matt. 23:29-32, 37).

Religious establishments, no less than political establishments, evidently can get caught up in vain attempts to keep from God what belongs to God: the hopes, dreams, souls of neighbors, strangers, friends, enemies. Today, among us Christians, they can do that by trying to make the church what God will not let it be: a monument to the brave past kept now as a safe haven for just the "right kind of people," not all whom Christ calls to himself through faith and repentance, but simply "my kind of people," as the saying goes. They can do that by indulging in a sentimental search for that garden, apart, where Jesus "walks with me, and talks with me, and tells me I am his own." Never mind that the last stanza of that gospel song of the early twentieth century — my mother's favorite — reads: "But he bids me go; through the voice of woe, his voice to me is calling."[18] Where do we hear that voice right now: in Bosnia, in Somalia, in the Sudan, high in the hills among the rural poor of Appalachia, just down the block and around the corner from any city or suburban church, in the pews we sit in, in some pastor's study? Once again, from the *Sermon on the Mount:* "I tell you, unless your righteousness exceeds that of the Scribes and Pharisees, you will never enter the kingdom of heaven" (Matt. 5:20).

When Jesus spoke his parable of the talents, Passover was just two days away. And Jesus said of it: "The Son of Man will be handed over to be crucified" (Matt. 26:2). Jesus was on his way to courtyards and courtrooms of controversy. He was on his way to a singular place in history, a place marked in the creeds, hymns, and prayers of the church that still follows after him — at a distance. He was on his way to a cross and a crown of thorns, and no one-talent mentality had any hope of stopping him. Peter tried to stop him, with all his one-talent might: "God forbid it, Lord! This must never happen to you" (Matt. 16:22). But his Lord replied, "Get behind me, Satan!" (Matt. 16:23). Talk about name calling!

Believe it: the parables are not our way of getting hold of God. Instead, as the Roman Catholic biblical scholar Sandra Schneiders has said, the parables are God's way of getting hold of us.[19] And as John Donne pointed out somewhere ages ago: "It is a terrible thing to fall into the hands of the living God. But what must it be to fall out of God's hands? To be secluded eternally, eternally, eternally from the sight of God?" That at last is the real "outer darkness" spoken of in Matthew's account of Jesus' parable of the talents, and throughout his account of the gospel: an eternity of "weeping and gnashing of teeth" (Matt. 25:30), as tedious as it is godless.

Caution won't cut it, for the kingdom of heaven "is as if a man, going on a journey, summoned his slaves, and entrusted his property to them" (Matt. 25:14). And what if it is not to slaves, but to friends that Jesus speaks: "I do not call you [slaves] any longer, because the [slave] does not know what the master is doing; but [I call] you friends, because I have made known to you everything that I have heard from

18. C. Austin Miles, "In the Garden," in *Hymns for the Family of God* (Nashville, TN: Paragon Associates, 1976), p. 588.

19. Sandra Schneiders, "Scripture as the Word of God," *Princeton Seminary Bulletin* 14, no. 1 (1993): pp. 18-35.

my Father" (John 15:15)? And what if what is entrusted to Jesus' friends is not property (some greedy master's indifferent wealth) but God's own life? Do we dare to believe it: God's own life vouchsafed to us in every moment of our own life — whatever comes of it?

Listen: "To be on top of the earth . . . breathing the clean air of heaven in some great, creative period of the human epic and to know nothing about it! . . . To eat and sleep and stretch and plod along through magnificent years of extremity and ruin, peril and birth: and to see nothing, hear nothing; sense nothing but Monday, Tuesday, Wednesday, Thursday, Friday, Saturday, Sunday . . . until you could scream."[20] That is one way to manage life, I suppose, but it is not life with God. Life with God is a venture of faith, with a promise in it that "[t]he utmost reward of daring should be still to dare."[21] It is life worth the living, too, and five talents, two talents, or one, our lives shall prove it.

> For your name's sake, deny us peace with the world as it is and with ourselves as we are, O God, that we may have peace with you through our Lord, Jesus Christ. Let us inherit the kingdom of heaven and not the outer darkness, the rule of God and not the rule of mammon and of self; and to you, and to you alone, be glory, majesty, dominion, and authority, before all time, and now, and forever. Amen.

20. Paul E. Scherer, "Luke 19:12-27: Exposition," in *The Interpreter's Bible*, vol. 8, p. 329.

21. Robert Frost, "The Trial by Existence," in *The Poetry of Robert Frost*, p. 19.

Wilhelmina's House Is Clean

Text: Luke 10:38-42

Visit us in the midst of our distractions, our God and Christ,
and as you spoke to Martha and to Mary, speak to us that word
we must hear and heed if we are to have a life worth the living.
This we ask for your mercy's sake. Amen.

Wilhelmina's house is clean. That is what you notice first when you go into it. And no matter how often you go into it, or when, it always looks the same. Even years ago when her husband was still alive and her children still were with her, her house was clean. It is amazing that that should have been so, for keeping the house clean then was anything but easy. The children played and fought and made a mess as children do at home, no matter what their age. And her husband smoked — a lot — and as most smokers do, he flicked his ashes carelessly about and stubbed his butts in ashtrays in every room. He used the toilet bowl at times too. But unlike some of the more uncouth types I've met, he did not stick his butts wet-end-up in egg yolks. Even if he did, however, it would not have mattered much in Wilhelmina's house, because such things as egg yolks, broken crusts of toast, jelly-stained knives, and coffee-ringed cups never survived the first two minutes past breakfast. Everything was cleared from the table, scraped, rinsed, washed, wiped, and put away before the morning newspaper was finished or the last grumbled words of any of the breakfasters were spoken. All meals were like that. Wilhelmina's house was clean, is clean, every room of it, cellar and attic included.

Wilhelmina's house is elegant also. Thick carpeting stretches wall to wall in every room. Small crystal chandeliers hang from the ceiling in the main hallway and the dining room. The windows are dressed with exquisite curtains and drapes. The walls are papered tastefully, expensively. Two family portraits hang opposite the stairway in the main hall and greet you with centuries-old smiles whether you come in the

160

front door or the back. A visitor's bench beneath the portraits is wooden, aged, worn, but polished, and if you are visiting Wilhelmina only for a few minutes, you will sit there and talk or transact business. All the rest of the rooms in the house are furnished with just the right pieces in just the right places. The theme is colonial and certain of the appointments are authentic. Wilhelmina never studied home decor. But her instincts are sure. She is a person of taste.

Wilhelmina also knows how to cook. Her specialty is the buffet: succulent roast beef — rare or well done — baked Virginia ham, potato salad prepared with mayonnaise and sour cream, vegetable casseroles, home-baked beans, carrot strips, celery strips stuffed with cream cheese, pickles, olives, punch, coffee, tea, freshly baked biscuits, homemade apple pie, and rich, dark Philadelphia chocolate cake. If you've never had that cake, you should visit Wilhelmina and try it. She'll not give you the recipe though. It's her specialty, her secret. It will go to the grave with her, be sure of that; and it will make people miss her. Wilhelmina wants to be missed. Wilhelmina wants to be wanted.

Maybe that is why Wilhelmina works so hard, even now, when there is no husband around to help and there are no children in need of help. She doesn't have to work. She has a Bell System pension, a social security check, a check from her husband's pension fund, fees from a tenant — there is a small apartment attached to her house — and dividend income from investments made in her earlier years as a telephone operator. Still, she doesn't rest. She doesn't know how to rest. Late into the night Wilhelmina worries about how she will cope with tomorrow, and before tomorrow dawns, the light in her kitchen is lit, the left front burner of her stove is on, and her two eggs are frying hard in an old cast iron pan. She will eat her eggs standing at the kitchen counter, swallowing them down hurriedly with bites of buttered toast and sips of black, unsugared coffee. "I can't be late," Wilhelmina thinks. Wilhelmina never is late. She was on time always at her switchboard when she had one, and she is on time now at her clerical assistant's terminal. "You do two days' work in one," her boss is fond of telling her. And Wilhelmina glows and believes him.

Wilhelmina works hard even when you might think she should be relaxing and enjoying herself. Whenever she has one of her party buffets, for example, you would expect her to sit down and to take her ease from time to time, wouldn't you? Relatives and friends she may not have seen for months, however, only get a fleeting word or two from her as she works her way dutifully from room to room, making sure that everybody is comfortable, that every glass or cup is full, that every plate is kept replenished from the always lavishly spread dining room table. And of course there is the picking up. Wilhelmina gathers empty trays and bowls, used utensils, dishes, coasters, ashtrays, all through the hours of entertainment. That way everything is ready to be washed and put away just as soon as the company leaves. Wilhelmina is efficient. Wilhelmina keeps her house clean. Wilhelmina tries hard to keep everything in order, to keep everybody happy. Wilhelmina is not happy herself.

You can tell that by what she says when everybody is gone. She fusses and fumes and grumbles out loud to herself as she works: "You'd think those kids would stay and help me out with all there is to do around here. But they don't. They just hurry off and leave me. What am I to them? Just a place for them to come and to get together, that's all. They don't touch a dish. They don't lift a finger. They just sit there and argue with each other in words I can't even understand. They think they're smart. Did I send them to college for this? Did I work my fingers to the bone for this? Why should I bother with them? That's what I'd like to know. They don't appreciate it, any of it. Selfish, that's what they are, lazy. Their father in the grave and me all alone, and what do they care? WHAT DO THEY CARE! They take what I give them and go on their way as though they were all that mattered, as though I were nothing but their servant.

"Look at this house I'm left with, will you? Just look at it! Everything is upset. Nothing is where it belongs. But can I take off and leave it? Can I just sit and look at it? Not on your life! Oh no, not me! Good old mom, she'll do it. Good old mom, she'll get the work done. All my life I've worked, morning, noon, and night. And what have I to show for it? Where have I gotten to ever? Another night of cleaning up, that's what I have to look forward to, and a day of invoice preparation and mailing, eight full hours' worth, tomorrow. I'm sick of it; just sick of it! Do you hear me? I'm sick of going and going and going. I'm so sick of it I could scream."

Wilhelmina does not scream. Instead she does the knives and forks and dishes. Each piece of silver is washed and dried by hand, and each is placed carefully in a chemically treated cloth wrapping that preserves its lustre. The silver is old and ornate. It doesn't have a single scratch. Wilhelmina cares for what she possesses as much as a mother might care for her only child. Wilhelmina cares for her china. Each piece of that also gets washed by hand just the same as the silver. Then the china is put away in the bottom right drawer of the dining room service. The plates are stacked carefully with pieces of soft flannel between them, and the cups and saucers are set alongside in precise rows. At last she gathers up the serving platters and bowls, the pots and pans and ovenware, scrubs each item to a faultless gleam, and places each where it belongs. With the wiping of the countertop, tabletop, stove top, the oven and refrigerator doors, the kitchen is done, perfectly restored. It looks as though no one had ever used it. Soon the vacuuming, straightening, and dusting will be done and the whole house, as the kitchen, will be set in order. Hardly have Wilhelmina's children and visitors gone than every trace of their even having been there is removed. Wilhelmina may have had a party, but Wilhelmina's house still is clean.

Wilhelmina's house is clean and empty. Her husband is gone from it. Her children are gone from it. Wilhelmina has it all to herself. Her parties hold no joy for her. Wilhelmina's work holds no meaning. Wilhelmina's sleep, what she gets of it, is dreamless as the sleep of death. Wilhelmina's life seems hardly worth the living. Sometimes Wilhelmina wishes she could die. Pray for Wilhelmina. Wilhelmina needs your prayers. Pray that Wilhelmina may find her God, herself, some peace. Pray with me now.

We pray for Wilhelmina, O God, not for the Wilhelmina of fiction, but for the Wilhelmina who could be anyone of us: the Wilhelmina whose agonies lie locked and frozen in neatly ordered habits of life and work, the Wilhelmina too busy with life to enjoy it, the Wilhelmina distracted with much serving, the Wilhelmina too out of touch with self, with others, and with you even to know how to pray. Help poor Wilhelmina, for she cannot help herself. Speak to her by name, as in Christ Jesus you spoke to Martha and to Mary long ago. Give to Wilhelmina your word of peace, which the world can neither give nor take away. Save Wilhelmina from her anger and her busyness. Save her from her servitude. Save her for yourself. Save us for yourself, for Jesus' sake. Amen.

The Answer to Our Greatest Need

Text: Psalms 42–43

Whether in pleasure or in pain, whether in happiness or in despair, we could not pray to you, O God, except as you have invited us to pray in your word. So speak your word to us now, and grant that we may receive it, and find in it courage to pray without ceasing, that, in everything, we may find our need of you met in him who is your Word and your prayer on our behalf, even Jesus Christ our Lord. Amen.

"As a deer longs for flowing streams, so my soul longs for you, O God. My soul thirsts for God, for the living God" (Ps. 42:1-2a). It is not the prayer of a happy man. It is the prayer of someone who is angry and anxious for cause. He has been banished — who knows why? — to a wild mountain country where the river Jordan takes its rise. Each day he wakes up to the antiphonal crashing of waterfalls, "deep calls to deep at the thunder of your cataracts" (Ps. 42:7) and to the taunting of oppressors, a taunting he cannot get out of his mind: "Where is your God?" (Ps. 42:3b).

Echoes of the psalmist's lament can be heard in the cries of children dunned with abusive language, pestered, bullied, mocked: "Sticks and stones may break my bones but words will never hurt me." It is more plea than assertion. It is said to keep from crying. What comes to mind, from a decade back, is the young California AIDS victim and his family, harassed out of town by their neighbors. Where was their God? Then, too, there may be the memory of that cruel moment when our own need of God was ridiculed by someone who felt no such need. So the need grew stronger, more insistent, even desperate; and it seemed no passage of Scripture, no sermon, no prayer, no hymn, no anthem, no requiem mass could meet it. On his death bed, Rudyard Kipling was asked by his nurse, "Is there anything you need?" The poet and spinner

164

of tales replied, "I need God."[22] The psalmist therefore prays not only for himself, but for us all: "My soul thirsts for God, for the living God" (Ps. 42:2a).

The need of God is not brought on by dire circumstance. It is brought on by the vivid remembrance of what it is like truly to live, and to praise God. "These things I remember, as I pour out my soul: how I went with the throng, and led them in procession to the house of God, with glad shouts and songs of thanksgiving, a multitude keeping festival" (Ps. 42:4). But what if the pain becomes so severe that there is barely a memory of anything, including worship? What if the pain itself is nearly all there is, hour after hour, day after day, year in and year out? Anna Akhmatova, in her poem "Requiem," suggests what such pain must be like. She says of the Stalinist years in the former Soviet Union that they were "a time when only the dead smiled, happy in their peace,"[23] delivered from their wars.

Not all wars are bruited across such a vast terrain. Some are waged within the confines of a single soul. "Do not go gentle into that good night," Dylan Thomas cried out, as it were, at his father's bier; "rage, rage against the dying of the light."[24] Our psalmist rages: "Vindicate me, O God, and defend my cause against an ungodly people; from those who are deceitful and unjust deliver me!" (Ps. 43:1). He does not bear his pain in stoic silence. He storms his way through it with tears and prayers, his jaw set, his fists clenched, maybe.

Rage can have its reasons. When euphemisms such as "ethnic cleansing" are used — as they were by Serbian forces clearing Muslim Croats out of their own cities — it is time for loud lamentation, isn't it? Who will not lament attempts to enlist the one true God as a tribal deity to bless this or that clan, or race, or class or cause or nation? Closer to home: when someone you know hits rock bottom in a world that seems too often indifferent to its failures, and to its poorest, and weakest, and loneliest, and when even God seems not to care, "Why have you

22. Told by Strother A. Campbell, *Grit to Grapple with Life* (Nashville, TN: Broadman, 1942), p. 38, and quoted in George Arthur Buttrick, *Sermons Preached in a University Church* (Nashville: Abingdon, 1959), p. 157.

23. Anna Akhmatova, "Requiem 1935-1940," in *A Book of Women Poets from Antiquity to Now,* ed. Aliki Barnstone and Willis Barnstone (New York: Shocken Books, 1980), p. 378.

24. Dylan Thomas, "Do Not Go Gentle into that Good Night," in *The Collected Poems of Dylan Thomas* (New York: New Directions Publishers, 1957), p. 128.

cast me off?" (Ps. 43:2a) some poor soul shouts. Then it is time to take up the prayer of the psalmist; isn't that so? Then it is time to hurl some thunder of your own toward heaven.

No sad psalmist ever was meant to pray alone. Instead, the people of God were given the responsibility to pray with him, and to take up his prayer for him if at last his voice gave out. So we have in our Bible a psalter full of lamentation, an ancient hymnody to remind us of our need of God, and of the solidarity we have with all who share that need.

It is hard not to want to praise God when once you have known what that praise is all about. Therefore our psalmist sings out of the thick of his troubles: "By day the LORD commands his steadfast love, and at night his song is with me, a prayer to the God of my life" (Ps. 42:8). He can no more quiet that song of praise than he can silence the taunting of his oppressors or stop his own tears. It is with him. It surrounds him. It has hold of him. It will not let him go. His wounded body aches with the singing of it. Harassed and injured people across millennia have known that ache: African Americans, once purchased for slavery, then singing, praying their way toward freedom or death — they never knew which — "Nobody knows the trouble I've seen, nobody knows but Jesus; nobody knows the trouble I've seen, Glory! Hallelujah!"[25] Lamentation is not the opposite of praise to God. It is what needs to be done in order to praise God "when life tumbles in."[26] Hear the psalmist again: "Why are you cast down, O my soul, and why are you disquieted within me? Hope in God; for I shall again praise him, my help and my God" (Ps. 42:5-6, 11; 43:5).

In singing his song, the psalmist is not begging special favors from God. He is not asking for a way through life henceforth cleared of anything that could bruise him. "The thousand natural shocks that flesh is heir to"[27] have been shocks to him no less than to anybody else; and they will be. Beyond that, to paraphrase Langston Hughes, "life for [him] ain't been no crystal stair."[28] Even the vindication he seeks and the

---

25. "Nobody Knows the Trouble I've Seen" (spiritual). See Mark and Anne Oberndorfer, eds., *The New American Song Book* (Chicago: Hall and McCreary, 1941).

26. Arthur John Gossip, "But When Life Tumbles In, What Then?" in Andrew Watterson Blackwood, *The Protestant Pulpit* (Nashville, TN: Abingdon Press, 1947), p. 198.

27. Shakespeare, *Hamlet, Prince of Denmark*, act 3, sc. 1, lns. 62-63.

28. Langston Hughes, "Mother to Son," in *American Negro Poetry*, ed. Arna Bontemps (New York: Hill and Wang, 1963), p. 67.

deliverance from oppressors he has every right to demand are not sought as ends in themselves. The psalmist wants vindication and deliverance so that he once again can praise God free of restraint: "O send out your light and your truth; let them lead me; let them bring me to your holy hill and to your dwelling. Then I will go to the altar of God, to God my exceeding joy; and I will praise you with the harp, O God, my God" (Ps. 43:34).

When you have sung the majestic and humorous, romantic and antic, thoroughly human and nearly divine music of Haydn's *Creation* — a work Robert Shaw once called an achievement of genius that comes once in a millennium — you could not be blamed for hoping to get over a case of laryngitis so that you could sing it again. When you have burst into tears at the subtle beauty of a delicate Renoir gown rustling across a canvas, you could not be faulted for hoping to see it again, and again, and again. And the prose of Flannery O'Connor, and the poetry of Elizabeth Barrett Browning:

> How do I love thee? Let me count the ways.
> I love thee to the depth and breadth and height
> My soul can reach, when feeling out of sight
> For the ends of Being and ideal Grace. . . .[29]

Does anyone really think the world would be richer if no one ever read such works — or the Bible that inspired them?

Above all, what of the lives you and I have known, the flawed loves that have made us what we are, for better or worse? Is there no remembrance of any of them worth clinging to? Have we no hope for them beyond their return to dust? The "Shorter Catechism" asserts that humanity's chief end is to glorify God and to enjoy God forever.[30] Human need of God therefore is not a sign of weakness; it is a sign of strength. It is our reason for being. No need of Haydn? No need of Renoir? No need of Flannery O'Connor? No need of Elizabeth Barrett Browning? No need of Scripture? No need of you, or of me, or of those who have loved us — or tried to — often beyond their strength? No

29. Elizabeth Barrett Browning, "How Do I Love Thee?" in *Immortal Poems of the English Language,* ed. Oscar Williams (New York: Washington Square Press, 1952), p. 349.

30. "The Shorter Catechism," in *The Book of Confessions* (Louisville, KY: Presbyterian Church [U.S.A.], 1994), C.7.001, p. 181.

need of God? The mind boggles. More than anything, more than life as
we know it, we need God; and we needn't be ashamed of that. It is the
measure of our stature as human beings. "As a deer longs for flowing
streams, so my soul longs for you, O God. My soul thirsts for God, for
the living God" (Ps. 42:1-2a).

But what of the living God? Is there any evidence that God cares
that we need him? When people cry to God, does God hear? When
they sing and shout their praise, does it matter at all? As for the
psalmist, we haven't the slightest clue whether or how his specific
requests were answered. Perhaps he was vindicated. Perhaps he was
delivered from "those who are deceitful and unjust" (Ps. 43:1b). Perhaps, at last, he did get back to Jerusalem, to the temple, to the altar
of God, his "exceeding joy" (Ps. 43:4). Or perhaps just as likely —
perhaps more likely — he was left in the wilderness with his hopes and
his prayers and his pain until the end of his days. That could have
happened. It has happened often enough. And if, in fact, that is what
happened, would we have to conclude that the psalmist got no answer
from God, that God was deaf to him, indifferent to him, or — worse
yet — powerless to do anything for him? Some would say so. Others,
however, including our psalmist, would not say so; for they know that
vindication and deliverance and Jerusalem and the temple and the altar
are not answers to prayer in any worthwhile sense of the term if they
are themselves godless. If the soul truly "thirsts for God, for the living
God" (Ps. 42:2), only God will do.

Therefore we pray to God to bear our reproach with us and for
us if we cannot simply be rid of it. And we cannot simply be rid of
it. We pray to God to see us through the valley of the shadow if there
is no way around it. And, at last, there is no way around it for anybody.
We pray to God to fill our prayers with the breath of his own Spirit,
to give voice to our lament, as to our praise, when our voices give
out. And God does: on the lips of Jesus — Psalm 22, from the cross,
another prayer of lament on its way to praise — "My God, my God,
why have you forsaken me?" (Ps. 22:1). We pray to God to fill our
mortal flesh with divine glory, until the tears that have been our food
day and night (Ps. 42:3) turn to Eucharist and song. When the soul
"thirsts for God, for the living God" (Ps. 42:2), God will answer. God
will give the divine self, as God has given the divine self, in an agony
of bliss, of heavenly joy.

Why are you cast down, O my soul,
    and why are you disquieted within me?
Hope in God; for I shall again praise him,
    my help and my God. (Ps. 43:5)

We turn to you in our need, O God, glad to know that already you have provided for it. We thank you for the psalmist who has voiced our need so well, and for the Christ who has met our need so fully. Keep us ever alert to your presence, vouchsafed to us in Christ in the best of times and in the worst, that we may have courage to pray without ceasing and to live in hope. Amen.

Bibliography of Works Cited

Allen, Diogenes. *Christian Belief in a Postmodern World: The Full Wealth of Conviction.* Louisville, KY: Westminster/John Knox Press, 1989.

Anderson, Bernhard W. "The Kingdom, the Power, and the Glory: The Sovereignty of God in the Bible." *Theology Today* 53, no. 1 (April 1996).

Apczynski, John V. *Doers of the Word.* Dissertation Series 18. Missoula, MT: Scholars Press, 1977.

Auden, W. H. *Selected Poetry of W. H. Auden.* New York: Random House (The Modern Library), 1958.

Augustine, *Confessions of St. Augustine.* Trans. Edward B. Pusey. London: Collier-Macmillan, Ltd, 1961.

Bacon, Wallace A. *The Art of Interpretation.* New York: Holt, Rinehart and Winston, 1972.

Baillie, Donald M. *The Theology of the Sacraments and Other Papers.* New York: Charles Scribner's Sons, 1957.

Barth, Karl. *Homiletics.* Louisville, KY: Westminster/John Knox Press, 1991.

———. *The Humanity of God.* Richmond, VA: John Knox Press, 1960.

———. *Church Dogmatics.* I/1. Trans. G. T. Thomson. Edinburgh: T & T Clark, 1936.

———. *Church Dogmatics.* I/2. Trans. G. T. Thomson and Harold Knight. Edinburgh: T & T Clark, 1956.

Bartow, Charles L. "Speaking the Text and Preaching the Gospel." *Homosexuality and Christian Community.* Ed. Choon-Leong Seow. Louisville, KY: Westminster/John Knox Press, 1996.

———. *The Preaching Moment: A Guide to Sermon Delivery.* Dubuque, IA: Kendall/Hunt Publishing Co., 1995.

———. "In Service to the Servants of the Word: Teaching Speech at Princeton Seminary." *Princeton Seminary Bulletin* 13, no. 3 (1992).

————. *Effective Speech Communication in Leading Worship.* Nashville, TN: Abingdon Press, 1988.

————. *An Evaluation of Student Preaching in the Basic Homiletics Courses at Princeton Theological Seminary: A Farmerian Approach to Homiletical Criticism.* Ph.D. dissertation, New York University, 1971.

Beardsley, Monroe C. "Right Readings and Good Readings." *Literature in Performance* 1, no. 1 (Nov. 1980).

Bender, John, and David E. Wellbery. "Rhetoricality: On the Modernist Return of Rhetoric." *The Ends of Rhetoric: History, Theory, Practice.* Ed. John Bender and David E. Wellbery. Stanford, CA: Stanford University Press, 1990.

Berger, Peter L. *The Sacred Canopy: Elements of a Sociological Theory of Religion.* New York: Doubleday (Anchor Books), 1967.

Bergson, Henri. *The Creative Mind.* Trans. Mabelle L. Andison. New York: Philosophical Library, 1946.

Berleant, Arnold. *Art and Engagement.* Philadelphia: Temple University Press, 1991.

Berry, Wendell. *Standing By Words.* New York: Farrar, Straus and Giroux, 1983.

Bonhoeffer, Dietrich. *Letters and Papers from Prison.* Ed. Eberhard Bethge. Trans. Reginald H. Fuller. New York: Macmillan, 1953.

The Book of Common Worship. Philadelphia: Presbyterian Church in the U.S.A., 1946.

The Book of Confessions. The Constitution of the Presbyterian Church (U.S.A.), Pt. 1. Louisville, KY: Presbyterian Church (U.S.A.), 1994.

The Book of Order. The Constitution of the Presbyterian Church (U.S.A.), Pt. 2. Louisville, KY: Office of the General Assembly, 1995.

Booth, Wayne C. *The Rhetoric of Fiction.* 2nd ed. Chicago: University of Chicago Press, 1983.

————. *Critical Understanding: The Powers and Limits of Pluralism.* Chicago: University of Chicago Press, 1979.

Bouwsma, William J. "Calvinism as *Theologica Rhetorica.*" *Protocol Colloquy* 54, 28 September 1986. Ed. Wilhelm Wuellner. Berkeley, CA: Center for Hermeneutical Studies in Hellenistic and Modern Culture (Graduate Theological Union and the University of California at Berkeley).

Bozarth-Campbell, Alla. *The Word's Body: An Incarnational Aesthetic of Interpretation.* Tuskaloosa, AL: The University of Alabama Press, 1979.

Brower, William. "Advent." Unpublished Poem, 1970.

Browning, Robert. *Browning's Complete Poetical Works.* Ed. Horace E. Scudder. Boston: Houghton Mifflin Co., 1895.

Brueggemann, Walter. "Preaching as Reimagination." *Theology Today* 52, no. 3 (October 1995).

————. *The Message of the Psalms: A Theological Commentary.* Minneapolis, MN: Augsburg Publishing House, 1984.

————. *Praying the Psalms.* Winona, MN: St. Mary's Press, 1982.

Buber, Martin. *I and Thou.* New York: Charles Scribner's Sons, 1937.

Burke, Kenneth. *On Symbols and Society.* Ed. Joseph R. Gusfield. Chicago: The University of Chicago Press, 1989.

————. *A Rhetoric of Motives.* Berkeley, CA: University of California Press, 1969.

————. *A Grammar of Motives.* Englewood Cliffs, NJ: Prentice-Hall, 1945.

Buttrick, David. "Who Hears the Sermon on the Mount?" *Studia Homiletica* 1 (1995).

————. *A Captive Voice: The Liberation of Preaching.* Louisville, KY: Westminster/John Knox Press, 1994.

Buttrick, George Arthur. *Sermons Preached in a University Church.* Nashville, TN: Abingdon Press, 1959.

Caird, G. B. *New Testament Theology.* Completed and ed. by L. D. Hurst. New York: Oxford University Press, 1994.

Calvin, John. *Institutes of the Christian Religion.* Ed. John T. McNeill, Jr. Trans. Ford Lewis Battles. Philadelphia: Westminster Press, 1960.

Carter, Elton S. and Iline Fife. "The Critical Approach." *An Introduction to Graduate Study in Speech and Theatre.* Ed. Clyde W. Dow. East Lansing, MI: Michigan State University Press, 1961.

Childers, Jana Lynn. "A Critical Analysis of the Homiletical Theory and Practice of Browne Barr: First Congregational Church, Berkeley, 1960-1977." Ph.D. dissertation, The Graduate Theological Union, Berkeley, CA, 1992.

————. "One Stone Upon Another." *And Blessed Is She: Sermons by Women.* Ed. David Albert Farmer and Edwina Hunter. San Francisco: Harper & Row, 1990.

Conrad, Joseph. *A Conrad Argosy.* Ed. William McFee. Garden City, NY: Doubleday, Doran & Co., 1942.

Coote, Robert B. and Mary P. *Power, Politics and the Making of the Bible: An Introduction.* Minneapolis, MN: Fortress Press, 1990.

Craddock, Fred B. *Preaching.* Nashville, TN: Abingdon Press, 1985.

Craigie, Peter C. *Psalms 1–50.* Word Biblical Commentary, vol. 19. Waco, TX: Word Books, 1993.

Cunningham, David S. *Faithful Persuasion: In Aid of a Rhetoric of Christian Theology.* Notre Dame, IN: University of Notre Dame Press, 1991.

Curry, S. S. *The Province of Expression.* Boston: School of Expression, 1891.

Davis, Ellen F. "Holy Preaching: Ethical Interpretation and Practical Imagination." *Reclaiming Faith: Essays on Orthodoxy in the Episcopal Church and the Baltimore Declaration.* Ed. Ephraim Radner and George R. Sumner. Grand Rapids, MI: William B. Eerdmans Publishing Co., 1993.

Davis, John D., and Henry Snyder Gehman. *The Westminster Dictionary of the Bible*. Philadelphia: Westminster Press, 1944.

Dodd, C. H. *The Apostolic Preaching and Its Developments*. London: Hodder and Stoughton, 1936.

Donne, John. *Devotions upon Emergent Occasions*. Ed. Anthony Raspa. Montreal & London: McGill-Queens University Press, 1975.

Douglass, Jane Dempsey. *Women, Freedom and Calvin*. Philadelphia: Westminster Press, 1985.

Dowey, Edward A. *The Knowledge of God in Calvin's Theology*. Grand Rapids, MI: Wm. B. Eerdmans Publishing Co., 1994.

————. "The Reforming Tradition: Presbyterians and Mainstream Protestantism: A Review." *Princeton Seminary Bulletin* 14 (1993).

Eisenson, Jon, J. Jeffry Auer, and John V. Irwin. *The Psychology of Communication*. New York: Appleton Century-Crofts, 1963.

Eliot, T. S. *The Complete Poems and Plays, 1909–1950*. New York: Harcourt, Brace and World, Inc., 1952.

Encyclopedia Judaica. New York: Macmillan, 1971.

Ettema, James Stewart. "Discourse That Is Closer to Silence than to Talk: The Politics and Possibilities of Reporting on Victims of War." *Critical Studies in Mass Communication* 2, no. 1 (March 1994).

Farmer, H. H. *The Servant of the Word*. Philadelphia: Fortress Press, 1964.

————. *Revelation and Religion*. New York: Harper and Bros., 1954.

————. *God and Men*. New York: Abingdon-Cokesbury Press, 1947.

Farrer, Austin. *The Glass of Vision*. Westminster, England: Dacre Press, 1948.

Forsyth, P. T. *Positive Preaching and the Modern Mind*. 1907 Beecher Lectures. Grand Rapids, MI: Baker Book House, 1980.

Frost, Robert. *The Poetry of Robert Frost*. Ed. Edward Connery Latham. New York: Holt, Rinehart and Winston, 1969.

Gaventa, Beverly Roberts. "Our Mother St. Paul: Toward the Recovery of a Neglected Theme." *Princeton Seminary Bulletin* 17, no. 1 (Feb. 1996).

Geiger, Don. *The Sound, Sense and Performance of Literature*. Chicago: Scott, Foresman Co., 1963.

Gerstenberger, Erhard S. *Psalms Part I with an Introduction to Cultic Poetry*. Grand Rapids, MI: Wm. B. Eerdmans Publishing Co., 1988.

Gillespie, Thomas W. "A Generous Orthodoxy." *The Princeton Seminary Bulletin* 16, no. 3 (1995).

Goldingay, John. *Models for Interpretation of Scripture*. Grand Rapids, MI: Wm. B. Eerdmans Publishing Co., 1995.

Green, Garrett. "The Gender of God and the Theology of Metaphor." *Speaking the Christian God: The Holy Trinity and the Challenge of Feminism*. Ed. Alvin F. Kimel, Jr. Grand Rapids, MI: Wm. B. Eerdmans Publishing Co., 1992.

————. *Imagining God: Theology and the Religious Imagination*. San Francisco: Harper and Row Publishers, 1989.

Gunton, Colin. "Proteus and Procrustes." *Speaking the Christian God: The Holy Trinity and the Challenge of Feminism*. Ed. Alvin F. Kimel, Jr. Grand Rapids, MI: Wm. B. Eerdmans Publishing Co., 1992.

Guthrie, Shirley C. *Christian Doctrine*. Atlanta: John Knox Press, 1968.

Gutiérrez, Gustavo. *A Theology of Liberation*. Maryknoll, NY: Orbis Books, 1973.

Hawkins, Peter S. *The Language of Grace: Flannery O'Connor, Walker Percy and Iris Murdoch*. Cambridge: Cowley Publications, 1983.

Hendry, George S. *The Westminster Confession for Today: A Contemporary Interpretation of the Confession of Faith*. Richmond, VA: John Knox Press, 1960.

————. *The Holy Spirit in Christian Theology*. Philadelphia: Westminster Press, 1956.

Herbert, George. *The Life and Works of George Herbert*. Ed. and ann. by George Herbert Palmer. Boston: Houghton Mifflin & Co., 1905.

Hirsch, E. D., Jr. *Validity in Interpretation*. New Haven: Yale University Press, 1967.

Hossfeld, F. L., and E. Zenger. *Die Psalmen I*. Würzburg: Echter Verlag, 1993.

Hughes, Langston. *The Big Sea: An Autobiography*. New York: Hill and Wang, 1940.

Jacks, G. Robert. *Getting the Word Across*. Grand Rapids, MI: Wm. B. Eerdmans Publishing Co., 1995.

Jenson, Blanche A. "The Movement and the Story: Whatever Happened to 'Her'?" *Speaking the Christian God: The Holy Trinity and the Challenge of Feminism*. Ed. Alvin F. Kimel, Jr. Grand Rapids, MI: William B. Eerdmans Publishing Co., 1992.

Johnson, Elizabeth A. *She Who Is: The Mystery of God in Feminist Theological Discourse*. New York: Crossroad Publishing Co., 1994.

Johnson, Mark. *The Body in the Mind: The Bodily Basis of Meaning, Imagination and Reason*. Chicago: University of Chicago Press, 1987.

Kavanaugh, Aidan. *On Liturgical Theology*. New York: Pueblo, 1981.

Kay, James F. *Christus Praesens: A Reconsideration of Rudolf Bultmann's Christology*. Grand Rapids: Wm. B. Eerdmans Publishing Co., 1994.

Keck, Leander E. *The Church Confident*. Nashville, TN: Abingdon Press, 1993.

————. *The Bible in the Pulpit: The Renewal of Biblical Preaching*. Nashville, TN: Abingdon Press, 1978.

Kennedy, Rodney. *The Creative Power of Metaphor: A Rhetorical Homiletics*. Lanham, MD: University Press of America, 1993.

Ketels, Violet B. "Václav Havel on Language." *Quinnipiac Schweitzer Journal* 1, no. 2 (Fall/Winter 1994-95).

Knohl, Israel. "Between Voice and Silence: The Relationship Between Prayer and Temple Cult." *Journal of Biblical Literature* 115, no. 1 (1996).

Krause, Hans-Joachim. *Psalms 1–59: A Commentary.* Trans. Hilton C. Oswald. Minneapolis, MN: Augsburg Publishing House, 1988.

Kunitz, Stanley. "Three Floors." *Strong Measures: Contemporary American Poetry in Traditional Forms.* Ed. Philip Dacey and David Jauss. New York: Harper and Row, 1986.

Lathrop, Gordon. *Holy Things: A Liturgical Theology.* Minneapolis, MN: Fortress Press, 1993.

Lee, Charlotte I. *Oral Interpretation.* 4th ed. Boston: Houghton Mifflin Co., 1974.

———. *Oral Reading of the Scriptures.* New York: Houghton Mifflin Co., 1974.

Leith, John H. *The Reformed Imperative.* Philadelphia: Westminster Press, 1988.

Leonick, Michael D. "Forever Amber." *Time,* February 12, 1996.

Long, Beverly Whitaker, and Mary Frances HopKins. *Performing Literature: An Introduction to Oral Interpretation.* Englewood Cliffs, NJ: Prentice-Hall, 1982.

Long, Thomas G. "Living with the Bible." *Homosexuality and Christian Community.* Ed. Choon-Leong Seow. Louisville, KY: Westminster/John Knox Press, 1996.

———. "And How Shall They Hear? The Listener in Contemporary Preaching." *Listening to the Word: Studies in Honor of Fred B. Craddock.* Ed. Gail R. O'Day and Thomas G. Long. Nashville, TN: Abingdon Press, 1993.

———. *Preaching and the Literary Forms of the Bible.* Philadelphia: Fortress Press, 1989.

———. *The Witness of Preaching.* Louisville, KY: Westminster/John Knox Press, 1989.

Lyas, Colin. "Personal Qualities and the Intentional Fallacy." *Aesthetics: A Critical Anthology.* Ed. George Dickie, Richard Sclafani, and Ronald Roblin. New York: St. Martin's Press, 1989.

McClure, John S. *The Four Codes of Preaching: Rhetorical Strategies.* Minneapolis, MN: Fortress Press, 1991.

McFague, Sallie. *Metaphorical Theology: Models of God in Religious Language.* Philadelphia: Fortress Press, 1982.

———. *Speaking in Parables: A Study in Metaphor and Theology.* Philadelphia: Fortress Press, 1975.

McLuhan, Marshall. *Understanding Media: The Extensions of Man.* New York: The New American Library (Signet Books), 1964.

McNaughton, Marie Thomas. "Not for Sale." *Meat and Poultry* 39, no. 9 (September 1993).

Massa, Conrad H. "Toward a Contemporary Theology of Preaching." Ph.D. dissertation, Princeton Theological Seminary, 1960.

Mays, James L. *Psalms.* Interpretation: A Biblical Commentary for Teaching and Preaching. Louisville, KY: John Knox Press, 1994.

Metzger, Bruce M. *The New Testament: Its Background, Growth and Content.* Nashville, TN: Abingdon Press, 1965.

Migliore, Daniel L. *Called to Freedom: Liberation Theology and the Future of Christian Doctrine.* Philadelphia: Westminster Press, 1980.

Miller, Patrick D. "Editorial." *Theology Today* 53, no. 1 (April 1996).

Moltmann, Jürgen. *The Crucified God: The Cross of Christ as the Foundation and Criticism of Christian Theology.* San Francisco: Harper & Row, 1974.

Morrow, Lance. "Fifteen Cheers for Abstinence." *Time,* Oct. 2, 1995.

Mulholland, John. "Witchcraft." *The World Book Encyclopedia,* vol. 20. Chicago: Field Enterprise Educational Corporation, 1966.

Nelson, John S., Allan Megill, and Donald N. McClosky, eds. *The Rhetoric of the Human Sciences: Language and Argument in Scholarship and Public Affairs.* Madison, WI: The University of Wisconsin Press, 1987.

Nemerov, Howard. *The Collected Poems of Howard Nemerov.* Chicago: University of Chicago Press, 1977.

The New Oxford Annotated Bible with Apocrypha. Ed. Bruce M. Metzger and Roland E. Murphy. New York: Oxford University Press, 1991.

Nichols, Marie H. *Rhetoric and Criticism.* Baton Rouge, LA: Louisiana State University Press, 1967.

Noller, Annett. *Feministische Hermeneutik: Wege einer neuen Schriftauslegung.* Neukirchen-Vluyn: Neukirchener, 1995.

O'Connor, Flannery. "Revelation." *The Complete Stories.* New York: Farrar, Straus and Giroux, 1982.

O'Neill, Eugene. *A Moon for the Misbegotten.* New York: Random House, 1952.

Ong, Walter J., S.J. *The Presence of the Word: Some Prolegomena for Cultural and Religious History.* New York: Simon and Schuster, 1970.

Panko, Steven M. *Martin Buber.* Waco, TX: Word Books, 1976.

Pearson, Hesketh. *Oscar Wilde: His Life and Wit.* New York: Harper and Brothers, 1946.

Pelias, Ronald J. *Performance Studies: The Interpretation of Aesthetic Texts.* New York: St. Martin's Press, 1992.

Pelikan, Jaroslav. *The Melody of Theology: A Philosophical Dictionary.* Cambridge, MA: Harvard University Press, 1988.

Pentz, Rebecca. "Jesus as Sophia." *The Reformed Journal* 38 (December 1988).

Polanyi, Michael. *The Tacit Dimension.* Garden City, NY: Doubleday and Co. (Anchor Books), 1967.

Prakash, Perumala Surya. *The Preaching of Sadhu Sundar Singh: A Homiletic Analysis of Independent Preaching and Personal Christianity.* Bangalore, India: Wordmakers, 1991.

Prickett, Stephen. *Words and the Word: Language, Hermeneutics and Biblical Interpretation*. New York: Cambridge University Press, 1986.

Quinn, Arthur. *Figures of Speech: 60 Ways to Turn a Phrase*. Salt Lake City: Gibbs M. Smith, Inc., 1982.

Radner, Ephraim, and George R. Sumner, eds. *Reclaiming Faith: Essays on Orthodoxy in the Episcopal Church and the Baltimore Declaration*. Grand Rapids, MI: Wm. B. Eerdmans Publishing Co., 1993.

Reist, Benjamin A. *A Reading of Calvin's Institutes*. Louisville, KY: Westminster/John Knox Press, 1991.

Ricoeur, Paul. "The Hermeneutics of Testimony." *Essays on Biblical Interpretation*. Ed. Lewis S. Mudge. Philadelphia: Fortress Press, 1980.

————. "Biblical Hermeneutics." *Semeia: An Experimental Journal for Biblical Criticism* 4 (1975).

————. *The Conflict of Interpretations: Essays in Hermeneutics*. Ed. Don Ihde. Evanston, IL: Northwestern University Press, 1974.

Rigby, Cynthia L. "Freedom to Be Human: Limits, Possibilities and the Sovereignty of God." *Theology Today* 53, no. 1 (April 1996).

Rohler, Lloyd. *Ralph Waldo Emerson: Preacher and Lecturer*. Westport, CT: Greenwood Press, 1995.

Rorty, Richard. *Contingency, Irony and Solidarity*. New York: Cambridge University Press, 1989.

Rosenblatt, Louise M. *Literature as Exploration*. New York: The Modern Language Association of America, 1983.

————. "Act 1, Scene 1: Enter the Reader." *Literature in Performance* 1, no. 2 (April 1981).

————. *The Reader, the Text, the Poem: The Transactional Theory of Literary Work*. Carbondale, IL: Southern Illinois University Press, 1978.

Russell, Letty M. *Church in the Round: Feminist Interpretation of the Church*. Louisville, KY: Westminster/John Knox Press, 1993.

————, ed. *Feminist Interpretation of the Bible*. Philadelphia: Westminster Press, 1985.

Sanders, James A. *God Has a Story Too: Sermons in Context*. Philadelphia: Fortress Press, 1979.

Schechner, Richard. *Performance Theory*. New York: Routledge, 1988.

Scherer, Paul E. *For We Have This Treasure*. Grand Rapids, MI: Baker Book House, 1979.

————. *The Word God Sent*. Grand Rapids, MI: Baker Book House, 1977.

————. *Worship Resources for the Christian Year*. Ed. Charles L. Wallis. New York: Harper and Brothers, 1954.

————. "The Gospel According to St. Luke: Exposition." *The Interpreter's Bible*, vol. 8. Ed. George Arthur Buttrick. Nashville, TN: Abingdon Press, 1952.

178 BIBLIOGRAPHY OF WORKS CITED

————. "Luke 19:12-27: Exposition." *The Interpreter's Bible*, vol. 8. Ed. George Arthur Buttrick. Nashville, TN: Abingdon Press, 1952.

Schickel, Richard. Review of Harold Pinter's *Old Times. Time*, January 23, 1984.

Schleiermacher, Friedrich. *Servant of the Word: Selected Sermons of Friedrich Schleiermacher.* Trans. with an intro. by Dawn DeVries. Philadelphia: Fortress Press, 1987.

Schmit, Clayton J. "Feeling and Form in Worship." Ph.D. dissertation, The Graduate Theological Union, Berkeley, CA, 1994.

Schneiders, Sandra. "Scripture as the Word of God." *The Princeton Seminary Bulletin* 14, no. 1 (1993).

Schüssler-Fiorenza, Elisabeth. *In Memory of Her: A Feminist Theological Reconstruction of Christian Origins.* New York: Crossroad Publishing Co., 1983.

Schweizer, Eduard. *The Good News According to Matthew.* Atlanta: John Knox Press, 1975.

Sellers, James E. *The Outsider and the Word of God: A Study in Christian Communication.* Nashville, TN: Abingdon Press, 1961.

Seow, Choon-Leong, ed. *Homosexuality and Christian Community.* Louisville, KY: Westminster/John Knox Press, 1996.

Simons, Herbert W., ed. *The Rhetorical Turn: Invention and Persuasion in the Conduct of Inquiry.* Chicago: The University of Chicago Press, 1990.

Sittler, Joseph. *Essays on Nature and Grace.* Philadelphia: Fortress Press, 1972.

————. *The Ecology of Faith: The New Situation in Preaching.* Philadelphia: Muhlenberg Press, 1961.

Sloane, Thomas O. *Donne, Milton, and the End of Humanist Rhetoric.* Berkeley, CA: The University of California Press, 1985.

Sobrino, Jon, S.J. *Christology at the Crossroads: A Latin American Approach.* Trans. John Drury. Maryknoll, NY: Orbis Books, 1976.

Soskice, Janet Martin. "Can a Feminist Call God 'Father'?" *Speaking the Christian God: The Holy Trinity and the Challenge of Feminism.* Ed. Alvin F. Kimel, Jr. Grand Rapids, MI: Wm. B. Eerdmans Publishing Co., 1992.

Starbuck, Scott R. A. "And What Had Kings? The Reappropriation of Court Oracles Among the Royal Psalms of the Hebrew Psalter." Ph.D. dissertation, Princeton Theological Seminary, 1996.

Stern, Carol Simpson, and Bruce Henderson. *Performance: Texts and Contexts.* New York: Longman, 1993.

Taylor, Gardner C. "The Sweet Torture of Sunday Morning." *Leadership* 2, no. 3 (Summer 1981).

Taylor, William R. "Commentary on Psalm 27." *The Interpreter's Bible,* vol. 4. Ed. George Arthur Buttrick. Nashville, TN: Abingdon Press, 1955.

Terrien, Samuel. *The Psalms and Their Meaning for Today.* New York: Bobbs-Merrill, 1952.

Thielicke, Helmut. *Nihilism: Its Origin and Nature — With a Christian Answer.*

Trans. John W. Doberstein. New York: Harper & Brothers Publishers, 1961.

————. *Between God and Satan.* Trans. C. C. Barber. Grand Rapids, MI: Wm. B. Eerdmans Publishing Co., 1958.

Thomas, Dylan. "Do Not Go Gentle into that Good Night." *The Collected Poems of Dylan Thomas.* New York: New Directions Publishers, 1957.

Tisdale, Nora Tubbs. *Preaching as Local Theology and Folk Art.* Minneapolis, MN: Fortress Press, 1996.

Tracy, David. *Plurality and Ambiguity: Hermeneutics, Religion, Hope.* San Francisco: Harper & Row, 1987.

————. *The Analogical Imagination: Christian Theology and the Culture of Pluralism.* New York: Crossroad Publishing Co., 1981.

Turner, Victor. *From Ritual to Theatre: The Human Seriousness of Play.* New York: PAJ Publications, 1982.

————. *The Anthropology of Performance.* New York: PAJ Publications, 1982.

Van Huyssteen, Wentzel. *Theology and the Justification of Faith: Constructing Theories in Systematic Theology.* Grand Rapids, MI: Wm. B. Eerdmans Publishing Co., 1981.

Ward, Richard F. *Speaking from the Heart: Preaching with Passion.* Nashville, TN: Abingdon Press, 1992.

Webb, Stephen H. *Re-figuring Theology: The Rhetoric of Karl Barth.* Albany, NY: State University of New York Press, 1991.

Westermann, Claus. *Praise and Lament in the Psalms.* Trans. Keith R. Crim and Richard N. Soulen. Atlanta: John Knox Press, 1981.

Wilder, Amos N. *Early Christian Rhetoric: The Language of the Gospels.* Cambridge, MA: Harvard University Press, 1971.

Wilson, Paul Scott. *The Practice of Preaching.* Nashville, TN: Abingdon Press, 1995.

Winter, Miriam Therese. "I AM Has Sent Me to You." *Princeton Seminary Bulletin* 16, no. 2 (1995).

Wood, Charles M. *The Formation of Christian Understanding: An Essay in Theological Hermeneutics.* Philadelphia: Westminster Press, 1981.

Yordon, Judy E. *Roles in Interpretation.* 3rd ed. Madison, WI: W. B. Brown and Benchmark, 1993.

Index of Subjects and Names

Index of Scriptural Quotations and Allusions